To Be or Not To Be DEVELOPED

About the Nature and Causes of Development

REIDULF MOLVAER

AFRICA WORLD PRESS
TRENTON | LONDON | CAPE TOWN | NAIROBI | ADDIS ABABA | ASMARA | IBADAN | NEW DELHI

AFRICA WORLD PRESS
541 West Ingham Avenue | Suite B
Trenton, New Jersey 08638

Cover & Book design: LiteBook Prepress Services

Cataloging-in-Publication Data may be obtained from the Library of Congress.

ISBNs: 978-1-56902-836-0 (HB)
978-1-56902-837-7 (PB)

To my sons
Ralph, Arnold, David and Michael
with love, respect and admiration

CONTENTS

Preface vii

1. What development means 1

2. Characteristics of developed countries 13

3. Blind alleys 33

4. Developed areas 83

5. How modern development started 91

6. How development has spread 131

7. Are there different paths to development? 151

8. Common features of the development process 165

9. A development model for Africa 201

Conclusion 249

Addendum: Dynamic Functionalism as Social Theory 255

Appendix: Various uses of the sociodynamic model 277

PREFACE

Development is the universal quest of our time. But how is development achieved? Many answers have been given to this question.

In the not so distant past, people in the West tended to think that modern development could take place only in societies with a Western-style culture, a Western mentality, a Western ethos. In developing countries, many thought that modernisation and development meant Westernisation. However, contrary to this belief, development has today spread to many parts of the globe, and non-Western areas may one day perhaps take the lead in development. This has kindled the hope worldwide that development is within the reach of all.

As developed countries now present many faces, it also seems likely that societies in pursuit of development do not have to put their people in a strait-jacket made abroad in order to achieve their aims but that they can develop without abandoning their identity and many deeply cherished national values and customs.

How to get there

What leads to development is not easy to define. It is evident that not all countries committed to development are equally successful in reaching their goals. This makes it necessary to go on trying to explain the process - to discover what contributes to development and what obstacles must be overcome for a country in order to develop. This book is presented as a contribution to the debate about these questions.

The ideas presented here have matured over many years, at least since I first went to Africa in 1965, and some of them have even more distant roots. They have taken shape on the basis of innumerable observations as well as much reading all this time, both in the course of 20 years of participation in practical development work and during periods of purely academic pursuits. This combination of theory and practice, with the opportunity to check ideas in the field, has made me realise the inadequacy of many common theories and explanations of development as well as the unsuitability of practices based upon them. The proof of the pudding is the eating, and as present development efforts have not led to real development in most of the Third World, there must be something wrong with the very assumptions these efforts are based upon. In this book I attempt to present alternative approaches.

Paradise lost, over the horizon, or round the corner?

I admit that I am not an unreserved admirer of all aspects of modern development and regret to see the havoc wrought in many developing countries by their efforts at development. A wealth of social, cultural and spiritual values that have contributed to the enrichment of life for people there, as well as much priceless traditional wisdom, have been sacrificed in the name of development - needlessly so. It is implied in the theory of development advanced in this book that it is possible and indeed desirable to keep, strengthen and enrich many aspects of national cultures in the process of development, although many changes will take place - and there will also be a tendency to imitate other, more developed countries, especially in externals. Co-operation for development within a country should be possible between those who are reluctant to give up precious past values and those who set less store by accumulated lore. In that way, development goals, and not only economic ones, may be attained more quickly and with less strife and pain.

Many words, few new ideas

The literature about development is vast, and it is increasing at a brisk pace. It is a hotchpotch ranging from pure guesswork to efforts showing great theoretical ingenuity and practical insight - and generally much good will and many good intentions. But alas, we know that the road to hell is also paved with good intentions: the proof is the state of development in much of the Third World. It is evident that the problems of development have not been "solved" for the least developed countries, either by development theorisers or by practitioners in the field. New approaches are needed, approaches that take account of a very wide range of social forces, as every aspect of human life is in some way related to development.

Many theories of development have inspired costly experiments that have plunged large parts of the world into new depths of poverty and underdevelopment. Repeated reference to the unworkable theories underlying such experiments would make this book more directly polemical (and theoretical) than it is meant to be, except by implication. I prefer to deal with the problems as I see them without spending too much time discussing obsolete theories, and my own theoretical foundations will become evident as we go along. What is of value is what can be put into practice. Good theory is practical.

The arguments in this book are based on central events in human history and development processes which can easily be checked. Obscure social, economic or political happenings in a country (or in the West), however "cleverly" they are interpreted, cannot explain the most epoch-making event in modern history - the breakthrough of "the modern". I therefore stick to essentials related to the argument and argue from well-known facts that can easily be verified. Bibliographic footnotes are thus rather few.[1] Detailed references serve no purpose

---

1 Professionals and students will easily find their way to the relevant literature. I refer other readers to a few books summing up certain aspects of the debate. Most of these are "mainstream" sources that should be accessible also in developing countries at a reasonable price (very many of them are Penguin books or otherwise paperbacks available from London).

here, and they are not necessary in order to understand these questions, which are not primarily academic but of vital practical interest and importance to so many people whose life and welfare depend on the "solution" found to the elusive "problem of development".

Why more words?

Many years of work and pondering, with attendant headaches and heartaches, have given birth to this book. Development cannot be reduced to a question of economic policies, institution building, class or capital formation, investment, the acquisition of skills and techniques, a desire to develop, hard work, communications and infrastructure, etc. The problem is indeed many-sided and wide-ranging. One could thus go on thinking and studying and observing without ever being able to answer all the relevant questions. However, at one stage anyone who wants to make a contribution to this issue must draw the line and "publish and (perhaps) be damned", although the problem may actually be felt to be: "I'll be damned if I don't".

In view of the serious economic crisis in most developing countries at present, this may be the right time to bring new viewpoints forward. Fresh ideas and different practical approaches are needed. Only theories founded on social, cultural, political and economic realities in developing countries should be taken seriously.

Fantasies and facts

Some development theories (popular in academic circles in the Third World) dwell much on the origins and causes of present predicaments and then abandon the analysis when "blame" for the ills has been

---

They have not necessarily influenced my own thinking, and they do not reflect my views on development except in some details: the main points and overall conclusions in this book are my own.

allocated. This is of no use to those in most urgent need of help, and it tends to justify and prolong age-old inertia.

Others (strong ideologists) dream of a Great Event or a system that will change it all, in spite of clear evidence that no such panacea has ever been found. All such once-and-for-all "solutions" have plunged developing countries into deeper and deeper misery.

Many theories formulated by people with deep knowledge of practical development problems and of the Third World have not been of any practical use because they reflect a hidebound, unrealistic and impractical ideological bias.

Some theories of development have tended to be purely speculative, with weak foundations in Third World realities or even the history of developed countries, or both. They limit their purview to the present workings of industrialised societies without investigating how they came to be as they are. Obviously theories not related to decisive contemporary and historical facts and factors are of no practical value.

In outlining an alternative development model, one must not forget that development can take on many faces and present striking differences from one society to another in many respects. Still, no development theory is of practical interest unless it is based on identified characteristics of developed societies; and what is essential in this regard may prove to be more uniform than what meets the eye at a first or even a second glance. A really valid theory of development should make it possible (1) to predict what is likely to happen as a result of various development strategies, and (2) to formulate and implement strategies that promote real development. Any valid and useful development theory must have universal applicability; otherwise it has no value or validity whatsoever.

Development takes place when a country's total population is prepared for it and have fulfilled the necessary "preconditions for development". A relevant development theory and model must state the necessary preconditions for development and show how they are established. When the necessary preconditions are realised, nothing can stop the development process; development will then eventually take place, although measures can be taken both to slow down and to speed up the process.

This book is about the road that leads to development.

Reidulf Molvaer
Oslo, 2024.

Chapter 1

WHAT DEVELOPMENT MEANS

Defining development

Many terms have been used for "development", such as progress, growth, evolution, industrialisation, modernisation, Westernisation, change, rapid change, radical change, revolution, self-reliance, etc. Different emphases and views may decide one's preference for any one of these terms; however, "development" is still the most common and "popular" one. A certain view of history as unfolding according to strict and unalterable laws may be implied in the strict meaning of this word, but without committing myself to any such view, I shall use the term here as convenient, since it is used by people of many persuasions and not only by those with ideological commitment to one particular philosophy of history.

What a definition of development must do

There has been much speculation whether there are different "paths" to development. This will be discussed in a later chapter of this book (chapter 7).

To be of any use, a theory of development must be able to explain the following three points:

- why and how development has occurred anywhere in the world, under whatever social, economic or political system;

- why development has been comprehensive in some countries, partial in some, and a failure in others; and
- why countries that were once at the forefront in the development race now seem to be lagging behind. (This can be explained without a pompous exposition of "the rise and fall of civilisations", but something has to be said about this topic too.)

What's in a name?

Countries that have not developed very far in an economic or technical sense are called less (or the least) developed countries, or developing countries (although some of them are not developing at all, and others are developing at a much slower rate than developed or "industrialised" countries), or underdeveloped countries (which is in fact a good and precise term and full of "promise" as it implies that these countries have many untapped human and natural resources and that they can therefore advance beyond their present state of development; but unfortunately the term has fallen into disfavour in developing countries), the Third World, the South, or poor countries, and so on. I may use any of these terms in more or less the same sense.

"Developed" countries can of course also develop further (and are generally in the process of doing so all the time), but it is a valid question to ask whether it is beneficial for people living in these countries if development goes on unchecked (as "growth") at any cost (- it is probably not a good idea). The term "industrialised nations" is much used, but it is misleading as it focuses the attention too strongly upon a single aspect of the development of these nations, and such a one-sided description can put people and nations in search of development on the wrong track. This will be discussed later. However, I may use the term in a broad sense, as a high level of industrialisation is of course one of the distinctive features of developed societies. "The West" is used as a convenient (but imprecise) term for the countries that developed first.

"The North" is now much in fashion as a designation of the most developed parts of the world, but the term is as imprecise as "the West".

The outstanding feature of "developed" countries is that they have advanced economically and technically further than other countries, and they have distributed wealth and extended social services to "the masses". However, this does not necessarily mean that they are ahead of others in other respects, for example humanly, socially, culturally, artistically, morally, in their ability to create happy and contented citizens, and so on - although this may of course also be the case. Development provides material wealth but does not always and everywhere lead to the "good life" or the "good society" for all. On the other hand, it is not impossible that developed countries may be the ones that give the greatest happiness to the greatest number of people. This is not the primary question addressed in this book. Here we shall concentrate on how development is achieved for societies that want to develop. Value judgements on which societies are best must be part of another discussion.

Why develop?

Many traditional values will be lost or transformed when societies modernise, and these values are often at the heart of these societies - what many of their members cherish most. Why then accept changes that endanger these values? For many the choice is easy, but I shall here mention three reasons why even people with strong ties to past traditions may find it advantageous to change and to "progress":

(1) Probably the majority of people in less developed countries want the things or products that development brings: better houses, a greater variety of clothes, better health care and education, nourishing or "interesting" foods and drinks, cars, radios, television sets, and so on. Some have just as strong a desire for things that bring no improvement at all: weapons,

cigarettes, strong drinks, drugs, pornography, etc. Many may only wish to obtain "things" without giving up old values or traditions. But modern change does not work quite like that: with modern goods and services come certain new lifestyles, "imported" values, a rather different outlook on many things in life, and for many a new view of life altogether. All this will start (and is in fact part of) the process of modifying many "traditions". But, as we shall see, this need not destroy national identities or basic cultural values: many essentials of each culture can live on and actually be strengthened the further a country develops.

(2) Unless the poorest and weakest countries in the world develop, they will be exploited and dominated by more developed countries. In the process, they will be even more impoverished, and their cultures will be "contaminated" and diluted by stronger and more expansive "universal" cultures. With the intention of preventing that this should happen, many resist modernisation. However, it may be that the very resistance to change accelerates the process of decay of national cultures, as it produces conflict, and during intense conflicts one has little or no control over how society is transformed. Outside pressures may become relentless and bring change anyway. By facing up to and adapting to modern reality, poor countries can exercise at least some measure of control over their own development instead of only submitting to the imposition of perhaps the worst aspects of an alien civilisation. With a totally negative attitude to change, one may also find that it is the least valuable aspects of one's own culture that survive the longest, usually in a degenerate form.

(3) Rich countries "export" some aspects of "modernity" to underdeveloped countries whether these latter like it or not.

Such "imports" may appear under many labels. When they show their most human face, they will be presented as, for example, "human rights", "democracy", or "progress". As these are widely held to be universal ("natural") values and rights, it is implied that they should be enjoyed by all. They may pop up piecemeal and relate to health services, population planning, sufficient food and a balanced diet, literacy and education, freedom from arbitrary justice, freedom of religion and of speech, multi-party democracy, women's liberation, and so on. Even where such "ideas" are just tolerated but still felt as outside interference, they will inevitably be the starting point of many more, and more wide-ranging changes. When put into practice, they will of necessity be the precursors of "modernisation" in all areas of life. No society has been able to reject or resist indefinitely the "intrusion" of these "universal values". By taking a positive attitude to them, developing societies may exercise a high degree of control over their own development. But however praiseworthy such ideas and values are, they are not identical with development, as we shall see. They are more often the products rather than the preconditions of development.

Only by meeting "modernity" head-on and by "taking control" will poor countries be able to steer the development in line with, and so as to serve, their own interests. In this way they can in large measure be masters of their own destiny.

What is there in it for me?

Together with new products, services, ideas (brought along with modern education and the "information explosion") and ways of doing things, a new mentality follows suit. It is not possible to acquire a plethora of modern things and skills without also gradually acquiring modern thoughts, however unconsciously this mental transformation may be taking place. In most cases it is a slow process, maturing over many years; in fact, it usually takes generations.

It is not possible to remain with the same outlook on life in all respects if the conditions of life change dramatically. However, we shall first define development in relation to the things, services and skills people get or acquire as a result of development, and then later mention the ideas and values that may follow in its wake.[1]

There are different views concerning details of what is basic, materially speaking, in the achievement of development, but there is fairly general agreement that at least the following goods and services must be extended to practically everyone in a country if one shall be able to say that this country is developed (these are thus the "signs and symptoms" of development):

- enough food and water for normal growth and healthy development of each individual;
- sufficient clothes that give adequate protection of the body against cold and disease, and which make it possible to observe the accepted codes of decency in the society in which one lives;

---

1 General books on development, development economics, development sociology or comparative sociology usually contain a discussion of what development means in material and non-material terms. "Standard of living" used to be an accepted measure of the quality of life; but now "quality of life" has become the fashionable term for the measure of "success" in ways not indicated by the standard of living. The change in terminology came as a result of the failure of development efforts to raise the standard of living of people in developing countries, a fact uncomfortable to live with. It could have been an eye-opener. Improved "quality of life" in its fashionable sense, e.g. increased longevity, may indicate prolonged misery, a "slower death" as it were.

- shelter that provides reasonable comfort and protection of one's physical and mental health against harmful environmental influences;
- modern health care for all;
- nation-wide sanitary services and hygienic conditions of life;
- universal primary education, at least to the level of being permanently literate;
- employment that enables individuals or heads of households to provide the basic needs of those dependent on the income from or outcome of such work.

In addition to these "concrete" aspects of development, there are some more intangible ones that are also basic: a feeling or realisation of greater freedom of the spirit and body, leading to enhanced dignity and self-respect, and involving relative freedom to *choose*, for example:

- one's work and career more or less according to one's ability and aptitude,
- the place to live (limited by economic power and availability but not by race or "class"),
- a life partner (by mutual - not parental or other - choice, and with the same freedom for women as for men),
- marital status,
- (perhaps, in our time,) approximate family size.

It is important to have the freedom to use one's talents and skills in meaningful ways so as to be able to lead a satisfying life, and to have one's choices respected and one's contribution to society appreciated without essential discrimination between "respectable" and "degrading" work, such as, for example, between "mental" and "manual" work.

At the base of these freedoms lies the principle of power-sharing. When a country is genuinely developing, absolute and arbitrary power gradually erodes. Instead, democratic institutions are strengthened, not only on paper or as a "front", but as a genuine manifestation of real power-sharing and increasing influence of ordinary citizens on elected authorities. This is so because the same human qualities that help to bring about development also contribute to the rise of democratic forms of government suitable for modern, developed societies. The rule of law and a balance of powers, with accountability for power-holders, will gradually evolve as a country develops. The opposite trend is an indication of a glide into (renewed or further) underdevelopment.

Not only bits and pieces

An important aspect of true development is its comprehensiveness and durability. A country may find a source of wealth that makes it possible for the government of that country to provide for its citizens all the goods and services considered criteria of development. But chance may reduce the value of what they offer for sale on the world market, or the source may be exhausted, and the country is back in the same situation as before the lucky strike was made. If that country has not developed other ways of meeting the challenges of the modern world, it can hardly be called developed.

Development has been achieved in a country when the population of that country has been (en)able(d) to exploit a number of the resources of the country so as to make sustained development possible over a long period of time. On the other hand, it cannot be maintained that this is the case in a country that has become and remains dependent on only one or two sources of wealth that may give it a brief surface impression of modernity.

In fact, development may not be wealth as much as the ability of a people to make the most of the potentials and resources at hand, ideally without overexploiting them so that they will be depleted to the detriment of future generations.

Do countries or people develop?

Another point to note about development is that it has not really been achieved unless it has come to involve and benefit the majority of the people in a country. If the wealth - however great - of a country has been produced without the help of the majority of the population, and is perhaps even concentrated in a few hands while the majority of the population lives in poverty and want, that country cannot reasonably be defined as developed.

A country may, on the other hand, have great wealth that may be pretty well distributed among its citizens. But if the economic life of the country is kept up by means of the labour of a foreign work force, or if the economy is entirely or largely in the hands of foreigners, it is not justified to regard that country as developed. Such a situation occurs when the supply of goods and services in a country is provided by immigrant labourers or a foreign commercial or productive "class", while the government satisfies the basic needs of "genuine" citizens by extracting wealth from resident foreigners (or nationals of foreign extraction considered a community apart) in the form of taxes and duties on their products and services or joint ownership (perhaps by law) in productive enterprises owned and/or run by them, without, however, making the citizens of the country masters in their own house by giving them the responsibility for meeting their own needs through their own efforts.

*

How big a majority is "enough"?

For a country to develop and be developed, the majority of the population must take part in, contribute to, and benefit from the development process. The size of this majority can only be arbitrarily determined, and I would suggest that it must comprise at least seventy-five per cent (three-quarters) of the population of a country, and the more the better.

This percentage should also increase as development gathers momentum. To be of any real and lasting value, the benefits of development must be perceived by the vast majority of the population as greater material, social and mental well-being than would be the case if modern development had not taken place in their country.

More than money and things

Development cannot be measured only by external criteria. The mental outlook and the ways in which the talents and skills of people are used or find outlet are basic to development. The necessary conditions for development may be influenced by certain social and political measures for their full application to the development process. Obstacles may be put in the way of rapid development, and obstacles to development may be removed by persons and institutions interested in guiding the course or pace of development. However, the same human qualities that are needed to get development started can also influence these conditions and create the circumstances favourable for development. Creating conditions conducive to development may be hard and full of conflict in some countries and rather smooth in others. Governments may support or try to hinder development efforts, but they do not in the long run have the last word in the matter. It is the people who develop a country, not the leaders.

*

Development is a complicated phenomenon, and its investigation and explication have engaged a great number of politicians, social scientists, economists, philosophers, development workers and "ordinary" citizens in many countries for decades. Perhaps more than anyone else, people in underdeveloped countries who hope and long for the benefits of modern development are concerned to understand the processes that lead to the desired goal, so that they can take the necessary measures to improve their lot.

This book aims to contribute to the elucidation of the problems of development and to point to the path to follow in order to get "there": to become a modern, developed society. However, it does not put the responsibility for the development of a country into the hands of any "vanguard" or group of experts (or any development agency) but in the hands of the whole population of a country in search of development.

CHAPTER 2

CHARACTERISTICS OF DEVELOPED COUNTRIES

Before defining the development process itself, it may be helpful to take a broad look at developed countries so as to arrive at a definition of what a developed country is. This could clear up some misconceptions of the nature of developed countries that may have obscured the understanding of development and also led to misguided attempts at development.

In the next chapter we shall have more to say about some misguided attempts at development in the hope of reducing the temptation to enter blind alleys. In chapter 8 we shall try to sum up the salient features of the development process and chart the way to modern development. Our aim in this chapter is to get a bird's-eye view of the situation in clearly developed countries, leaving debatable cases aside for the time being (see also chapter 4).[1]

The great acceleration

Modern development has roots going back many hundred years (we shall have more to say about this in chapter 5). An increasing acceleration towards "modern society" began in Europe after AD 1500, and this "wave" led to the Industrial Revolution, which first took off in England

1 Any standard textbook of sociology or the sociology of development sets out the main features of developed societies. They will also have references to more specialised works. As a starter, P. Worsley (ed.), *Introducing Sociology* will do.

from the end of the 18th century and then spread to other areas, a process still going on; but the process took somewhat different forms under varying conditions.

In chapter 4, a broader picture will be given of developed societies. We shall then also discuss why they are so called and also say something about marginal cases. Here we shall first of all note the more striking and essential features of a modern society. On the basis of such outstanding characteristics, we shall be able to determine more precisely what can be called a developed country and why.

Where has there been rapid development?

There is no serious disagreement that modern development started in the West, and practically everyone would agree to call western Europe and North America (the United States and Canada) developed.

There is also general agreement that parts of east Asia, Australia and New Zealand are developed. Japan is the prime example of an Asian country that has achieved a very high level of development, and some other countries in the region (South Korea, Hong Kong, Taiwan and Singapore) are not so very far behind.

Among the former socialist countries, most would probably count Russia and some other parts of eastern Europe as developed, although they were much more successful in heavy industry than in consumer and service industries and agriculture. Besides, the quality of goods produced in eastern and western Europe differed and still differ greatly. China may call itself "socialist", but it gives the impression of progressing in the direction of a modern developed society, although it still has a long way to go.

There may be other societies to consider (e.g. Israel, South Africa, some Latin American and some other Asian countries), but the examples mentioned are sufficient to give concrete illustrations of what we in the main mean by a developed country.

What is special about developed societies?

1. Overall use of the "mother tongue"

An aspect of development that needs to be paid special attention to is the fact that in *every* developed country in the world the, or a, local national language is used as the principal means of communication in all areas, including education.

The position given to one's native or national language reflects the respect one has for oneself and one's own and the spiritual independence a country has. Perhaps it is precisely with the self-respect, self-esteem and self-confidence shown by one's attitude to and use of the mother tongue that modern development starts.

The gradual (however incomplete and imperfect) formation of national units (i.e. states) in Europe corresponding more or less to linguistic units was an important (but not calculated) preparation and precondition for modern development. Whether states other than nation-states can serve the same purpose, and whether nations can be "built", are questions we shall discuss later; but we shall mention already now that no state that is not approaching the status of a nation-state has ever achieved modern development.

Countries that try to develop through merely or primarily imitating developed countries may be misguided enough to adopt too much from the country they have chosen as their model, even to the extent of adopting a foreign language as the "official" means of communication. This can lead them about as far forward as Europe came when Latin was the language of prestige: it did not develop very much. Only an elite can learn a foreign or dead language well enough to benefit greatly from it. Most people will not become fluent in it, and they will not be in a position to make the best use of modern tools in the kitchen, the farm or the work place, nor of medicines and modern services, etc., if instructions are given in a foreign language.

That all have the opportunity and ability to benefit from modern inventions and services is an essential aspect of a modern society.

Development results from the involvement of the majority of the population in the development process. Without the active involvement and co-operation of a reasonably educated (at least permanently and confidently literate) mass of people, a country cannot develop. The efforts of elites to develop a country without a popular base have proved again and again to end in confusion and disaster. In the process, financial resources are squandered while the economic advance is practically nil. People who regard themselves as "vanguards" in the development process have often, when frustrated in their ambitions, tried to find support in the mob - people without sufficient qualifications to think and act democratically or to understand what development means. These crowds can easily be stirred to violent action by emotional appeals to their "interests". However, mob movements (e.g. revolutions) tend to be destructive, and mobs often end up turning on their leaders and "devouring" them. Nobody's aims are achieved, except perhaps for a short transitional period before further decline sets in.

Development depends on the active, voluntary (not forced) participation of a reasonably enlightened populace. Those who thus contribute to development will also be able to benefit from development - in spite of appearances to the contrary: a time lag that may delay a reasonably fair distribution of gains for a limited period (see later).

For the masses to get involved and participate in development, they must be able to communicate meaningfully with each other, i.e. use the same language, which in practice means: a national language must be understood and used by the whole nation.

2. Nations and states

Because the national language is so important for education and communication in development, it is worth noting that the move towards the creation of nation-states (with state boundaries more or less coinciding with language boundaries) took place in Europe at about the same time as modern development came under way. The formation of nation-states and modern development were in all likelihood two linked factors in one general movement towards modernisation. Multilingual Switzerland and bilingual Belgium, as well as the division of the speakers of German into several states, may seem like "anomalies" in a general trend and process. But these countries have been able to benefit from having close ties with the countries they share common languages with. The parallel formation of nation-states and economic and technical progress is not as crude as to *identify* the nation-state with a developed country. But this historical process is an indication of the normal condition under which development takes place: development has usually begun and taken off in the "natural" grouping of people in nation-states. Perhaps other state-formations ("built nations") can serve the same purpose. Even nation-states have been melting pots, creating or giving birth to "nations" made up of many "tribes" or language groups that have coalesced.[2] Although some (e.g. Ferdinand Tönnies) see the need to communicate easily in a common language as the last vestiges of a pre-modern "community" (*Gemeinschaft*),[3] no modern society can in fact function well without it. It is at the end of the process of forming societies containing people who can communicate easily with each other that modern development has - and can - become a reality.

Emil Durkheim thought that each society can establish social values and structures (on a religious or ethical basis) which will suit that society, and that it is a necessity for a society to have such moral "laws"

---

2 Cf. Peter Worsley, *The Three Worlds. Culture and Development*, chapter IV, and Benedict Anderson, *Imagined Communities. Reflections on the Origin and Spread of Nationalism.*

3 Cf. Ferdinand Tönnies, *Community and Association.*

("discipline") to exist.[4] This explains also indirectly why societies begin to dissolve and decay: the moral basis disappears, and as a result, social and family ties weaken, workers' morale slackens, ultimate values are overtaken by (perhaps) a seemingly rigid "scientific" attitude (so that one does not for example accept what cannot be scientifically proved - and values *cannot* be thus proved), educational and child rearing principles disintegrate, etc. Common values bind a society together and are thus of importance also for development, as modern societies depend on what Durkheim called "organic solidarity".

With the disappearance of a "national" orientation (based on "national" values), one basis of development disappears or becomes diffuse, so that development may slow down, come to a halt or be reversed, a process that is now beginning to show in some highly developed societies.

Ideal and reality

The ideal of internationalism - which is of course good and praiseworthy in almost every respect - seems to be so abstract for most people that the idea is not capable of uniting them in co-operative ways that will contribute to the enhancement of economic development. The fact that fanatical nationalism (Nazism, Fascism, Apartheid, etc.) is not only inhuman but confrontational and in the end self-destructive is not a valid argument against the concept and the creation of the nation-state as a boost to development. A healthy kind of "nationalism" is for most people a natural expression of patriotism and love of one's country and culture. Thus understood, it is not an expression of hostility and aggressiveness towards others - not more than international sports events are. Nationalism can have positive rather than negative features, expressing

---

4 Cf. Emil Durkheim, *The Elementary Forms of the Religious Life* and *Professional Ethics and Civic Morals*, and summarised in *Sociology and Philosophy*.

love, not hatred or feelings of superiority. It is a "natural" feeling that can make for unity and smooth co-operation. This benefits development.

The essential thing about a nation in modern society is that it comprises people with (or using) a common language and only secondarily a common culture generally; common "blood" or race should not come into the picture at all (and common history is a purely mental construct).[5] The nation in this sense has for developed countries in most cases proved to be a unit of fair size for state-formation and development: big enough for modern development to take place (with some lilliputian states surviving in friendly surroundings), and rarely so large as to be ungovernable.[6]

---

5 In reality the definition of a nation is not so neat and tidy as the above may give the impression of. Every nation absorbs members "coming in" from "outside", through for example immigration or intermarriage. These should be counted as full members of the nation they want to belong to. In general, a nation is made up of people speaking the same language. A nation-state would also normally be in a connected (contiguous) area. English speakers living as far apart as England, Ireland, the USA, Canada, Australia and New Zealand could not in the long run be one state. That German speakers were divided into separate states may have historical roots in attempts to preserve a balance of power in Europe. The linguistic unity of the Chinese is more a question of having a common *written* language, spoken in many ways that are not mutually intelligible. Other considerations may sometimes be of greater importance than nationality. Still, a simple general definition of a nation could be: "a group of people who speak the same language", and if they constitute a state, this will be a nation-state. Ethnicity is a word that connotes the aspect of "common blood" or race and should perhaps not be used in the same sense as nationality as specified above.

6 It is not possible to be specific about what is the ideal or optimal or reasonable size of a state, or what size a state must be to be governable. England could rule its colonies, including more than all English speakers, at one time in the past. That is not possible today. The Soviet Union was

In the Third World (perhaps especially in Africa), many nations or nationalities or "tribes" are so small that they would find it difficult to develop on their own (as nation-states) in competitive and unfriendly surroundings. In such cases, it may be a reasonable solution to unite with other nations or nationalities to form viable (perhaps federal) states of reasonable size for close co-operation in development, although efforts should also be made to preserve different cultural values and customs of each nationality ("tribe") that are no obstacle to development. "Nation-building" in the sense indicated (almost artificially creating one nation out of a number of adjacent nationalities) is probably a necessary phenomenon under such circumstances. Many (but far from all) neighbouring nations have much in common culturally and socially. The sacrifices they may have to make for the sake of achieving a "built" (or artificially created) nation or country (a conglomeration of nationalities) may therefore not (always) be destructive of their own identity, although such alliances will tend to modify cultures to various degrees.

It is of the utmost importance for developing countries that a language (or perhaps two) spoken as the mother tongue(s) within that state is (are) chosen as the state ("national" and "official") language(s) and used daily, in education, the mass media, for state and private business and so on.[7] Such a language must be heard and used every day in its

---

governable for several decades but then became ungovernable. The same may happen elsewhere, for instance in the United States or Brazil, Sudan or Zaire, China or India. The present trend of uniting several independent states into common markets or political unions ("regionalism" - the formation of regional units based on "common culture" and/or contiguity) may work (for a time), but then again it may not. History will tell.

7 In multilingual countries, one solution could be to teach the national language chosen from among the vernaculars plus the vernacular of any specific area in about equal proportions, and to have school textbooks in

natural setting (especially being used by people who have it as their mother tongue) and in a variety of contexts. No borrowed (foreign) language can serve this purpose in nation-building and development.

It may not be such a big effort to adopt a language other than one's mother-tongue when this language is used daily, naturally, correctly, fluently and massively in one's immediate surroundings (as has, for example, been the case for most immigrants to the United States). This is not the case when a foreign (extraneous) language is chosen as the national or official language. In that case, understanding, education, logic, rationality, precision, intellectual growth, communication and social, cultural and economic development suffer. This is certainly an obstacle to modern economic development and prevents it from reaching beyond a low point. A country that has chosen a foreign "national" or official language will have the greatest difficulties in getting ahead in its development efforts (unless, of course, it changes its language policy). It has stumbled over the first hurdle. It will not get very far in modern development as long as it pursues it in this way.

Basic to modern development is clear, easy and precise communication between people who live and work together.

3. Democratic ideas and modes of interaction

It was only after the everyday language of the people (instead of classical languages - mostly Latin in Europe) became the normal means of education at all levels, as well as of general public information and communication in all areas of life, that modern development really took

---

all subjects in both languages and used in an equal mixture, or perhaps have the books in the national language and teach the subject orally in the vernacular. So as not to give an unfair advantage to those whose vernacular is the national language, such people could be taught one of the other important languages in the country, according to their preference or dependent on the availability of teachers.

off. This was and is also a necessary condition for people to acquire sufficient knowledge to form "educated" opinions based on reasonably precise information. Education is the basis of a proper understanding of modern society. The possibility of full participation in political and social life has come within the reach of the masses as a result of modern linguistic and educational policies.

Wide dissemination of books and newspapers and extensive use of radio and television have meant a great breakthrough for people who earlier relied on authoritarian pronouncements or sermons for information and opinions. With the modern information order, people have been enabled to form their own opinions on solid grounds and take decisions and make choices based on personal insight. With the rise of "pluralistic societies" (i.e., societies with more than one "culture" or form of religion or political party, etc.), people have been more or less forced to "take sides" and make fundamental choices.

As people become gradually better informed and are able to exchange educated ideas - privately and publicly - in their own language, they naturally demand to have a say in the way affairs affecting their lives are conducted. The realisation of alternatives to the status quo leads to demands for democracy and institutions expressing the new intellectual climate. The practice of democracy takes shape alongside social and economic development. They are in fact two sides of the same coin.

To put it another way: the knowledge, skills and attitudes needed for economic development are the same as those that pave the way for modern democracy. The two are so closely interconnected that one is not in the long run possible without the other. But that does not justify the conclusion so commonly drawn today, that one causes the other. Formal multi-party democratic procedures do not automatically lead to modern development. On the other hand, the use of force to prevent the expression of democratic ideas and the formation of democratic institutions may delay development for some time. But when people are truly ready (enabled, "educated", with the necessary "capacity") for development, they are also truly ready for democracy, and nothing can for long stand in the way of the ultimate realisation of both goals: development and democracy.

At least lip service has normally to be paid to the ideal of development, and nowadays also of democracy, even where democratic freedoms are suppressed in practice. The attainment of modern development is ultimately incompatible with the suppression of democratic freedom. One hopeful universal sign of the times is the great emphasis placed on education in any society pursuing any kind of development goals. As a result of modern education (of the "right sort"), people will sooner or later come to demand, and get, increasing democratic rights in any truly (even only slightly) developing country. They will get them more or less at the same pace as they begin to achieve the goals of development. This is so because development and democracy go hand in hand.

4. Do it yourself

Every developed country has developed through its own efforts. Foreign rule or direction or aid has never developed a country. In fact, such efforts distort and delay genuine development if a country is not ready (properly "equipped") to develop on its own. When it is ready, aid and "expert advice" may speed up the development process - if wisdom and honesty prevail.

Even when a country is truly developing or already developed and has acquired the knowledge, skills and attitudes necessary for development, it can experience temporary economic setbacks (depression) or face acute problems (drought, war or some other disaster) that make further development difficult or impossible for a time. In such a situation, outside help can ease recovery. On the other hand, we have no example showing that external aid has initiated true development. Aid may even be detrimental to sustained progress and development if it takes the form of "imposing" development from outside on an unwilling populace.

To achieve development, the knowledge, mental outlook, attitudes and skills of people in developing countries must in many cases change drastically, and people must have been properly "prepared". It is the combination of a number of factors that will breed the *efficiency* and *scientific spirit* that are important marks of developed countries. It is not enough to train a lot of people in the skills required for development and let them retain the old turns of mind. Furthermore, in developing countries we often see that old customs and beliefs are destroyed without being replaced by a progressive outlook, etc. This will not in itself contribute to a country's development (although a "vacuum" may sometimes have to be created before it is filled with new contents). Highly skilled workers not mentally prepared for modern society will often (perhaps unwittingly but just as often on purpose) obstruct the development process (in attempts to gain personal advantages). People who have lost their links with the past without having found or been given anything to replace old beliefs and customs often become very destructive elements in a society.

If political power is in the hands of people without a progressive outlook and progressive policies, well educated and motivated people are often not made proper use of. The "brain drain" in developing countries mostly takes place in those countries themselves, as so few of the best equipped "brains" are ever given a real chance to apply acquired skills and knowledge to the benefit of the country. Thus they may (probably rightly so) feel that they can be more useful in countries that have already developed or at least started on the road to genuine development than "at home".

A country in search of development needs to (learn to) do the things necessary for development *by itself*, by equipping and making good use of its people in all areas of life.

5. The role of government

The pervasive influence and the tasks of national governments increase with the advance towards modernisation and corresponds roughly to its level of development, although there are disagreements on the "right", the "left", and the "centre" of politics about the exact role of government in economic, social, and cultural life.

Prior to "modern development", affairs of state were mostly concerned with internal security and foreign policy, finances to run the state apparatus, and so on. But the governments of developed countries, and now increasingly also of developing ones, have taken on, or been forced to take on, responsibilities for income distribution, the care of children, the old and infirm, education, information, culture, sports, roads and other infrastructure, and much more. At the same time, defence and the maintenance of law and order as well as state finances generally have become much more complex. Governments are charged with the responsibility of safeguarding and enhancing the welfare of its citizens through various regulations regarding industry, trade, the exploitation of national resources, etc., in addition to supplying social and other services.

Developed and strictly capitalist societies try ("ideally") to reduce government power and involvement in the conduct or direction of the economic life of the country. This may sometimes have led to high levels of production and wealth, but (at least initially) it has also created large impoverished groups in the population; however, the distribution of wealth has gradually improved even in the most capitalist developed countries. On the other hand, developed countries with a strong socialist leaning tried to obtain state ownership and regulation of as much as possible of the economic life. This led to reasonably fair distribution, but (as strict socialism was an attempt at development without true democracy) also to low productivity, and most products were of poor quality.

In capitalist Japan too, the state plays an important role in economic life, but on the whole it stimulates rather than hampers entrepreneurial efforts.

Social democracies have tried a middle road with a "mixed" economy, where the state runs (and pays for) many services (e.g., education, health services, communications), but at the same times it leaves the means of production largely in private hands. In this way, these countries have mostly succeeded in keeping productivity at a high level, at the same time as they have been able to distribute wealth reasonably equitably and to maintain a decent standard of public services.

Governments in developed countries usually handle the responsibilities following in the wake of modern development fairly well. On the other hand, no country can develop by just imitating a developed country's state apparatus (the structure of its "bureaucracy"). What is a consequence cannot become a cause of development. By taking on the tasks of modern governments and by establishing elaborate and costly bureaucracies but without developing, many governments of poor countries have brought their countries to the brink of ruin. This is not a sign of development, however laudable many such efforts are.

6. The role of capital

Capital is accumulated and invested for *productive* purposes to a higher degree in developed countries than elsewhere. When capital is invested and this results in high levels of productivity, status symbols may be acquired as signs of success; but although status symbols may be signs of development, they can never be its cause, and status symbols that are too costly in relation to a nation's wealth are obstacles to development.

In underdeveloped countries, status symbols are often rated so highly as to retard development and may take priority over investment in productive enterprises. This may be the case both with individuals and governments. Investments may there also be made in the acquisition of land rather than for the improvement of its yield; or in houses, which give rent but produce nothing. The "progressive" exceptions are commonly still too few to make much difference with respect to the modernisation of these countries. Much wealth may also be spent to ensure "the welfare on one's soul", for example contributions to the erection of sanctuaries, to keep a priesthood happy, to obtain objects (sacred relics, amulets, etc.) thought to be beneficial for one's body or soul, and so on. This was also the case in developed countries before they developed, but such expenditures have little or no place in modern society even when people retain their religious beliefs. In developing countries they are, however, still a drain on the economy. All this reduces the chances of accumulating capital that can get development processes started, especially if such things are done at the expense of for example popular education which is important in laying a foundation on which modern societies can be built.

Capital is needed for development, but it is not a *sufficient* condition, nor is its size as important as *how it is used*.

That capital by itself is not enough to start development can be seen in most of today's oil-rich countries as well as from the history of Europe a few centuries ago. It was in the poorer areas of north-western Europe that modern development started, and the relative poverty there may have been a spur to develop: fellowship in misery and in being exploited may have joined people together for effective co-operation so as to make them more independent and manage their own affairs. In the end they overtook the better off areas in production, wealth and power.

It is not capital as such but the use to which it is put that makes such a big difference. Only when the people of a country have "qualified" for modern development can capital be put to proper use so as to start or enhance development.

7. Division of labour

There is a high degree of work specialisation in developed countries.[8] This is required by the nature of the goods produced and the services rendered. It is made possible by a high level of training and education

---

8 Emil Durkheim used the terms "organic solidarity" for social (especially labour) relations prevailing in modern societies and "mechanical solidarity"

in these countries. It derives from and leads to a quality of labour that is very important for development: goal-oriented, practical efficiency, or "rationality" in Max Weber's terminology.[9] (This is very different from the purely "logical" rationality that was the focus of interest of for example Vilfredo Pareto[10]: this is of only limited relevance for development as such logical rationality is an elite phenomenon, whereas development depends on the participation of masses of people with practical - i.e. goal-oriented - common sense and sound basic education.)

The division of labour in "complex societies" has led to strong sectoral *interdependence* (what Emil Durkheim called "organic solidarity") of various groups. In this way, each group learns to do its limited tasks efficiently and "professionally", and here know-how is very important. Nobody can do *all* the tasks needed in a modern society; therefore. one has both to specialise and to rely on others for what one cannot provide by oneself. Within government itself, this is seen in bureaucratic efficiency, in line with impersonal "rules", taking the place of more personal relations prevailing in less developed societies (this topic has been much discussed after Max Weber published his classic analysis of modern bureaucracy, *The Theory of Social and Economic Organisation*).

The division of labour does not necessarily lead to "alienation" and boredom, and it is not only a loss to the worker. There can be great pleasure in the achievements of professional workers. Besides, nobody can become expert in every aspect of complicated production processes or other areas of modern life. A jack of all trades (or of all aspects of a complicated production process) is rarely happier than an expert. It may actually be so that workers of all kinds (from farmers

---

for those in less developed ones. See his book *The Division of Labour in Society*.

9 Cf. Max Weber, *The Protestant Ethic and the Spirit of Capitalism* and *The Theory of Social and Economic Organisation*.

10 Cf. Vilfredo Pareto, *The Mind and Society*.

and factory hands to university professors and managers of industry) in developed countries find greater job-satisfaction than people in less developed societies with fewer opportunities for initiative, innovation, creativity and choice, and where the division of labour is generally less sharp. However, job-satisfaction does not necessarily mean satisfaction or happiness in other areas of life - although very often it does.

As many developing countries have introduced modern work routines in order to speed up their development, it should be stressed that high productivity based on work specialisation and differentiation of tasks is a consequence of development, but the division of labour is itself not a cause of, and cannot as such bring about, development.

8. Comprehensive development

It is important to note that development in highly developed societies is *comprehensive* and overall, and that it affects all areas of life.

The belief that *industrialisation* is the basis and chief characteristic of a modern society has led some countries (both "socialist" and underdeveloped ones) to invest heavily in machine industry and less in agriculture and consumer and service industries, or in industry generally rather than in agriculture, or vice versa, but not in all areas of economic life at once. This has given rise to societies with halting and uneven development or, in the worst cases, no development at all. Such efforts at development have resulted in shortages of many commodities and services - and (especially in socialist countries) in endless queuing and much dissatisfaction (or worse: in acquiescence and corruption). Industrialisation is only one aspect of modern development, and if other economic and social sectors are neglected, genuine development is hampered and delayed. The same can be said generally if only one sector of production is stressed to the exclusion of all or most others.

Those who view industry as the principal basis of modern development are likely to see massive *urbanisation* also as necessary for development. As a consequence, more services and a higher standard of living are supplied for town dwellers than for the rural population, to the extent of leaving the latter to suffer neglect and be paid poorly for their products, with the result that rural productivity declines. This situation does not help development but retards it.

The arguments for the need of rapid industrialisation and urbanisation in order to achieve development focus too narrowly on only one aspects of modern societies, and there is thus a risk of failing to take the total situation into account.

Similar objections can be made against concentrating too heavily on *trade*. Trade skims off the surplus of production but it does not get development started, nor does it in itself promote development. A well developed country may look like "a nation of shopkeepers", but this should not lead one to conclude that what is a result of development is a cause.

The major economic advances preceding and laying the basis of the Industrial Revolution were made in *agriculture*. This provides a useful perspective on development: industrialisation without well developed agriculture makes for lopsided development; and heavy urbanisation (accompanied by mass unemployment and depopulated agricultural areas) puts the economy out of balance and makes poor use of (marginalises or removes from productive life) much of the available workforce.

A developed country is not developed in only one sector. On the contrary: in developed countries we find both the most advanced agricultural methods, the most sophisticated technology and precision in both consumer and heavy industry, and the most efficient service apparatus, including education, health services, transport and communications. The quality of all these sectors of developed societies increases with the level of development. Modern development is by its very nature comprehensive and all-embracing.

Development is, however, not only a question of economics, technology and science. In developed countries we also find the greatest number of cultural institutions, and a large proportion of the population can enjoy and take part in a wide variety of cultural activities. Less developed countries may also have a rich culture and may be even more artistic than developed countries. But developed countries have more culture to offer *all* their people just because they have developed. It is worth pointing to the high level of development of *national* cultures in developed societies, in addition to strong international interaction and widespread borrowings from others. Countries in pursuit of development may neglect their own culture in an attempt to imitate developed countries too closely; but this is probably a mistake, harmful to development.

Popular countrywide participation in development processes and respect for one's own and others' culture and identity are important features of true and comprehensive development.

9. Distribution of wealth

With modern development, ways are sooner or later found to distribute wealth more equitably, although big differences remain. This process is due to the gradual political changes that accompany development. With the growth of education and people's ability to state and make their demands, such a development seems a natural and inevitable outcome of democratic processes. But it shall not be denied that much wealth can be concentrated in few hands also in developed countries, and this was particularly so in the early stages of modern development (and this process seems to repeat itself, for example in the United States and Japan: *nouveaux riches* countries produce many *nouveaux riches* people).

However, the number of destitute people seems to diminish as a country develops, and the proportion of absolutely poor people is much smaller in developed societies than in developing ones.

CHAPTER 3

BLIND ALLEYS

When modern development occurred, it took everyone by surprise. Nobody had planned it. Nobody had expected it. Nobody had ever seen anything like it. It was a new and unparalleled phenomenon in world history. Subsequent attempts at explaining what had taken place have naturally been many. It was important for people who lived through the Industrial Revolution to understand what was happening to them and to their societies, and today it is important for people who want to develop to understand this process.

Economic theory at the time contributed nothing to start modern development nor to direct it once it had come under way. It tried to explain what was already a fact, and also to formulate general, universally valid laws of economic development. But fully satisfactory explanations have still not been given, and therefore attempts at elucidating what took place, and why, have occupied many minds ever since. Early explanations of how development came and comes about have not satisfied enquiring minds of later generations. More contemporary explanations have not found general acceptance either. Still, the belief persists that what worked once can happen again, and that what worked for some can work for all. In other words: there is a universal belief and hope that since some countries have developed, all can develop - if only one can discover the mechanism that leads to and sustains progress.

Early explanations of rapid economic development were more parochial than modern ones, but one should of course not blame contemporaries of the events of the first Industrial Revolution for their limited vision and experience. Even today it is difficult to take all the facts into account in attempts to explain development and modernisation. However, the search for answers and explanations goes on and will go on as long as people aspire to a better material and social life.

Development theorists and development workers are today struggling with the same old questions: What is development? What brings it about? How did developed countries manage to develop? What preconditions must be fulfilled for development to take place? If we can answer these questions correctly, we have of course laid the basis for replication of the development process anywhere in the world. The answers may affect the lives of millions of people. For many, this problem is a matter of life and death.

Before attempting to explain development, we shall in this chapter look at some theories and views of development that are not fitting the facts and therefore not helpful for nations trying to find ways to develop. When development policies and practices have been based on such views or theories, the result has not been development; at best, a few useful or indifferent changes have taken place, at worst, much damage has been done and the development process retarded. What follows is thus a catalogue of errors, a map of the blind alleys that have been followed by some countries that have failed to develop, or misleading development theories that developing countries have sometimes been urged to adopt as their basis when they formulate their development policies.[1]

---

1 Those interested in a systematic survey of past development theories can find good summaries in H. W. Arndt, *Economic Development. The History of an Idea* and C. P. Oman and G. Wignaraja, *The Postwar Evolution of Development Thinking*. Although earlier development theories have not promoted development in the Third World, familiarity with them can help prevent a repetition of past mistakes. Many of these theories hold an inherent

1. Development is not a result of political or religious ideologies

(A) Once upon a time in Christendom

At present, political and economic questions are at the forefront of the development debate, and the religious aspect is hardly heard. We shall soon enter the discussion from a political and economic angle but first point to another side of the question. When modern development first took off, there were questions of a different nature that occupied many minds, such as: Where did development first occur? What were the main characteristics of these early developed societies? Why did development take place there and not (yet) elsewhere? Many of the attempted answers had a religious and cultural tinge, and it is of interest even today to elucidate these points.

It was not Europe as a whole that first developed. It was north-western Europe; and from there development spread to North America and elsewhere. It was noted that development was initially practically confined to predominantly Protestant countries. This led many to speculate that it was something in the Protestant ethic (or other aspects of Protestantism) that led to development, and that the Protestant ethic (or ethos, or spirit), or something like it, was a necessary precondition for modern development to take place.

This argument had great force at a time when religion was of prime importance to people, and it found many supporters as long as only the West developed along modern lines. But when development later took place in non-Protestant countries such as Japan, Israel, Russia, France, and so on, this explanation could no longer be adhered to.

Still, the fact that modern development started in Protestant countries in the West may give us some clues to understanding what

---

fascination that may be seductive - and they have seduced many on to false tracks.

development is and how the process evolves; but it is important to discuss the question so as to avoid drawing the same erroneous conclusions as previous generations did.

The relationship between development and Protestantism has been presented in distorted ways, and we need to take a new look at the whole problem. By focusing too narrowly on the religious (or ethical) aspects or the economic theories of (early) Protestantism, the debate on the Protestant impetus towards development has led many to draw conclusions that are not at all helpful in explaining development in more general terms.

If we can discover why development occurred first in Protestant countries, we shall also see that the relevant principles are of a non-religious nature and can be applied and replicated in any country or culture, of whatever or of no religious bent. We can then discover that the basic traits of development are of a universal nature, and that there is only one known way to development. This will be a major theme in chapters 5, 7 and 8, and no more shall be said about the matter for the time being.

(B) Politics without God

Political ideologies have not (any more than religious ones) given satisfactory explanations of modern economic development.

When rapid development took off in north-western Europe, nobody was ready for it. Governments had never, anywhere, known or had responsibilities for economic developments of this kind or on this scale, and they did not know how best to deal with the situation. At first they interfered little with the changes that were taking place, and they did not, and could not, give much direction to these events.

Going it alone?

Modern development naturally occurred under the impetus and control of people who could *do* things. This included a wide range of people with a variety of talents and capabilities. Some give prime place to the so-called entrepreneurs, but in fact, the entrepreneurs only took the lead. Without a large group of people who were by that time prepared and capable of doing the different tasks that needed doing, the entrepreneurs alone could have done little or nothing to bring modern development about. Entrepreneurs existed in all countries before modern development took off. Something else was needed, in addition to leaders of industry and other enterprises, for modern economic development to take off. A whole new social fabric had to have taken shape to fit the times, and the entrepreneurs were just one - admittedly important - part of the total pattern.

It is therefore misleading to overemphasise the importance of entrepreneurs in development. Entrepreneurs are ubiquitous, but on their own they have never been able to bring about rapid development. Other conditions have to be fulfilled before this can take place, before the talents of entrepreneurs can be fully utilised to assist and lead the development process.

Guess who: The broad masses

The first precondition for modern development to take place is the presence of a *mass* of people with sufficient qualifications to do the work required. It is an advantage if people can choose the kind of work they like and can do well and that needs to be done in a modern or modernising society. Some enthusiasm for and pride in one's work or one's job or the finished product is a great stimulus in the development process, although much drudgery is involved in many tasks. If one's welfare depends on what one is doing, this will normally ensure a certain level of work discipline (keeping time, keeping up production levels quantitatively and qualitatively, etc.). On the other hand, in a well-functioning society, jobs may not be so plentiful that there are no workers to do the numerous uninteresting routine jobs necessary in modern industry, etc.

Workers with the necessary qualifications to take part in the development process do best when someone else has the responsibility for the management and the business side of an enterprise. On the other hand, employers (entrepreneurs) can do little without a qualified work force and are therefore not more "important" for development than ordinary workers. They all need each other. All contribute something of value.

The money-spinners

When people with capital see that they can make more money through investment in certain enterprises, they are of course likely to use their capital in this way. This is what happened during the early stages of the Industrial Revolution. But capital alone never could and never can bring modern development about without a broad mass of people with the necessary (mental and technical) qualifications to do the various kinds of work that must be done in a modern society.

Capital is always needed for large-scale development. In the "first" Industrial Revolution (c. 1780-1830), such capital was mainly in private hands. As the state hardly knew how to handle the new and unexpected situation, it left modern development to those who obviously had been able to get it going: the market forces and private capital and initiative. It is a misnomer to call such countries "capitalist", as capital is just as much needed in countries with strict state control of the economy. Development is also a question of who can make the best use of both capital, human and physical resources and the situation ("the market forces").

Interpretations after the fact

The start of development in Europe laid the basis for later political differences.

Because development had started under the direction and drive of private citizens and with capital in private hands, many politicians then and later were afraid to change this pattern and wanted to preserve it. This laid the basis for a conservative philosophy in politics and economics.

Leaders of modern development enterprises soon got strong influence over governments, and these governments came to see it as one of their principal tasks to secure the best conditions for modern development and the growth of the economy. As long as the most developed countries had the upper hand in economic and commercial terms, they naturally fought for free trade, free movement of capital and people, and a free hand for the leaders in the development process to do what they thought would accelerate development and bring high profits. In theory, they tried to give the impression, and perhaps believed, that this was to the advantage of all, that it would benefit and develop also other parts of the world. Liberal trade and other *laissez-faire* policies were seen as advantageous, even essential, for development.

Many are so afraid to change anything in the way things were done - and *worked* - in the past that they develop a very conservative attitude in political, social and economic matters.

The mass of people that had contributed so much to make this development possible had at first little say in what was going on. While the economy grew, their wages did not grow at the same rate. Much poverty resulted. What constituted "fair pay" for work done came up as a new problem, and a high rate of inflation made wages lag behind prices. "Just" wages became a social and ethical question fiercely debated. Till then, nobody had thought much about the regulation of working conditions (labour laws). The new industrial life brought with it many new hazards to the life and health of the workers. These problems had to be tackled and solved.

The same people who had acquired the skills and mental attitudes necessary for modern development did, however, gradually find ways of airing their concerns and grievances (although not as fast and as forcefully as this happens in free societies today). They also found leaders who fought for the workers, for their "rights".

The fight for better conditions for the workers had at first often a religious colouring. But the exhortation to be "charitable" to workers was generally tempered by religious awe and submissiveness in relation to the authorities, and this in many cases hampered the work to improve the life of the workers. Non-religious voices became louder, and soon they were the ones most listened to in the struggle for a better life for the workers.

Some (the radicals, advocating changes "from the roots") wanted to change practically everything in society, from top to bottom. Some of them were religious people, but most radicals were anti-clerical socialists who wanted to get rid of the influence of the church and religion altogether. Some wanted to reduce the influence of state authorities and give a greater say to the workers in matters that affected them most. Others, on a similar ideological basis, wanted the society as a whole (or a radical government) to control all aspects of life, including, of course, capital and capital movements (the uses to which capital was put). They argued that the impersonal (and presumably disinterested) state should take charge of most aspects of (public) social life, and especially the economy ("the material base"), which they considered to be the factor that gave shape to all other aspects of life.

These political movements rose as a *result* of modern development, but they did not bring economic development about, which is beyond their capacity. Still, their proponents sought to influence and control it. The most fanatical and narrow-minded of them believed that they had the full and final explanation of what modern development was all about, and they wanted to turn consequences of development into a cause of development, and in this spirit they also tried, and still try, to advise developing countries on how to progress. Of course it does not work.

It is a misconception that development can be made to happen by the introduction of any political or economic system based on any theory of development or of government or of the state. Many developing countries have tried to solve their economic and development problems by changing from one political or economic system to another, but these changes have made no or little difference. Something else is needed for development to take off.

Development and democracy

The people who contributed most to modern development (that is, the workers and entrepreneurs of all categories, and not the economists, planners or politicians) were gradually able to influence governments to such an extent that at least the most basic of their demands were met. Their contribution to development was thus being equalled by their influence on politics. Governments became gradually more democratic. Modern development and democracy grew hand in hand, although the former was usually ahead of the latter.

The acquisition of the mentality and the abilities needed for modern development enabled people to gradually shape politics to their advantage. Therefore workers (and people generally) in free, democratic countries are better off than workers (and people on the whole) in any other part of the world.

"There must be a quicker way"

From the start of modern times, many people have been dissatisfied with the pace and the extent and the nature of the changes that have taken place in modern economic and social life. They have wanted to speed up and radicalise the process. Various solutions have been proposed and tried.

Some (mostly middle-class intellectuals) have found the root of all evils in the ("class") structure of existing society and want to change this - not slowly and through negotiated processes but through violent overthrow of the existing order. This is the revolutionary way.

If we look at the major revolutions in the world (the French of 1789,[2] the Russian of 1917,[3] the Chinese[4] and the Vietnamese[5] of the 1940s, and other lesser ones more or less in imitation of these[6] - and some caricatures of them), certain features emerge.

The countries where they occurred had in the development race fallen or were falling behind the most advanced countries in the world or countries in their immediate vicinity. Small groups of people had developed a modern attitude, or an appetite for modernity, and were eager for their countries to develop fast and catch up with the more advanced ones. However, they did not want, or did not "have the time", to take the same slow laborious path that had been followed by every single one of the more advanced societies. They were in a hurry. One means of achieving their aims was agitation in order to get popular support. In many cases they succeeded in gaining power, largely with the support of the crowds (the mob), whom they manipulated to serve their purposes. Many revolutionaries were great idealists, having the cause of the masses at heart; others were just greedy for power.

Those who wanted to obtain the fruits of development (and development itself) very quickly, proved to be chasing the wind. These revolutionaries were pursuing a goal not possible to attain in this way. The means employed did not serve their aims, except where the only real aim was political power. The desire for development was not matched by proper understanding of what development implies. As neither these leaders nor the population in their countries were equipped to bring development about, it did not materialise. After the existing political

---

2 Cf. Simon Schama, *Citizens. A Chronicle of the French Revolution.*

3 Cf. E. C. Carr, *A Story of Soviet Russia* (especially the volumes on the Bolshevik revolution), and Richard Pipes, *The Russian Revolution.*

4 Cf. Witold Rodzínski, *The Walled Kingdom.*

5 Cf. Stein Tønnesson, *The Vietnamese Revolution of 1945.*

6 Cf. e.g. René Lefort, *Ethiopia: A Heretical Revolution?*

and social structures were destroyed, little happened to speed up development. The countries that underwent this experience remained for long in poverty and underdevelopment.

In France, the Revolution ended in tyranny and dictatorship. Of lasting value it produced fine declarations that were, however, put into practice first of all in countries that did not "need" or experience violent revolutions. Aspirations outstripped the potentials for progress.

Inchoate development in Russia and China might without revolutions have been just as rapid after conservative opposition had been overcome. The upheavals that did occur may have jerked these giant countries out of centuries-long "traditional" inertia, but once this "awakening" had taken place, development might have proceeded at a more rapid pace and led to higher levels of development if these countries had abandoned their revolutionary rhetoric and philosophy (and socialist economic policies) at an early stage.

A few socialist countries may in the short term possibly have benefited from social upheavals termed revolutions. In most places, though, revolution has led to economic chaos and much misery, with development becoming an empty word (as their use of words like "freedom", "peace" and "democracy"). This has especially been the case with revolutions (socialist or not) in the poorest parts of the Third World.

"Off with his head" - the suicidal class struggle

The call for a "class struggle" has, wherever it has taken place on an ideological basis, led to stagnation and underdevelopment. If one group of people profits very much and others are impoverished as a result of modern development, advanced countries have found ways of regulating these differences through peaceful, democratic processes, although many serious economic imbalances and injustices remain. The solutions found, however imperfect, have on the whole improved the lot of the poor in these countries.

But suppressing and eradicating one group or "class" that has contributed substantially to modern development always harms development.[7] There are ways of regulating economic activities without eliminating valuable contributors and without letting a few people get away with all the spoils. Entrepreneurs without qualified workers can do little for development, no more than workers without good leaders (talented and innovative entrepreneurs, etc.). To take the "spoils" from actual contributors to development and instead give them as privileges to unproductive ideologues has certainly not done anything good for progress!

"No private property in Paradise"

The means of production ought of course to be in the hands of and controlled by those who can make the best use of them and manage them properly; that is, those who can both achieve the highest possible levels of productivity and services (without harming the welfare and interests of workers), and also maintain the productive instruments well for efficiency and long life. In some cases, that may be done by the state, which often does well in running hospitals, transportation systems, educational institutions, etc. In other cases, private owners do best, for example in the production of goods and supplying services

7 An important argument for the class struggle was for Marx the belief that the "surplus value" of labour was "expropriated" by the employers. Obviously, it is shared between workers (who get the lion's share) and employers (who appear to get more because fewer share their share). This has stimulated demand and supply and benefited all parties, whereas the Marxian class struggle (to eliminate entrepreneurs and private owners of means of production) has impoverished everyone involved. There would be no market for most products if employers took all the profits, as too few would have money to buy anything except life necessities and thus make production of most goods profitable.

for profit, and so on. There are ways to regulate equitably the distribution of wealth and prevent the exploitation of workers other than by a change of ownership of the means of production. State ownership of all such means is a recipe for failure, harmful to productivity and standards and the welfare of workers. This has been amply demonstrated in 20th century history.

Some private owners of means of production are able to dodge many economic control mechanisms. However regrettable, this has had a less harmful effect on economic life than the pervasive inefficiency (and corruption) prevailing where the state has owned all the means of production. If people can deal with this question by democratic means and with a view to what serves everyone (workers, employers and the state) best, ways can normally be found that lead to greater general welfare instead of inefficiency, exploitation, servitude and great inequality.

"Greedy pigs!"

One thing should be emphasised about developed, so-called capitalist countries, where most of the means of production are in private hands: naked greed for monetary gain (the economic profit motive as the highest principle for personal and social conduct) is not the most prominent characteristic of most of the inhabitants in these societies. There are greedy people in these societies as in any other society (although it would not be strange if this is less the case in rich developed than in poor developing countries where the struggle for survival is fiercer); but most people have values above purely material ones. Some people will of course measure their success primarily in monetary terms: such people are found in all communities at all times. The "spirit of capitalism" is universal, and perhaps this also is most noticeable among people in poor countries.

A much more salient feature than greed in the life of people in developed "capitalist" countries is the fact that people have and use all chances to make the most of their talents and aptitudes. They usually want to pursue careers that give them feelings of personal satisfaction. They want work that will enrich their lives in terms other than purely material ones - in spite of exceptions: there are those who will never be satisfied, as well as unfortunate people not able to do what they would most like to do for a living. However, the "exceptions to the rule" are fewer in developed countries than in any other part of the world, and the exceptions grow fewer with the level of development, in spite of recurrent periods of unemployment and labour problems that limit choice.

People born and bred in developed "capitalist" countries rarely choose their careers only with an eye to where the money is. The strongest motive in the choice of a career is, for the vast majority, to be able to do what they find most interesting and can do best. However, within the range of possibilities offered, after these primary requirements are fulfilled, most people would opt for the best paid job obtainable in their chosen field. On the other hand, those who cannot get jobs they like may well regard the salary as the highest motivation for doing their job. For the unemployed too, money will loom high on their scale of priorities.

Doubtless there are many people in all developed countries who go for the money in the first place, but it is rather seldom one hears this argument for choosing a career. Most people in these countries will not give the profit motive as the basis of their choice of work. On the other hand, the pursuit of monetary gain is certainly a strong element in organisational activities, of productive enterprises, trade unions, etc. No doubt people want their businesses to succeed, and they want to be paid fairly and preferably well. But that is not the whole story.

So-called capitalism is a social, economic and political "system" where capital is largely in the hands of people who can manage capital well and where market forces set most of the economic rules, but not without many restrictions and control mechanisms. In developed countries, private owners try to increase their capital through capable management and hard work.

There is no reason why the state cannot or should not take part in normal competition in economic life and establish and run enterprises (without giving itself unfair advantages). If it can do this better than private people, the state is a fully legitimate competitor in development activities. But if the state fails to produce to acceptable standards (quantitatively and qualitatively and at affordable prices), it will be outdone by other, "free" competitors, and in that case it ought to hand over its "means of production" to people capable of using them better. However, if private owners of means of production misuse them and manipulate the market so as to exploit both workers and ordinary customers, the state may be a valid alternative producer for the open and free market.

Entrepreneurs may love money, but probably most of all they love to do what they are doing, or they like to try out new things. They normally have an innovative and adventurous spirit and are willing to take risks. This is an important aspect and element in the drive towards progress. Greed or the profit motive is not the only (perhaps not even the primary) force that keeps capitalist societies going, although the hunger for material things is increasing as earlier social and cultural values (that helped progress) are crumbling. Capital accumulation is only one aspect of capitalist societies, and perhaps not even the most important one. Human freedom to live the life of one's choice and human dignity are probably the features people there value most. Even competition is there more of a competition with oneself - to use one's potential to the full, or in meaningful competitive co-operation *with* others, rather than against others. This is very different from the competitive spirit of succeeding at the expense of others - by getting the next person down, which is more common in countries where only a few succeed in reaching financial security and reasonable comfort.

The pen is (sometimes) mightier than the sword

In earlier centuries, rich communities were often raided by poorer communities as a means of redistributing wealth. In the last couple of centuries, ideologies advocating implacable class struggles have served a similar purpose. In both cases, such means of redistribution have left poverty in their wake, even for the "raiders" - after a short spell of enjoying their booty: it is not a basis for permanent prosperity.

As violent conflicts may become rather outmoded and inefficient means of redistributing wealth, ideologically inspired conflicts may perhaps again increase, unless nations develop to a level where they are able to resolve their differences (and especially their economic ones) by other, peaceful political and diplomatic means. Economic adjustment and fair distribution of wealth among the nations of the world may be one of the most effective means of avoiding violent conflict and war and establishing lasting peaceful international relations.[8]

Whereas violent raids on rich communities had the simple aim of plunder, ideological struggles promise not only fair distribution of wealth but also greater development and welfare. This is, however, a delusion: no ideology has ever contributed anything to economic development. Ideologies may be useful for other purposes, but development does not follow in their wake. The most recent world-wide ideological craze, Marxism, made class hatred and armed struggle respectable means in the pursuit of development and welfare for all. In reality, it only made the way harder for a lot of people.

---

8 This idea was the reason why the United Nations established some of its specialised agencies. The fact that they have not worked as expected is no good reason for not trying to do better.

2. Development is not a moral or ethical issue

Candy for chums?

As we shall see in later chapters, there are aspects of behaviour (discipline, a willingness to follow instructions, punctuality, honesty, predictability) that are (at least partly) ethical and which do have an impact on development. On the other hand, it is difficult to identify a set of moral rules, or an ethical system as such, that might be said to have had any decisive impact on the development process.[9]

The point is raised here because of the prominence some (particularly earlier) sociologists have given to claims for a "Protestant ethic" and for "bourgeois values" in relation to development; and also in order to relate questions of human rights and "values" to development.

Human "rights", such as democracy and other freedoms, are strongly stressed in all developed societies, and these issues increase in importance with the level of development. This is of course very good. But the question needs also to be put into perspective, and then we find that these values have never been a cause of economic development. In fact, they can hardly even be said to have been consequences of development. On the contrary, "modern" human freedoms and values grow parallel with economic development, but because the time "fit" is not perfect, the one preceding the other may appear as its cause or precondition.[10] As we shall see, human "rights" (such as democracy) and

---

9 That some ethical systems with a religious base promote certain aspects of development (discipline, hard work, co-operation, etc.) shall not be denied. However, development has taken off in societies (the West, the Confucian sphere, Israel) that had this moral and religious base long before modern development started. Therefore, it is clear that development did not start on this base alone.

10 It is not difficult to understand this time-lag between development and democracy. In pre-democratic societies, members of a "ruling class"

economic development have the same causes, and it is therefore in vain to promote one of them (for example human rights or democracy) in the hope that the other (economic development) will automatically follow. One should of course fight for human rights for humane reasons, and some such rights can of course be respected without development; however, multi-party democracy does not function in underdeveloped countries in the same way as it does in developed ones. The foundations of democracy and of modern development are laid at the same time and have the same causes. They are true and genuine bedfellows. Although development does not go far without democracy and democracy does not function well without development, the one is not cause or consequence of the other: they both have the same cause.

Lutherics and Calvinacs[11]

Since modern development first occurred in Protestant countries, it has been speculated that there may be something in the Protestant ethic that promotes development. It is, however, difficult to discover or "prove"

---

hold power, and when a country develops, they will often try to steer development to their advantage. This may hold up democratic developments for some time. But as people find means of organising themselves, they will also be able to gain control of institutions of power, and democracy will come into operation. Democracy may appear to be a result of economic development due to this time-difference. Many in developing countries therefore seem to expect economic development to follow automatically upon the introduction of democratic institutions, and "donors" seem even more certain of this connection; but this is a fallacy.

11 In many cases references are made in this book to culture areas by using religious terms. This may give undue prominence to the religious aspect of some cultures, but I do not know more adequate terms. The "Lutherans" and "Calvinists" referred to may denote no more than people born and bred in a culture area dominated in the religious (but not only the religious)

that there is any such ethical impulse in the direction of modern development in Protestantism (at least in its original form, that is, as it found expression in the centuries before the Industrial Revolution - the only period that is of significance in this context). There are of course plenty of exhortations to co-operation and hard work from the Reformation onwards, but this is hardly an innovation of Protestantism. This is an aspect of Christian teaching generally, and it is found in non-Christian religions and cultures as well. At a more recent stage in history, socialist ethics has stressed the importance of and obligation to hard work and discipline, etc., perhaps even more so than Protestantism, but this did not make it possible for socialist countries to develop to the same level as Protestant countries (e.g., socialism did not drag Protestant East Germany out of an underdeveloped past - rather the contrary: East Germany would have done much better without socialism).

Protestantism did not primarily come with a new ethic in relation to work.[12] It was something else than the Protestant ethic that made it possible for Protestant countries to be the first to develop in a modern sense. Innovations in fields that were not primarily religious had, however, a strong and lasting influence on the development of Protestant countries.

In relation to the question of a possible link between the Protestant ethic and development, it has been suggested by several students of the problem (and especially by Max Weber and social scientists following in his footsteps) that Protestants (mostly strict Calvinists) who believed firmly in divine predestination (that is, that God had "predestined" or chosen some people to be saved and enter heaven and destined others to eternal damnation in hell) were eager to find signs of God's favour and "election" of them to eternal life and bliss; and this desire urged

field by Lutheran or Calvinist ideas (hence my unorthodox terms for them). This had, however, consequences also for non-religious aspects of life.

12 An interesting introduction to this and related questions is still R. H. Tawney's classic study, *Religion and the Rise of Capitalism*.

them to be successful, as this was thought to indicate God's blessing and thus their election to eternal life in heaven. While striving to be successful, people would of necessity display characteristics beneficial for development: hard work, thrift, discipline, foresight, investment for further and increased production, the pursuit of education and excellence in all fields. Although beneficial for development, the motivation for these exertions was religious: the desire to save one's soul. Thus, it was argued, religious goals created an ethical orientation that led to development; belief shaped personalities that could bring development about; development was the outcome of moral pursuits (on religious grounds) that had unexpected economic consequences - unexpected and unsought by the whole of society.

This line of arguing has intrigued many minds ever since Weber gave shape to these ideas (he gave clear and scientific form to these thoughts, but most of them were in fact not new by the time he wrote his famous book, *The Protestant Ethic and the Spirit of Capitalism*; nobody had done this so well and convincingly as he did).

Halfway through this book, Weber had to explain the success of Protestants (especially German Lutheran Pietists) who rejected the belief in the eternal and unchangeable election ("predestination") by God of some for salvation (heaven) and others for perdition (hell). For this he had to find another explanation than for the first group (the strict Calvinists). He observed that both these groups of Protestants worked hard in the "calling" (work) they thought God had given them, at the same time as they rejected "the world" and practised a kind of secular ("innerworldly") asceticism. Some (the Calvinists) did it in order to find proof of God's favour and blessing through success, others (the Lutherans) more in gratitude for blessings received and as a witness to non-believers of what God does to those who believe.[13]

---

13 Martin Luther (1483-1546) and John Calvin (1509-1564) agreed on essentials, but they also had their differences. Both were immensely

Both had "otherworldly" aspirations and values. Success was an important objective for both groups, but for different reasons. Since the pursuit of material success led to hard work, etc. (necessary preconditions for development), the Protestant ethic had paved the way for modern development: thus the argument ran.[14]

However, attitudes and beliefs that in this context were presented as specifically Protestant were not new at the time of the Protestant Reformation (let alone the Industrial Revolution). They were in fact formulated much earlier. The Old Testament expresses the view that success is a sign of God's favour,[15] and still it did not lead to modern economic development. All through the Middle Ages, the duty to work hard (also "in the world", such as in agriculture) and to be frugal, etc., were points stressed by many monastic orders, but this did not lead to any development that is in any way comparable to what took place during and after the Industrial Revolution.

Further afield, Confucian moral teaching and beliefs gave rise to a hard-working and "systematic" people, but China did not for that reason develop into a modern society. However, this "ethic" formed a firm foundation that later development efforts could build on. The ethic of hard work and strict discipline laid a partial basis for modern society, but it was and is not a *sufficient* cause of development, neither can it satisfactorily explain why and how modern development started or can start.

---

prolific writers. Most durable influence among Lutherans have Luther's *Small Catechism* and *Large Catechism* had (together with the *Augsburg Confession* written by Luther's friend and colleague, Philip Melanchton). Calvin is best remembered for his *Institutes of/Instruction in the Christian Religion.*

14 On modern responses to Weber's arguments, see e.g. S. N. Eisenstadt (ed.), *The Protestant Ethic and Modernisation.*

15 See for example Leviticus, chapter 26, and Deuteronomy, chapter 28. Cf. also the arguments of "the friends" in the Book of Job.

Early modern development did not involve only strict Lutherans and Calvinists, not any more than development in Japan and other east Asian countries in the Confucian culture area involves only adherents to strict Confucian principles. To answer the question why modern development started in Protestant countries, we shall have to look further than to the Protestant ethic; and development in east Asia must be explained by something more (or else) than the teachings of Confucius. This question will be further discussed in later chapters.

Anyone can be a prig

A certain lifestyle gradually evolved in countries that were the first to develop, and this lifestyle has (with modifications) spread to other developed countries. At least on the surface, it stresses "appearances" - that is, conformity to a certain (not well defined) moral code, good form, decency, refined manners, etc.[16] This lifestyle developed perhaps as a conscious attempt by the newly rich and their imitators to live like people of the "higher classes". Those who accept and live by these standards are very conscious of other people's views and opinions of them. This has been called the bourgeois lifestyle, reflecting a bourgeois ethic or bourgeois values - or perhaps just bourgeois success. (The bourgeoisie consisted of those who had become rich through trade and industry - by means of having "done" something and not only inherited wealth and social position, at least not in the "first generation". "Professional" people are also normally counted among the "bourgeois".)

It has been argued that the bourgeois lifestyle and bourgeois values are the result and expression of certain moral developments that some see as a necessary condition or accompaniment of modern development. Others think that they enslave the human mind and limit human

16 In developed countries, books on etiquette and "good manners" sell in great numbers. People love to enslave themselves to "proper form" (but many more before the upheavals of 1968 than after).

progress and freedom, and that it is only an aspect of the process of class formation. It should, however, be obvious that this lifestyle or ethic did not start modern economic development but was rather a result of it. It requires, in the first place, some degree of affluence to adopt a bourgeois lifestyle. Countries can start to develop long before people there can afford to adopt a "bourgeois" form of life. On the other hand, it is worth noting that the trend to adopt such a "finer" lifestyle soon spread world-wide in the wake of development, even to socialist countries, and it is even spreading in countries that do not develop.

Perhaps surprisingly, it is people who live in countries that developed long ago that have been best able to discard most of the superficial (and ridiculous) "bourgeois" symbols of affluence or success.

Bourgeois values and a bourgeois lifestyle may be superficial and ridiculous, binding people to other people's opinion of them, thus limiting their freedom. Still, this is primarily an external expression of an attitude and turn of mind that is accidental to development, in itself neither promoting nor delaying development.[17] Some people find it liberating to discard them; others feel free when they can afford to adopt these external forms, valuing them as symbols of liberation from grinding poverty and the necessity to live at what appears to them to be below the level of the bourgeoisie (the reasonably successful "middle class"). It was an aberration of some "progressive" intellectuals (they themselves as ridiculous as the bourgeoisie) to attach such great importance to this largely external phenomenon in relation to development.[18] This has served to befog the real issues rather than to clarify them.

---

17 People in developed countries seem to have lost the moral and ideological bases of conduct that prevailed in former times, but bourgeois forms persist in many circles. Such a shell without content can help keep up appearances of modernity, while in reality these societies (and their advanced status) may be undermined in the process.

18 Many members of the bourgeoisie have no other ethical values than "good form" ("appearances"), and the emptiness of their lives may of course

Who's human?

Developed countries have of late become very concerned about violations of human rights in developing countries. Aid for development may be made conditional on an improvement in the "human rights record" of recipients, especially concerning rights to free political and religious activities, free speech and free trade. These freedoms may be presented as such an essential part of development that aid without them is thought (or at least said) to serve no useful purpose. Of course, one can only support efforts at promoting and protecting human rights; but what is the real relationship between human rights and development?

Developed countries had, during the initial stages of their development, little respect for human values and human rights. The exploitation of labour (including child labour), slavery, colonialism, destruction of local cultures and industries in less developed countries, depletion of natural resources in colonies and elsewhere, trade wars, etc., were part of early development in what are today the most advanced countries. Only when this stage was passed and prosperity seemed secure could more attention be paid to human rights. Such an initial "anarchic" period is now denied developing countries.

Many "technical" aspects of human rights, such as insisting on worker protection, strict safety precautions, limited working hours, minimum wages, certain standards of machinery and products, etc., may have made it much harder for underdeveloped countries to develop than it was for the nations that have now reached an advanced stage of development. This has of course not escaped leaders in developing countries, and they feel that outside interference of this kind may be self-righteous and unjustified - and with at least some justification.

---

have a negative, destructive influence on their lives and their surroundings (family, etc.). That is, however, not a valid argument for characterising this special lifestyle as anti-developmental. Socialist, capitalist, escapist and "otherworldly" lifestyles may have equally "anti-developmental" tendencies.

However, this does of course not mean that such "demands" should be abandoned. Human rights have values *in themselves*, not because they promote development.

Demands of respect for human rights as a condition for development assistance usually rest on the assumption that Western-style multi-party democracy is a necessary precondition for development.[19] This is not supported by historical facts. Development and democracy are linked, but only in the sense that they are caused by the same factors and not so that one causes the other.

Without in any way criticising those who fight for human rights, it should be clearly stated that such values and rights did not play any role in the process of development when this came under way in the West. Many specific "rights" of this nature, for example a check on child exploitation, were rather the result of this process, not the cause, not even part of the cause.

Neither religious nor humanitarian ethics can be said to have caused the take-off into modern development. Ethical questions raised by both religious and humanitarian organisations after the fact should not confuse the matter at issue here, which is an investigation of the causes of modern development.

3. Development is not primarily a question of economics

Is the fault in the map or in the landscape?

Economic theories in relation to development have had a seductive allure for people who have been involved in development. A number

19 Some donor countries want to reduce their development aid and need some morally acceptable pretext for doing so. An outcry about human rights violations (although such violations were well known also previously) may serve their purpose well: they save money while retaining their air of benevolence and moral superiority.

of theories put forward have had the "luck" to be tried out with costly experiments in the field, wasting donor money and bringing chaos and disruption to recipient countries. One theory after another has been abandoned when found not to work, and new theories (or old ones with a facelift) are in line for experimentation. Fashionable economic development theories have failed to accelerate development. In fact, it seems that economic policies and practices of governments only superficially or marginally influence the process of development. Development has other causes.

The economic theories at the time of the Industrial Revolution and for quite some time after attempted to explain what was happening or had happened, and they were often formulated as general economic laws. But they did not in any case help to start or stimulate development. These theories and explanations did not influence the development process at the time; nor have they helped development to take off in other areas of the world.

Economic theories are supposed to have predictive value. They point to ways of speeding up development or of getting out of economic crises. Development economics[20] in particular tries to find and indicate ways for underdeveloped countries to develop.[21] None of the theories and prescriptions that have been tried have worked to the benefit of the poorest countries.

---

20 Development economics - an obscure and neglected branch of economics till the end of World War II - has become the queen of economics in the wake of world-wide efforts at development. Its dominant position in the field may, however, be challenged, considering its inability to improve the "quality of life" or the "standard of living".

21 Those who do not want to read very much about the topic could do with Walter Elkan, *An Introduction to Development Economics*, where the problems of development were already outlined. The enthusiasts could try to read Michael P Todaro, *Economic Development in the Third World.*

If and where rapid development has taken place, this has always been due to forces and factors outside the influence of economists. The best they can do is to try and explain what has already happened. They have not been very good at explaining development in *causal* terms that might help to meet and solve future crises or that have helped underdeveloped countries to develop.

No economic theory or economic system can bring about development. Modern development depends in every case on the state of the work force (including management), and if this work force is ready for development, development will take place. The most that economic theories and practices or systems can do is to some extent to facilitate and speed up or, on the other hand, to put obstacles in the way of and retard development. However, they cannot significantly influence the *fact* of development - whether it comes under way or not.

Let us look at some of the economic factors that have, incorrectly or only partly correctly, been considered necessary for development to take place.

"Capital will cap it all"

Capital is said to be needed for development to take place, and such capital must be invested for productive purposes and not used primarily for the acquisition of status symbols or non-productive possessions.

Two things should be pointed out in this connection: (1) When Europe started on the road to development, Europe was relatively poor, and (2) the parts of Europe that developed fastest were much poorer than some other parts of Europe that did not undergo the same development process. Portugal and Spain, for example, accumulated more wealth from their overseas possessions than England before the Industrial Revolution.

Capital is of course necessary for development, but it is not as essential in huge amounts as is sometimes thought; and the size of a nation's capital is not proportional to its level or pace of or potential for development. Rich countries may be poor at development. It is enough to consider the development of some oil-rich countries today to realise this.

Although capital has to be invested in order to be productive, investment itself does not promote development. Countries may build factories and dams and obtain agricultural and other machinery and still not develop. They may even become poorer in the process. Without a work force of the appropriate kind, no amount of capital or investment can bring about development. Significantly, development aid has not done more than "oil money" to start or speed up the process of development in underdeveloped countries not yet ready to "take off".

People and commodities

It has been suggested that exploitation helped Europe to develop. But while some areas of Europe developed, Spain and Portugal exploited many parts of the world much more than the countries where development did take place; and during the period of their greatest affluence, Spain and Portugal did not develop. Their wealth may even have plunged these countries further into underdevelopment. Furthermore, north-western Europe had been exploited by the richer south (especially Italy, with the headquarters of the Pope) till the very eve of the acceleration at the beginning of modern times (c. 1500); and resources were squandered on wars and the pleasures of kings and consorts and nobles long after.

At a later stage - after the first phase of development was a fact, developed countries may have exploited other countries more than the less developed countries of Europe did; but this does not explain development or underdevelopment. When north-western Europe had reached a certain level of development, they were more *able* to do what others tried just as hard to do (e.g., to exploit others) but with less success. The wish to exploit others was not less in less developed countries. Cruelty to slaves was not less in less successful slave trading nations than in those that succeeded in taking the lead in this trade. The thirst for colonies was not less among the less successful. International trade at the expense of others was the aim and aspiration as much among poor as among rich nations. However, those who won in the competition in all these areas were those who were most *capable* and successful also in other economic fields, that is, in development. It did not depend on their wish or mentality or national character but upon the *capacities* that had matured *before* they developed and the skills they perfected as they were developing.

New patches on old clothing?

As development is not and cannot be a part process (for instance, almost exclusively in the area of trade, or industry, or the exploitation of foreign lands, or agriculture, or urban or rural development), success in any and every area of development depends on the state of the work force, the mass of workers (including leaders, managers, entrepreneurs, and so on, but not depending on them: development is not an elite phenomenon). Where the work force is in good shape, suitable leaders will always be found. Leaders may be present without a work force qualified to promote development, but without a suitable work force, they alone cannot bring about development. "Natural" leaders will usually do a better job than those who attain leadership due not to talent but to class, family connections or wealth.

A place of one's own

Land "reform" (land distribution benefiting productivity) has been said to be a prerequisite for development where land is in the hands of people who cannot (or do not want to) make the most productive use of it. Of course, it is important for agriculture that land is used by people who can and want to cultivate it properly.

The "enclosure movement" (turning communally used grazing grounds into more productive "enclosed" land) in England at approximately the time of the early Industrial Revolution (or preceding it) is often mentioned as an example of a process that is thought to have led to more efficient development of agriculture (and the Industrial Revolution was mainly agricultural before industry became the more prominent or conspicuous feature of it). But this process (combined with modern forms of land use and production methods) has been replicated elsewhere and not led to development. Cause and effect, and phenomena occurring simultaneously, are easily confused in interpretations of the development process.

Almost any imaginable form of land ownership, use and distribution pattern has been attempted in developing countries, and it has made practically no difference to the rate or state of development. Obviously this is not the key to development.

Development in the agricultural sector as in any other area depends on the state of the work force, how the peasants or farmers are able to use the land, and not on the amount or even on the quality of the land they own or cultivate. Compare, for example, Israeli farmers who made the desert bloom, and Marxist ideologists who turned fertile areas into deserts.

In the sweat of thy brow

Hard work has been thought to be a key to development.

Reasonably hard work is of course needed for any enterprise to succeed, but hard work alone does not bring about development. Any observer will be able to find many hard workers in developing countries, but this has not led their countries out of a state of underdevelopment. On the other hand, it can be seriously doubted whether workers in developed countries (at least in the West) are so very hard-working.

However, one thing seems clear: the efficiency of work performed in developed countries is much greater than in developing countries, where long hours may give poor results in both quantitative and qualitative terms. Generally speaking, the quality of work, the way it is carried out, and the productivity of workers in all fields vary fundamentally between workers in developed and developing countries.

We come back to the same point as mentioned above: Development depends on the state and quality of the workforce. It is the shaping of this workforce that is the very foundation in getting development started, and the continued quality of this workforce is the very essence of development.

How do workers become efficient and productive? That is the crucial question in development. We shall discuss it from chapter 5 onwards.

4. Development does not depend on political power

Political parties and leaders in the developing world may have different aims, but practically all pay at least lip service to the ideal of modern development, and some mean it. But in spite of strenuous efforts, few have been able to score significant successes in this field.

Leading politicians may represent (others only use) a party supporting the policies of the government. Where the party plays the role of a vanguard in development, it faces the same problems as any elite group that tries to develop a country: it will not succeed for the simple reason that development is neither an elite nor a political phenomenon. Wherever development has taken off, it has done so because it has (so gradually that it is almost unnoticeable) become a "mass movement", having given shape to the mentality and the skills of the majority of the people.

Where political power is used to prepare the broad masses of the population for development in the correct and proper way (see chapters 5-9), political power can pave the way for development; but the use of power alone to force people to develop has always led to chaos, inefficiency and continued underdevelopment.

Some politicians are so impatient for progress (leaving aside those whose ambitions are purely personal power and wealth) that they seize power and rule on their own authority (usually supported by interest groups that receive certain benefits from such rule, for instance business people or the military). Military coups for the professed purpose of speeding up development have proliferated in the developing world. However, development is not among the blessings resulting from coups, take-overs, revolutions or authoritarian rule; but if people are "ready", almost any system can to some extent "work".

When a country (that is, its people) is ready for development, it will find the leaders it needs. Attempts at forcing the pace of development from above always fail. Politics and politicians are the fruits and products of circumstances prevailing in a country. Changes of government mainly through the use of force (coups, revolutions), deceit (election fraud) or corrupt dealings (bribery) only reflect the unpreparedness of these countries for development.

When the people of a country are ready to develop, politics will (gradually and eventually) take its shape from this readiness and become part of the development process. Politicians who do not favour this state of affairs (that development proceeds almost independently of them) will not be able to stop the process for long.

5. Not all kinds of education benefit development

Some kinds of education produce mainly grey hair

Many developing countries have put their trust in modern education. But in spite of the importance of education for development, it is not an automatic process that all education will necessarily lead to development. It depends on whether it is mass or mainly elite education, and on whether it is general education or mainly skills training, and on others things besides, as we shall see.

The view has been expressed that it makes a great difference to the development of a country if a section of the people there becomes literate. It is true that some mental activity is stimulated by the ability to read and write, but it does not always direct the mind in the direction of modern development. This can be seen in many countries with an old script and literature and where quite a number of people can read and write. More often than not, literate groups in such countries become interested in gaining and preserving privileges for themselves and will thus constitute conservative obstacles to development, as happened in China (Confucian schools), India (Sanskrit schools), Ethiopia (Geez church schools), Muslim countries (Koran schools using classical Arabic), Europe (when Latin was the language of education), etc. Something else is needed before literacy can become a tool for development.

It has been suggested that it was not until the invention of the printing press and the possibility of mass literacy that reading and writing skills became an important factor in development. It is of course true that printing has facilitated the transmission of knowledge and training in skills necessary for development; but it is not correct that popular literacy and the widespread habit of reading in themselves lead to rapid economic development. For one thing, modern development did not automatically and immediately result after the invention of modern printing (in the 15th century) and the mass circulation of books (especially from the 16th century onwards); and development did not progress evenly in all countries where books were printed and widely circulated and read, which should be the case if mass literacy and general access to books automatically lead to development. In some parts of the world where books are now being printed in large numbers and widely read, economic development seems even to be slowing down, so that they are becoming poorer than they were before "modern times" came upon them.

Reading skills and book production and distribution alone do not lead to development.

Pyramids built on sand

Developing countries have invested large sums in the education of their people, especially in the technical training of the smartest lot. There are today more engineers and other technical personnel and people generally with specialised skills in developing countries than these countries can make proper use of. Still, development has not been speeded up or taken off for this reason.

Technical education or skills training does not necessarily lead to development and may in some cases slow down the development process.

The reason for this is that the mass of the population in a country must be equipped for development if development is to take off. Training in skills is not enough. Developing countries have, on the whole, too many idle, useless, overqualified people. A country has in fact to be developed before it can make proper use of them.

This said, it should be stressed that the appropriate kind of education and training is absolutely essential in the development process. We shall come back to this crucial point later.

6. Not all kinds of rationality benefit development

Not all brains and not all brawn

It has been observed that people in developed countries tend to become increasingly rational and scientific in their thinking as well as in their work, that is, more efficient and productive. However, this is an ongoing process that is both cause and consequence of development.

Not very much new science was involved in the Industrial Revolution. Many of the scientific inventions used then had been made earlier and partly far away from this revolution; but before this event, people had not been able to make proper or full use of them for purposes of development. It was the emergence of people who knew what to do with already existing technology, plus a few new fairly simple inventions, that helped to give birth to the first modern developed nations.

Too great emphasis placed on intellectual rationalism and logic, and elitism generally, can become an obstacle to development.[22] Philosophers and social scientists in Europe who have stressed logical thinking and behaviour as a sign of modernisation have not as a rule come from the economically and technically most advanced countries. Some of them have ridiculed the British for being poor logicians and rather unimaginative, and for valuing "common sense" too highly; but it was probably their practical common sense that made it possible for the British to take the lead in early modern development. However, common sense alone is not a sufficient precondition for development, as seen from the fact that Britain now seems to be lagging behind some other nations in the development race - and besides, they probably had the same common sense even before they developed along modern lines. On the other hand, some late-comers to development in Europe are catching up because popular education and socialisation practices beneficial for modern development are replacing their former tradition-bound conservatism or (class-ridden) elitism.

There is a certain kind of rationality that has a positive influence on development, as pointed out by, for instance, Max Weber. This is the ability to work systematically towards an end and thus to achieve one's goal quickly and efficiently. This is perceived as a practical sense, an

---

22 Development can be held back by a very elitist educational system, which may have been the case in a few European countries. Some of the most developed countries may, on the other hand, have educational systems for the masses of rather "average" quality, but they are systems of *general* education, and that has made all the difference.

ability to get things done, rather than as purely theoretical or "logical" rationality. This peculiar practical sense is characteristic of people in developed societies and is in short supply in less developed ones. We shall later see how this sense or ability is developed.

Bureaucratic blunders

A modern bureaucracy has been seen as a precondition for development and as an example of a rational way of organising a country for development. But a bureaucracy that really benefits development can only grow up as a result of development, or parallel with it. The attempts of developing countries to speed up development through the creation of (usually overstaffed and inefficient) bureaucracies have evidently failed. As they exist today, these bureaucracies are, more often than not, serious obstacles to a country's development, and they also easily turn into centres serving only "class interests", full of corrupt practices.

The Main Chance for Number One

Individualism has also been seen as an advantage for development and as an expression of rationality. However, individualists can proliferate also in underdeveloped countries, although they may find the going tough. What characterises modern societies is rather greater freedom of choice for the individual, and thus individualistic behaviour may become easier to express and be more acceptable than in developing countries, where choices are more restricted and brakes on individualistic behaviour more numerous and stronger. Where choices are free, individual talents can be better used to the benefit of the country.

Individualism in developed countries is so visible because they have developed, but national development has not been brought about by individualism. After development has advanced rather far, full and proper use can be made of all individual talents, and individualism may as a result flourish more freely.

This topsy-turvy world

No country can develop by standing things on their head and by trying to turn results or consequences into causes. That is like the magic practice of attempting to create rain by making the sound of falling rain or by the sprinkling of a few drops of water. That only wastes precious water.

Imitation of the external structures of developed countries does not create development, but it wastes a lot of resources.

The kind of rationality that does stimulate development, and how it is acquired and applied, will be discussed later.

7. Development does not depend on intelligence or natural gifts or talents

What no one expected

When development did occur in the West, it took everyone by surprise, and first of all the Westerners themselves: this development was never planned or thought possible. People could hardly believe their eyes when rapid development took place at such a breathtaking pace. But when modern development was a reality, people began to seek for explanations of this unusual and unprecedented phenomenon.

"I must have deserved it"

One explanation put forward was that Westerners were more gifted or of a better moral fibre than other people, which is certainly not correct - and irrelevant even if it were.

There has never been any "proof" that people in developed countries have any gifts superior to any other people. In fact, modern research has shown that intelligence and other gifts seem to be very nearly equally distributed among any large groups of people. That is certainly true in the case of large nations.

Furthermore, and more to the point: research has shown that people use only a very small part of their intelligence and other natural gifts in daily life, including what goes into activities related to development. Most of the studies relevant to this specific problem have been carried out in developed countries, but the situation is hardly different in developing countries.

But we need geniuses, don't we?

Imaginative or creative intelligence is not particularly important for development, as routine tasks rather than creativity are characteristic of very many development processes. Actually, many less developed nations (and developed ones before they developed) may have produced greater artists and inventors and other geniuses than highly developed countries. And these geniuses were more conspicuous because they were more useful.

Geniuses are in greater "demand" in less developed than in highly developed societies because the latter can achieve their goals by other means. Developed countries can more efficiently and surely reach further development goals by systematic research than those relying on the lucky strike of a genius.

The seeming "preponderance" of geniuses in some less developed societies during certain periods is hardly due to an uneven distribution of such talents but to the fact that geniuses are more needed there than in developed countries. Practically all technical and other development problems arising can be, and are, solved in developed countries by the persistent efforts of gifted and dedicated scientists, workers and others, and no extraordinary genius is normally needed.[23] Because such dedicated, systematic search for solutions is rarer in developing countries, geniuses are more needed and come more easily to the fore. They have

---

23 Cf. David Dickson, *Alternative Technology and the Politics of Technical Change.*

therefore perhaps also greater opportunities to be noticed and to "sell" their unusual skills.

The race issue again

One of the more silly attempts at explaining modern development was and is to ascribe superior innate gifts to certain races. Besides being scientifically disproved, this also clearly goes against common sense. Very unequal development among, for instance, different groups of Semitic peoples shows how totally misguided such speculation about racial intelligence and talents is.

All races are equally gifted by nature. Every nation or race has the same capacity for development under the right conditions, conditions that can be created by people themselves anywhere in the world.

8. Development is not an ecological issue

As modern development first took off, and is still at the highest level, in temperate or cold areas of the world, and as development has been slowest in tropical areas, there has also been speculation that climate is a decisive factor for modern development to occur.[24]

Early human progress prior to modern development was made primarily in hotter climates. These seem therefore to have been the most favourable for progress, areas that are now largely underdeveloped (Egypt, Mesopotamia, Phoenicia, North Africa, parts of India and China and other areas).

Although tougher climates may have fostered some measure of frugality and forethought ("planning", e.g. to get through the winter), it may be easier to explain modern development in previously marginal areas by the very fact that they were in the periphery, far from

---

24 This may be reflected in the use of the terms North and South for developed and developing areas.

the centres of power and affluence, and that they were exploited by the centre. Their drive towards development could have resulted from, among other things, attempts at attaining equality with and greater independence from more "fortunate" countries.[25]

Although there might be certain factors serving to "predispose" some areas more than others for development, this certainly does not explain how all developed countries managed to develop. In no climate did development occur just for environmental reasons. If this had been the case, why did modern developed countries stay behind for so long (they were populated for millennia before they developed)? And why are not all countries with the same climate more or less equally developed?

The desire to develop is world-wide, but the ability to develop is strikingly different from region to region even under similar environmental conditions.

We shall come back to this problem when we discuss how modern development started and spread (chapters 5 and 6).

9. There are no laws of history necessitating development

Is development inevitable?

Some have tried to explain modern development as the result of immutable laws of historical or natural evolution.[26]

---

25 Some scholars have tried to explain the Protestant Reformation in purely economic terms: as an attempt to escape exploitation by Rome.

26 A development of Charles Darwin's scientific theories (concerning natural selection, the struggle for survival, and the survival of the fittest), in the form of "Social Darwinism", is the theoretical basis of such beliefs. Darwin himself drew such "social" and "cultural" conclusions from his scientific theories. They also fitted well into the Marxist concept of "progress". Christians had generally opposed Darwin's scientific theories,

Both socialists (primarily Karl Marx[27]) and capitalists (such as W. W. Rostow[28]) have put forward hypotheses of "laws" or "stages" of development that are thought to have universal validity. They are as easy to prove or disprove as the opposite theory (defended by, among others, Arnold Toynbee[29]), that history is cyclical (although Toynbee rejects this term to characterise his theory), with peaks and valleys along the way but with the same (or nearly the same) conditions occurring and vanishing again and again - progress and collapse alternating in eternal cycles.

There is no proof of such ideas, and they can never be verified or disproved. They are put forward on the basis of philosophical or ideological positions adopted for other reasons than scientific or historical evidence. They are not helpful in elucidating the process of development.

Under human control?

Modern development was and is not inevitable. It came about for reasons under human control. It started without being planned or calculated; but by studying and understanding what took and takes place in the process of development, situations leading to development can be replicated everywhere in the world. This is what we shall discuss in chapters 5 to 9.

---

but they often supported Social Darwinism, including the latent racism of this theory (for which they thought they had support in the story of Noah and his sons). Colonialism and Fascism were natural offshoots of Social Darwinism.

27 See especially *A Contribution to the Critique of Political Economy* and *Capital*, but also *The Communist Manifesto* (this last he wrote together with Friedrich Engels).

28 In *The Stages of Economic Growth: a non-Communist Manifesto.*

29 In *A Study of History.*

10. Development cannot be purely imitative

No tricks of the trade

In their desire to develop, many countries have looked to the West as a model in their development efforts. Japan is often cited as an example of a successful replication of Western development in a non-Western setting.

Much has been made of Japan's imitative skills. But so many others have failed in their attempts to develop in imitation of the West that it is obvious that imitation as such does not explain Japan's success. Borrowing technology from more advanced countries has undoubtedly speeded up the development process in Japan (why should they waste time re-inventing the wheel?); but they could never have successfully imitated or adapted borrowings from the West if they had not already themselves acquired the necessary preconditions for development.[30] They would almost certainly have reached the same level of development also with less imitation and fewer borrowings, although it would then have taken them more time. On the other hand, the realisation of Western success in developing (and the fact that no other part of the world had then developed) may have been a major contributing factor in Japan's decision to develop "along Western lines".

Most underdeveloped countries have failed to develop by imitating the West. Many would undoubtedly be glad to develop "by imitation" if they only could. But imitation alone will not do the trick.

Some eastern European countries developed by copying the economic, social and political model of the former Soviet Union. This development pattern was ideologically determined. Doubtless modern development would have taken place there too (as in Russia) with a

---

30 Russia (or the Soviet Union) also tried systematically to imitate and borrow Western technology but fell far behind Japan in their achievements. Most developing countries try unsuccessfully to imitate the West. Imitation cannot explain the *success* of Japan in doing what many others have tried.

different (non-socialist) orientation. This had already started before the communists took over. Most likely these countries would have developed at much greater speed and to much higher levels if they had not become socialist in the first place, although it might have taken them some more time to get under way.

To call formerly socialist countries "progressive" (usually as opposed to countries that had progressed much further) was an obvious misnomer. There may in fact be good reasons for calling them Less Progressive Countries. This applies to social, cultural and political development as well as to economic, scientific and technical development, in spite of some brilliant cultural and technical achievements.

On not losing one's soul

Development has taken place under different conditions, in various cultures and in all continents. A characteristic of *all* developed countries is that they have preserved the essence of their cultural and social identity, their own basic national character, and first of all their national languages. This touches on a fundamental question that we shall come back to in later chapters, with concrete examples.

11. Development does not depend on foreign aid

Wolves in sheep's clothing?

Development aid has, in spite of the best of intentions, in many cases been a waste of money. If that was all that could or needed to be said about it, not much harm would have been done. But foreign aid has also often retarded modern development and worked havoc in underdeveloped countries. One ought to be critical of its forms and uses if one wants to help poor and backward countries to develop. Global organisations do the most damage. However, bilateral aid and aid by or through non-governmental organisations (NGOs) can perhaps do some good (but not therefore always or necessarily promoting development), if aid policies and practices are "transparent" and above-board, and if accountability is stressed. In most cases, aid should also go directly to beneficiaries, i.e. the poor and needy, and not pass through state coffers in recipient countries. The control or monitoring of results must also be properly done. This is now rarely the case.

"Heads I win, tails you lose"

Foreign aid (including loans and favourable trade agreements) benefits mostly people who dominate and control a country's political and economic life. This dominant clique often uses its power and influence (increased by foreign aid) to oppress and exploit the general population to such an extent that colonial domination and exploitation appear mild and benevolent by comparison.

Political bribes

The only justification for much foreign aid as it is given today is that a donor country wants to be on good terms with the dominant class there so as to be able to have some influence over or "control" that country (and/or perhaps share in "the spoils" - such as profits from cheap raw materials - with those who exploit it at the local level). In order to camouflage one's intentions, much of the corrupting influence of aid is channelled through global development organisations.

Aid given with a truly humanitarian desire to help can in some cases be as corrupting as that given for overt political motives (political bribes in the form of aid). The "innocent" donors are either taken for a ride by the more sophisticated in both giving and receiving countries, or they are at a total loss about how to make development aid "work" as intended.

Aid that benefits only a few has a tendency to turn people in a country against the donor country. The poor in developing countries benefit much less than what was intended by the donors from development aid, and relative to those who benefit most, they seem clearly to become poorer and poorer the more aid a country receives.

Aid need not be subversive of development

There are of course ways to help poor people in poor countries if aid is properly "controlled". If one can be sure that aid is not misused and that it goes to those it is intended for, one can justify giving aid for at least the following purposes (although this is in fact not *development* aid strictly speaking except in one instance, namely aid for education):

(1) To help drought and famine-stricken countries to obtain food. However, one should keep in mind that such disasters are often created by misguided policies of governments, and that aid may contribute to hiding their misrule and prolonging their stay in power. Food aid may also discourage local initiatives for self-help through increased production in non-affected areas adjacent to famine-stricken regions.

(2) To help with serious and acute medical problems, and to set international health standards. However, many medical interventions from outside may also have done much harm (e.g. injections with non-sterile needles may have spread disease). Such damage is likely to be done again. One needs to know local cultures and conditions to minimise and perhaps avoid such harm.

(3) To assist countries in overcoming environmental problems that are becoming increasingly international in character.

(4) To stimulate universal education of the right kind. Modern education of one kind or another ought to reach the *whole* population so as to avoid elite and class formations of people who will mystify knowledge and monopolise power and the

> nation's wealth. Education must be of a kind that will overcome problems and practices that are obstacles to development and help people to develop their minds, attitudes and skills. This point is the most important of all, and the only one of the points mentioned here that relates directly to development, as it may contribute to laying a foundation for self-help.

Help should be given with the utmost care and in some cases perhaps some reluctance: it may well have harmful side-effects. And such help can be most effective and its harmful effects be least if it is properly monitored by people who must account to their governments or supporting bodies for how it is used. On the other hand, developing countries receiving aid should see to it that it is not primarily the interests of donors that are served when aid is given or received. And donors should see to it that agreed development objectives are achieved with the aid given.

Several bodies give aid: "private" charitable non-governmental organisations (NGOs), governments (bilaterally, directly from state coffer to state coffer, or indirectly through NGOs or international or global organisations), and international and global agencies. It seems that aid benefits development the less the bigger (and less transparent and manageable) an aid agency becomes.

NGOs are either religious or purely humanitarian. Religious bodies used to start schools and clinics in the "mission field" to teach converts (or potential converts) to read the Bible and other literature. Normally they opened elementary schools with religious instruction in the syllabus. Clinics were run to show Christian charity. This looked like a replication of what had happened in Europe prior to and laying the foundation for modern development. However, educating a small number of converts (church members) in underdeveloped countries is different from educating people in countries where the whole population was formally Christian. The "mission situation" made educated converts a minority, and when these got jobs, it opened opportunities for corruption for them that were not easy to resist. Mission-educated leaders formed elite groups that often monopolized power and wealth (after "independence" many others, not educated by churches or missions, joined the "club"). The result has not been development on the European model but rather class-formation, misrule and further under-development. What is needed in such countries is general education (in both senses), so that the educated cannot form exclusive exploiting cliques. Here development agencies with more money than the churches or mission bodies could make a tremendous contribution.

In recent decades, when development aid has become fashionable in the West, religious bodies have not built on their long experience; and in order not to seem to have a religious bias, non-religious development agencies have chosen to learn as little as possible from the experience of religious bodies. On the other hand: in order to appear modern, religious bodies have normally imitated the newcomers in the field, so that today there is little to distinguish the development work done by missions and non-religious bodies. The practice of religious NGOs to let their expatriate employees work for many years in one place made it possible for them to learn national languages, and sometimes they made efforts to understand local traditions and cultures. Their generally negative attitude to the latter made them poor guides in dealings with for example the economic problems of developing countries, but their insights in many other areas could have saved other NGOs from many mistakes. These opportunities were generally missed.

NGOs are most effective when they are relatively small and do not attract the greedy attention of local leaders. Emergency aid has often been effective. When an emergency is over, many NGOs turn into development agencies. They become part of the "development industry", and this may serve the interests of the employees as much as the interests of the poor in receiving countries. The long-term benefits of their activities vary, but many have potentials for becoming effective and useful agents of development if they build up experience and remain honest and stress "enabling" factors, especially education.

Governments mostly follow international development theories fashionable at any given time, although development theories and strategies frequently change. Results may be small,[31] and large funds are turned over to global organisations. If these fail, governments are not so open to blame. Global organisations (where donors and recipients of aid are equal partners) rarely report failures, as this might be interpreted as an "insult" of the "host countries". People who are concerned about results may find it difficult to work in such organisations, which therefore are often left with (in many cases well-educated) employees who are satisfied with following routines, the "mechanically faithful without attachment" or commitment. The resulting combination of indifference, incompetence and general negligence causes much unnecessary and preventable misery.

A big problem for global development agencies is the fact that donors and receiving governments have to agree on everything, including what to do and what to report. Thus, only (usually fictive) "successes" are reported, while the monitoring mechanisms do not function as intended, and accountability becomes an impossibility. More good results could perhaps be achieved if these agencies channelled their funds through small but efficient non-governmental organisations (NGOs). On the other hand, they could perhaps render some valuable service by facilitating the exchange of international experience through good research and the production of reliable reports, and by employing roving advisers who could bring useful knowledge to the attention of those who need it.[32]

---

31 They normally blame receiving countries for this, but in most cases the blame must be shared.

32 The United Nations was established to preserve world peace, and since economic inequalities between nations were seen as a potential cause of

Donor countries would probably achieve most if they gave more of their development aid through agencies (NGOs) that can reach the intended beneficiaries without being "robbed" by government officials or other "intermediaries". The agencies that can do something good with such aid are those that work in the areas mentioned above, and particularly those that have long-term objectives and stress enabling strategies (e.g. general education).

In government-to-government relations, advisers, experts and supervisors from developed countries could perhaps do useful work in developing countries. Each situation will have to determine the appropriateness of such arrangements. Foreign development agencies ought not to become big employers of local staff, which would turn these

---

future conflicts, specialised development(-oriented) agencies were added to remedy this. When Third World countries became the majority in the UN, its agencies and affiliated institutions became mechanisms for obtaining the "goodwill" (i.e. compliance - and dependency) of Third World leaders in matters related to international peace and order. About 90% of UN aid goes to this purpose, thus increasing the distance between rich and poor in poor countries, and the crumbs (c. 10%) that reach the poor and needy do not give them many lasting benefits. Criticism of the "inefficiency" of and harm done by such policies in relation to development and otherwise (as cogently done by, for example, Susan George) has no impact because the UN in this way in fact achieves what those who pull the strings (not its nominal leaders) want it to do. This is short-sighted and will weaken the UN also as peacekeeper when people in the Third World have had enough of realpolitik ("live and let die") posing as aid. UN agencies and affiliated institutions could best assist UN peace efforts in the long run (and also the long-term interests of rich as well as poor nations) by returning to their original aims and purposes. Economic differences are indeed a potential source of future conflicts. Besides, development is worth supporting for its own sake. But can a spanner in the works transform itself (or be transformed) into oil for the wheels of progress? Can the leopard (or leper) change his spots?

agencies into something more than just development agencies. When local staff is needed in foreign organisations, one could, where possible, use people already employed in their countries; these could be "on loan" to foreign development bodies for a time. Salaries and other benefits should be approximately the same as with their local employers, and they should have a guarantee that they can return to their former employment after a stint with a foreign development agency. Such "loan" arrangements should be for limited periods, so that these people do not lose contact with their previous employer, and so that people's opportunities are not reduced by their being taken out of their normal jobs for so long that they are "forgotten". Neither should they be able to settle so comfortably in the temporary job that they are reluctant to leave it and serve their own organisations - that would be unjustifiable "brain drain". In such ways, one could avoid that development agencies become disruptive elements in developing countries.

*

Tabula rasa

After this catalogue of false starts and misconceptions, we are ready to try to find out what development really is, how and why it started and spread and continues to spread, and what lessons we can learn from past processes (including errors), what principles we can deduce, what guidance we can find for countries in the process of developing or with the desire and determination to develop.

CHAPTER 4

DEVELOPED AREAS

In this chapter we shall mention the countries that are commonly classified as developed and briefly discuss features that have earned them this rank.

We were able to write chapter 2 before this one because we there kept in mind countries that everyone accepts as either highly developed or as clearly underdeveloped, without paying attention to doubtful border cases. Here we shall try to draw the dividing lines, discuss marginal cases, and look more closely at some of the criteria which have been thought to determine whether a country is developed or not.[1]

There is almost full agreement among writers on development issues, as well as among ordinary observers, which countries can be called developed and which are underdeveloped, with only a few marginal cases. There is also general agreement that development implies more than economics or per capita income or purchasing power - it comprises also the quality of life. In spite of the disagreements that do exist over the precise definition of development, disagreement is not significant about where it has taken place. Neither is there much doubt as to where developing nations look for inspiration, help and guidance when they want to develop.

1 Books on development and development economics will normally have a chapter related to this discussion.

1. It all started in "the West"

It is clear that modern development started (or began to take off) in Britain in the latter part of the 18th century. Then this kind of development spread quite rapidly to other countries on the European continent, initially limited to the north-western fringe, and moving much more slowly south and east.

Before, during and after the Industrial Revolution, about 50 million Europeans emigrated to America, Australia and South Africa.[2] In the wake of this emigration, development took place in those European dependencies occupied by people from the areas that had by then developed in Europe - and not (or only very slowly) in countries populated by migrants from less developed European countries. Thus, North America (the United States and Canada), Australia, New Zealand and South Africa developed, and the process continued when these countries became independent of the "mother country" - their development being neither caused nor impeded by their degree of "dependency" or independence. This is a further illustration of the fact that the level of development depends on the "capacity" or level of "enablement" of a people and on nothing else (such as, for example, climate or natural resources or dependency relations).

Only in recent times is for example Latin America (also occupied by European migrants but largely from underdeveloped areas) trying to catch up with the parts of the world that are ahead of them in the development race. A few of them seem to be "on course".

2 This was a higher number of migrants over a shorter period than the total number of slaves exported from Africa over several centuries. "Depopulation" of this nature is not a satisfactory explanation of underdevelopment.

2. What has Marx done for development?

Development began to spread and take off in Russia at the end of the 19th century, and this process continued till 1914, when it was retarded and stopped by the outbreak of the First World War and then further delayed by the Revolution of 1917. Only long after did it start up again, and then under state control. This centrally controlled development went on, after a fashion, till into the 1980s, with the help of much technology "borrowed" from the West. The collapse of communism started as economic collapse; then came the political collapse.

Development also gradually spread to other nations within, or dominated by, the Soviet Union. Countries that came under Soviet control in eastern Europe at the end of the Second World War had in many cases already taken the first steps towards modern development before they came into the Soviet sphere of influence. Development there continued with halting steps, and some will have difficulties counting it as real development. Several of these countries belong in fact to the Third World.

3. The "East Asia model"

After the Meiji Restoration in Japan in 1868, Japan sent many nationals to learn the technology of the West, and this knowledge they brought back home. This was the beginning of state-supported development there, a trend which has continued in Japan till this day.

Japan has become a model for other East Asian countries in pursuit of development. So far, four other East Asian countries are usually counted among developed nations, namely Taiwan, Hong Kong, South Korea and Singapore (all "Confucian" areas).

Modern development has to some extent come under way also in other Asian countries, such as China (Confucian) and perhaps Thailand (Buddhist), Indonesia (largely Muslim) and elsewhere, but still these countries have a long way to go. With the partial exception of China, these latter countries are hardly looked upon as prototypes of development.

4. Fascist development?

South Africa is a partly developed country, but due to its discriminatory policies and practices till recently and partly still (with or without a basis in law) and the exploitation of the majority of its people, few have so far wanted to develop on the South African model, at least not on the African continent - although exploitation and "class" differences may be even worse in other African countries, even if not so obviously based on colour or ethnic differences as it used to be in South Africa.

Fascist ideas and practices have, of course, historical parallels outside South Africa. American Indians were decimated in both North and South America. Black people were used as slaves particularly in America, but also in underdeveloped Arab lands. The aborigines of Australia and New Zealand were treated even worse than the Indians and the slaves in America. The self-destructive fascisms of Hitler, Mussolini and Franco are still in vivid memory. But that is the theme for another kind of debate.

Fascism is in the end self-defeating, because it is based on the dominance and suppression of people whose voluntary co-operation and contribution are needed for development to proceed smoothly. It has nowhere provided a sustainable model for development.

5. Meeting point of East and West

Israel is also a special case. Jews coming from Western countries are leaders in development in Israel, while those from Eastern countries are or were catching up with modern development trends at a slower pace. Still, Israel is generally counted among the highly developed countries of the world, in spite of an economy that is heavily dependent on outside support. For reasons of a mixed nature, few look upon Israel as a "model" for their development, but perhaps especially some African countries have received inspiration from development strategies applied in Israel, and many more could learn a lot from their approach to and handling of problems related to development.

6. Faith and development

When modern development was in its early stages, Protestant countries were the most developed. But it has spread to Catholic southern Europe, to Russia and some other Orthodox countries, and to East Asia, especially Japan - which is mainly Shinto but strongly influenced by Confucianism and other religious or ethical impulses.

Communist countries traditionally professed an atheist ("secular" or "materialist" or "scientific") ideology. Such an ideology is in reality also quite influential in many countries that officially profess adherence to a religious system or to be religiously neutral. On the other hand, religious influences were quite strong in some "atheist" countries.

These ideological or religious or cultural differences are only mentioned here, as they will come into the discussion again in chapters 5 and 6.

7. A weather forecasting development?

It has been pointed out that developed countries are in the temperate zones and that underdeveloped countries lie in the tropical zone (for which reason some call them just "tropical countries" as they find that this sounds less offensive than "underdeveloped countries", etc.). It has therefore been speculated that geography (climate, resources such as the quality of the soil, fertility, population density and so on) is related (positively or negatively) to development.

If this were the case, it does not explain why the countries that are now the most developed were for so many thousand years among the most backward and underdeveloped countries in the world. Neither does it explain the different levels of development among the various groups in South Africa; nor between Israel and its neighbours; nor between Kenya and Ethiopia. If this contention were true, it would also be hard to explain why countries with a temperate climate (riverine Egypt and Mesopotamia of old) were so far ahead of the rest of the world for so long in ancient times.

The relationship between development and geographical zones has to be explained differently. More about this will be said later.

8. The "Third World"

The countries not listed above among developed (or in some cases perhaps "intermediate") countries are the less developed, the underdeveloped, or developing countries (the "Third World" or "the South"). The Third World comprises most of the countries in the world, by far the majority of the world's population, and the areas where the population growth is fastest.

9. What does "the cargo" contain?

It is very difficult to give exact criteria for the division of the world into developing and underdeveloped countries, and I shall not try to give any dogmatic answers.

Average income, national wealth, energy consumption or longevity cannot be used as criteria. A country may find a single source of wealth (oil, diamonds, gold, etc.) that temporarily increases its income, wealth or energy consumption drastically, when it may also be possible to improve health services and nutritional standards and thus increase longevity considerably. But that is not enough to bring a country to the level of a developed country. Development has to be comprehensive and sustained or sustainable over a long period in a country if there shall be sufficient justification for calling it developed.

A country can also sink into sudden temporary poverty, as many European countries did during and after the Second World War. But they retained their skills and mental attitudes, and for this reason they could quickly rise again, and some modest outside assistance (the "Marshall Plan") could be used to good effect to help these countries on their feet again. This aid had an effect strikingly different from development aid to underdeveloped countries. Brief and transient spells of economic decline and hardship (which periodically do occur in all developed countries) do not reduce these countries to the status of underdeveloped countries.

Development is a many-sided process, and in this process it is not only the economy that develops. Also people change, and many social, cultural and political developments follow in the wake of economic and technical development. But more important in this context is it to note the fact that specific developments affecting the population at large must precede economic and technical development - that is largely what this book is about.

It should, however, also be said that these changes do not mean that people have to give up their identity or become "like Westerners". It is a mistake to think that one has to "sell one's soul" in order to develop.

Each country can develop along its own lines, although many of the changes associated with development seem to go in the same direction and may converge more and more, particularly in external behaviour, in products and their use. However, other countries can in this respect influence the West as the West has influenced the rest of the world. This is an ongoing process. There is change everywhere, also in the West, and what is Western society today will certainly have a different shape a hundred years from now - perhaps shaped primarily by influences from countries where the majority of the world's population lives. In any case, it seems that the process of development, which evolves along unpredictable lines, sets its mark on many facets of life in all societies affected by this process - but not so fundamentally that one is deprived of a choice of lifestyle.

Development is the creation of man, but it sets in motion forces that may at times be stronger than man. Thus it shapes to a large extent man in its own image. This shall only be pointed out here, and the evaluation of the phenomenon left to the reader. The price to be paid in order to achieve modern development in human and ethical terms may in the view of some be too high. But many feel that modern development also gives greater freedom of choice.

10. Is it worth it?

This book is not written in defence of development, and least of all of modern Western development in all its aspects. It only tries to explain what development is and how it comes about, or does not come about, and - more superficially - what it may lead to or has led to in terms other than economic or technical ones. The choice of what course to take is evidently up to the people of each country. Development is neither an unmitigated evil nor an undisputed good. Development increases economic efficiency and should (but does not always) give individuals the best chances to realise their inborn potentials, make use of their natural gifts, pursue their dreams, live life to the full.

Chapter 5

HOW MODERN DEVELOPMENT STARTED

As mentioned already, the Industrial Revolution started in Britain, and from there it soon spread to the countries on the north-western fringe of the European continent. The British dependencies that were largely peopled by immigrants from these early developed countries soon followed suit.

The expansion of modern development to other parts of Europe and the world was much slower; and the majority of the countries and peoples in the world are still far behind the most developed ones.[1]

The story of the Industrial Revolution and the spread of modern development is well enough known and shall not be repeated here.[2] We shall only attempt to explain the background and the fundamental causes of the economic and technical development that took place - how it became possible.[3]

---

1 By 1992 estimates, c. 77% of the world's population live in developing countries, where also 90% of the population increase takes place. C. 80% of the world's resources are consumed by c. 15% of the world's population in developed countries. (Information from the Earth Summit/UNCED in Rio de Janeiro in June 1992.)

2 Cf. *The Age of Revolution 1789-1848*, by Eric J. Hobsbawm.

3 Cf. *Reformation to Industrial Revolution*, by Christopher Hill.

An epoch-making event like the Industrial Revolution did not pop up accidentally without preparation. A fermenting and maturing preparatory period preceded it.

Development in areas outside north-western Europe has taken decades. In north-western Europe, where it all began, the preparatory phase was much longer. Although the first inklings of a "different" development can be traced back to ancient Greece (and outside Europe longer still: to influences from Egypt and Mesopotamia, etc.), the period of immediate interest here and the period of greatest explanatory power in this context is shorter.

A marked acceleration of events pointing towards modern development started in Europe around the year 1500. Strong stimuli for change came with the great discoveries, the Renaissance and Humanism. But exclusiveness and elitism characterised these "movements". A popular mass movement for change came in the wake the religious ferment that started with the Protestant Reformation. The non-religious aspects of this event are of special interest in our context: the evolution of individualism, entrepreneurship, nationalism and education in national languages - leading to greater general "enlightenment", and popular demands for a greater share in decision-making, resulting in the gradual development of democratic ideas and institutions, etc.

We have to study the roots of modern society by paying attention to *the great shift in north-western Europe from the sixteenth to the end of the eighteenth centuries*. This is the "pregnant" period that gave birth to the Industrial Revolution and modern society.[4]

---

4 Besides world history (e.g. J. M. Roberts's *History of the World* and W. H. McNeill's *The Rise of the West*) and the history of England (e.g. S. T. Bindoff's *Tudor England*, J. P. Kenyon's *Stuart England* and J. H. Plumb's *England in the Nineteenth Century*), one could profitably read some church history (e.g. O. Chadwick's *The Reformation* and G. R. Cragg's *The Church and the Age of Reason, 1648-1789*).

1. Protestantism and development[5]

It was observed long ago that modern development started in Protestant countries, and researchers are still trying to discover the reasons for this fact. We shall join this debate and make an effort to correct the most glaring misrepresentations of what happened - largely due to one person, Max Weber. He might have over-reacted to the misrepresentations of this event by Karl Marx and thus created his own distorted image of the causes of the Industrial Revolution.[6]

It may require studies of the history of developed countries - of their religious, philosophical, educational and economic development - to realise the inadequacy of some earlier explanations of the causes of modern development, not least within the "Weberian" tradition. The debate on the relationship between Protestantism and development took a wrong turn quite early in the debate.

The explanation of the occurrence of the Industrial Revolution is in fact less "mysterious" than many philosophers, economists, sociologists or historians have tried to make it. However, we shall have to review some of the old arguments in order to put the process into perspective. The most confusing thing is the fact that genuine and imagined causes of change and development were thoroughly mixed up in this debate. Therefore, Weber and his "school" have both many ardent defenders and many scathing detractors.

Weber's great learning and genius have made it impossible to ignore some of his arguments. On the other hand, economic and political

---

5 In this chapter and the next (and elsewhere in the book), there are references to various religions or forms of religion. For further information, interested readers could consult for example Ninian Smart's book *The Religious Experience of Mankind*, or his newer volume, *The World's Religions*. However, religion was of course only one aspect of various "culture areas".

6 See section 2 in chapter 3 and the last part of section 6 in this chapter on Weber's ideas.

disasters were needed to get rid of the destructive theories about development propagated by Karl Marx.[7]

If we concentrate on what relates to economic development in the Protestant Reformation and later Protestantism, namely the gradual development of personal traits and qualities, attitudes, mentalities, behaviour patterns and skills required for modern development, we can clearly see that it is not the Protestant religion or "ethic" that led to modern economic and technological development - and that Protestantism itself is not "capitalist".

Something different from the economic and work-related doctrines and aspirations of Protestants led to the Industrial Revolution and modern development. If Weber had been right in his interpretation of Protestantism and its relation to modern development, there would hardly be any other way to development than to become Protestant - which history has of course proved to be totally wrong.

In fact, the links between religion and development are indirect and not very obvious.

Protestants themselves were struck by the fact that their countries were the first to develop, and they soon explained this as the result of God's special blessing on them and proof of the superiority of their brand of Christianity. After that conclusion had been drawn, they soon also found it easy enough to devise ways to serve both God and Mammon, gaining a world while perhaps gradually losing their soul.

As modern man has realised that development is possible without religion, fewer and fewer people in pursuit of a better material life seem to feel the same appeal of religion as earlier generations did. Some may wonder what it has to offer man that the welfare state cannot give. Modern society is becoming more and more secular. See later.

---

7 Brief and well-written accounts of the main arguments of Karl Marx and Max Weber are given by Raymond Aron in *Main Currents in Sociological Thought*. See also A. J. P. Taylor's introduction to the Penguin edition of *The Communist Manifesto* on Marx's basic ideas.

2. Catholics and development

Catholics also realised that Protestants were more successful than them in developing their countries. This caused them early on to come out against modern development and modern forms of social life. This attitude characterised the "official" Catholic Church until fairly recently.[8] A result of this was that "progressive" people in Catholic countries found it natural to join hands with radical socialists and communists in order to achieve their economic and developmental goals. In recent times, many Catholic countries therefore had strong socialist or communist parties seeking more radical paths to development than has normally been the case in Protestant countries. Consequently, the appeal of the Catholic Church has also (like Protestantism, but for different reasons) tended to weaken for people in pursuit of greater welfare and modern development.

Rather late in the day, the Catholic Church has changed its mind and come up with slogans like, "Development means peace" (Pope Paul VI said, "Development is the new word for peace"); and since everyone is "of course" on the side of peace, the Catholic Church has also found it possible and indeed necessary to support modern development efforts and the aspirations of modern man for a better life in this world. However, ordinary people in Catholic countries had already (like Protestants) realised that they can develop without the church, and perhaps even faster without it. The number of merely nominal or lapsed Catholics has therefore increased tremendously. Most nominal Catholics, like Protestants, have decided that, if they have to make a choice, Mammon is more attractive than God, development is preferable to religion, and the enjoyments of the flesh (secular pleasures) are more alluring (and tangible) than those of the spirit - and can be had with greater certainty than the songs of heaven, the pie in the sky

8 Cf. Paul Johnson, *A History of Christianity*.

that requires bothersome piety, frugality and self-denial. Materialism is growing. But development has not stopped with the partial "collapse" of religion - it may even have accelerated, although there are indications that this growth may be temporary.

The religious aspects of early modern society do not, therefore, explain development as a causal factor; but some non-religious manifestations of especially the Protestant forms of religion do this to quite some extent.

The process of relative decline in the West at present may have causes of a complicated nature, one of them related to ethics with or without a religious basis. That is another question we shall have to come back to in another context.

3. The development question in Orthodox countries

The Orthodox churches are perhaps the most spiritual, other-worldly, mystic and conservative of all the Christian churches. They do not take any great interest in development, although they have had to take a stand to, and come out in favour of, many development issues recently, partly due to the pressures of modernity, but in many cases for reasons of "accommodation" with the secular state as most Orthodox Christians have experienced communist political surroundings in the past. However, any "internal" motivation to become involved with modern development is absent, or very weak, in the Orthodox churches: the spiritual, religious life has been their main preoccupation and concern till "the world" proved too strong also for them.

There may have been special reasons why governments in Orthodox countries so often opted for radical ideologies, strongly against religion (rather than regarding religion as merely irrelevant or "using" the church, as some others have done), in order to forge ahead with modern development. This happened in Russia and some other eastern European countries, and partly also in Greece, and more recently in Ethiopia.

It may have been the otherworldliness of the Orthodox churches that gave leaders there the impression that these churches were obstacles to modern development and that their influence had to be curtailed if their countries were to develop.

Instead of sticking to their merely spiritual guns, the Orthodox churches in these countries were more and more pressed to take part in the development debate and practical development work; and they also have followed the "fashionable" trends set by secular governments, agencies and development "theoreticians".

4. Development and religion today

Seemingly no church today gives any lead in development or in development thinking and analysis, nor in solving the moral problems of modern societies. Christians everywhere have in this respect (as in many others) become "followers", trying to modify and adapt their religious views (doctrines and practices) so as to be in tune with the times and not get further out of fashion (but which they do by this very attempt). Their role in the modern world is seemingly becoming increasingly marginalised and irrelevant.

5. Why development started in the Protestant West

We have to search carefully to discover the causes of the fact that modern development started in Protestant Europe. This observation may on the face of it give the impression that development at first had a religious basis.

We have to review briefly some historical developments in Europe all the way back to ancient Greece before we discuss the features of Protestantism that had economic consequences. We shall then be able to establish that these features are not, or are at most only indirectly, of a religious nature. Development may be possible without religion, or within a variety of religious contexts - but not without a moral base.

A glance at the past of "the West"

Greece learned from previously much more prosperous and advanced countries: Egypt, Mesopotamia, Phoenicia, Persia, India and other great civilisations in the tropical zone of the world, where the conditions for early development were better. But Greece did not only learn by imitation: it adapted and transformed whatever it took over, and it created a new civilisation, surpassing earlier civilisations in several spheres, such as art, literature, philosophy, learned pursuits, political organisation and science. The city-states gave the masses a share in the knowledge and art as well as the political life of these states. With its philosophy and art, Greece left a permanent mark on the European socio-cultural heritage.

When the centre of European civilisation moved to Rome and the Roman Empire, the Romans took over from Greek civilisation many features which they tried consciously to preserve and imitate, but also to adapt to their own ends and needs. The Romans had practical rather than theoretical inclinations and talents, and they made great advances in organisation, law, infrastructure and architecture.

When Christianity became a strong and dominant force in Europe, the Eastern churches kept more of the Greek philosophical heritage than the rest of Christendom. Thus the eastern churches tend towards speculation, introspection and philosophy. The Western churches took over more of the Roman spirit and emphasised questions of conduct, church organisation, authority, the relationship between the church and the state and its respective leaders (politics), etc. In the process, the West also gradually caught up with the East in some of the fields where the East had excelled, for example in the arts.

When the hold of the church on society loosened a bit during the couple of centuries before the Reformation, there was a blossoming of learning and the arts during the Renaissance and Humanism. These movements were not forward-looking but backward-looking, idealising the great periods of Athens and Rome, so much so that the movement was thought of as a renaissance (i.e., "rebirth") of the old cultures. In spite of the revival of art and learning and some new discoveries and inventions, and most significantly modern printing, the Renaissance remained an elite culture and movement, and it did not have a very wide and lasting influence on the masses, and it did not stimulate modern development. Some have tried to seek the roots of modern development in the Renaissance, but that is a futile search. If modern development could have been influenced by a movement like the Renaissance, it should rather have started during the periods it looked back to: the heyday of Greece and of Rome; or it should have started in southern Europe, where the Renaissance movement was strongest.

Before the great leap forward from around 1500 AD, other things happened in Europe that were of considerable importance: the crusades and the great discoveries.

Conquests of the (temporarily) conquered

The Crusades were attempts by Christian Europe to reconquer Jerusalem from the Muslims by force of arms. Thousands upon thousands of Christian Europeans took part in these crusades that lasted for a couple of centuries (the most important ones took place between 1095 and 1270 or 1291).

Although they were meant to serve Christian expansion and conquest, the crusades to the East also opened the eyes of thousands of Europeans to the greatness of cultures outside Europe and Christendom. It expanded their world view. The "insights" brought back to Christian Europe from the East changed Europe so much that it could not be quite the same again: some of its parochialism had gone.

In terms of "victories", the Christians "lost" in the Crusades, but the Muslims were so weakened that they eventually had to give up their last foothold in Spain in 1492; however, they left a permanent cultural mark on Europe.

Wider horizons

Of equal importance in expanding the horizons of Europeans were the great sea travels and discoveries that took place some time later than the crusades. Africa and Asia were explored, and America was "discovered" in 1492.

All this made cracks in the unitary organisation and world view of medieval Christendom and may have been decisive influences that eventually led to the splitting up and division of Europe marked by the Reformation of the early 16th century.

The earlier isolation of Europe was not conducive to competitive, open-minded, innovative and adventurous undertakings needed to stimulate people in the direction of modernity and progress.

However, one should not exaggerate the importance of these new influences for development, as they were strongest in southern Europe, which developed much more slowly than peripheral and "provincial" northern Europe. We shall come back to that.

Strength in disunity

There were thus several factors contributing to the break-up of the monolithic structure of narrow-minded medieval Europe. Chief among them were:

- the impressions received from the outside world through travel (the "crusades" and the "discoveries"),
- the impetus to gain knowledge, to explore new areas and new ideas, to seek and use opportunities for individual pursuits, to be free to think and take decisions without prior ecclesiastical approval, etc. (this "new wind" was stimulated by the Renaissance and Humanism),
- the impact of books and the "new learning" after the invention of the printing press in the 15th century,

- local circumstances, such as a new "nationalist" spirit, aroused by education and literature in national languages and as a centrifugal reaction because nations in the periphery of Christendom were being increasingly exploited by "the centre", especially Rome, the headquarters of the Pope and the Catholic Church.
- People in the periphery were advancing both economically and intellectually. In the later Middle Ages, the "progressive" nationalist movements of dissent were often centred around universities and university professors far away from Rome. (The dissident lay sects of "pious heretics" were usually geographically closer to the centre, Rome, and could thus be more easily tamed or suppressed.)

There were several dissenting voices before the Reformation, seeking a renewal of the Church, such as the professors John Wycliffe in England in the 14th century and John Huss in Bohemia a little bit later (he was burnt in 1415). The 16th century Reformers could thus build on a long tradition of dissent. The Reformation was the culmination of intellectual and social (and to some extent political) movements (religious, moral, and related to church organisation and authority) that practically all had gone in the same direction: a demand for a return to biblical Christianity.

The Reformation was thus born of the times. The demands for reform had to be of a religious nature in order to interest most people in those days, and the fight for change had to be conducted within the Church because the Church had taken control of all aspects of life by this time: kings and emperors had to be Christians; universities and other institutions of learning as well as all the staff had to declare their loyalty to the Church; nearly all were baptised, married and buried in the church; philosophy, art, architecture as well as daily life were totally dominated by the Church; practically everyone had to be a member of the Church and go to church regularly. Not unnaturally, any fundamental ideological or political, structural or organisational changes could be undertaken only after a fight with the clerical powers. That is also what happened.

Advantages of being peripheral

The questions at the forefront of the debate at the time of the Reformation were nearly all religious or moral, and only very marginally economic; and economic questions were discussed by theologians as moral issues.

Great amounts of money were at this time sent from northern Europe to Rome; and heavy fees were paid to churches everywhere, so as to keep clerics in state and to obtain their services. The many magnificent and not so magnificent churches and cathedrals also cost a lot of money which the believers had to come up with. All this was a cause of grave complaints in the countries where the Reformation movement took hold, and it may have had at least an indirect influence on the Reformation or its popular appeal. But still, when it comes to economic theory or practice, the medieval economic system was little affected by the Reformation.

The Reformers were not deep economic thinkers, and the few new thoughts they brought forward in this area (Calvin may for example have allowed the taking of interest on loans) did not amount to a new system or new economic thinking, and it cannot explain the great acceleration that came underway and which eventually led to the Industrial Revolution and modern development and the modern world. The explanation of that lies elsewhere, not in the economic theories or practices of the Reformers or their followers, the Protestants.

6. Is Protestantism capitalist?

We shall soon say something about the economic views and practices of early Protestantism; but first we have to refute erroneous views of the links between original Protestantism and capitalism, links that are supposed to explain why modern development started in Protestant countries.

Progressive in spite of themselves

The Reformers took practically no interest in economic matters and economic theory, and they thought that economic activities implied temptations to "sin" and loss of spirituality. They had no plans to change economic life or economic structures in their societies. They (and first of all Calvin, who wanted to regulate all of life according to biblical principles) were forced to take a stand on some pressing economic questions, but apart from that, hardly any new economic thinking can be traced to the Reformation. They stressed the importance and dignity of all kinds of "normal" work, as had many people before them. This was nothing new, and it did not bring about modern development.

It is probably right to say (with R. H. Tawney) that Luther was disgusted by commercial affairs and the capitalist spirit. He was certainly one of the least capitalistic persons of all times - to the near despair of his wife (he gave away their possessions, including highly valued wedding gifts, and he never worried or cared about material things).

In Calvin's teaching there was more understanding of some economic issues, and some have seen in his approach the beginning of a new view of and attitude to some economic questions; but it is an exaggeration to see in this a burgeoning new era. This matter was a side-issue also for Calvin, and it did not lay the foundation for the movement that culminated in the Industrial Revolution. Calvin said (in the *Institutes*) that God had made most Christians poor so as to keep them safe from the temptations and evils that follow in the wake of wealth. Luther was of the same opinion.

The Protestant churches were completely baffled by the Industrial Revolution and were not able to give any helpful advice or guidance under the circumstances or to influence it in any significant way.

Methodism may have helped people to cope with the worst horrors of the Industrial Revolution, but it did not otherwise alter its course or mitigate its brutality, and it may have retarded humanitarian reforms through its stress on obedience and patience and acceptance of one's worldly lot.[9]

The old with the new

It is true that the Reformers emphasised honesty, hard work, respect for authority (in economic life: respect for and obedience to one's employers), doing one's duty, etc. All this is beneficial for economic life, but it was not new with or exclusive to Protestantism. The early Protestants expected a person to remain in his or her "calling", "vocation", profession or "trade"; often one was born into this profession, and individual choice was extremely limited. The ideas of the Reformers in relation to these matters were largely inherited from the Middle Ages and represented nothing new. Several monastic institutions of earlier centuries had worked hard and done great things in agriculture, trade and so on, following their "calling"; but this did not bring about or lay (or even prepare) the foundation of any Industrial Revolution or modern economic development on a broad scale, as it happened a couple of centuries later. Neither did the Reformers start or wish to start any economic or industrial revolution: their concerns were spiritual.

The spirit of capitalism

The Reformation was anti-capitalistic.

The capitalist spirit has always existed everywhere. It is probably strongest in poor, underdeveloped countries as the poor worry most about the daily bread. As for the Reformers, they preached against worrying about tomorrow and against the profit-motive, usury, any kind of

9 Cf. E. P. Thompson, *The Making of the English Working Class*.

greed or exploitation, and they proclaimed the virtues of frugality, even poverty, and of giving things and money away. Hoarding and capital accumulation were absolutely foreign to their ideas, except as something evil, ugly, awful, dehumanising and sinful.

The Protestant Reformers would certainly have condemned the modern spirit of capitalism and what has come to be known as the Protestant ethic, if they had met the phenomenon. Protestant religious or ethical doctrines do not explain modern development, but other, non-religious aspects of the Reformation do.

The aspects of the Reformation that prepared the way for modern development and indeed made it possible have often been misunderstood and misrepresented, not least by Max Weber, whose views influenced the debate on development for quite some time, even today. We have already referred to this, but a brief recapitulation may be necessary for the line of argument.

Max Weber's idée fixe

Max Weber found that people in the developed Protestant world of his time, at the turn and beginning of the 20th century, were very hard-working and disciplined, and that they showed a unique kind of practical, goal-directed (as against a mainly theoretical, "logical") rationalism in their work. He thought that this was the main cause of modern development; and he saw this characteristic in people as the outcome of the teachings of (perhaps mostly modern) Protestantism.

The Calvinists believed that success in worldly affairs would prove that God was with them and blessed their work and undertaking, thus confirming that they were the chosen children of God. Equally hard-working, disciplined, practical, goal-oriented, "rational" Lutheran Pietists did not believe that God had decided beforehand who were to be his children. Their motive for working hard was largely to prove to others how God blesses those who believe in him, as a testimony and "call" to non-believers - or they may just have felt driven by their faith to do their "duty" with diligence and persistence, without thinking primarily about what others thought of them.

This was a "double" (in fact self-contradictory) argument for a link between hard work, etc., and development. But if contradictory arguments are used to prove the same thing, nothing is proved. This is what Weber did. On the one hand, he says that belief in eternal predestination formed modern workers who brought about modern development; on the other hand he says that those who denied eternal predestination had the same effect on development from very different motives.

In spite of the fame of Weber's book dealing with these questions, *The Protestant Ethic and the Spirit of Capitalism*, it is not a consistent, logical or well-argued book. Its influence is probably due - in addition to the dearth of ideas to explain modern development - to the great scholarship and original mind the author displays, the intriguing nature of his argument, and the field of study (Protestant theology - which few development theorists or sociologists take much interest in). And Protestant theologians do not seem to have taken much interest in understanding and explaining the problems of modern development and are thus unable to relate theology to development, so no corrective of Weber's arguments has come from them (and they probably wish that Weber were right).

Some of Weber's arguments are certainly valid, but the main thrust of his argument: that religious beliefs as such caused modern development, does not hold water. The link between Protestantism and modern economic development must be explained in other ways, as we shall see.

7. Development through plunder and exploitation?

It has been argued that the new wealth brought to Europe by trade and plunder after the great discoveries led to modern development. If that were true, it would not explain why this development started in

Protestant countries rather than in Spain or Portugal (Catholic countries), where in the early phase much more wealth was accumulated than in Britain.

Great wealth, whether obtained through plunder or from oil deposits or whatever, does not automatically lead to development. Unless people have acquired the attitudes and skills required for development, no amount of capital can by itself bring about modern development.

In this context it can be mentioned that wealth obtained by Third World countries through trade has not led to development, but rather to dependency and further underdevelopment. Just as in some rich underdeveloped countries, so has capital in many poor Third World countries fallen into the hands of small dominant groups of people (the new middle and upper classes) who neither invest in productive enterprises nor stimulate production nor promote modern development in other ways. Wealth in such cases increases the gap between rich and poor and keeps the poor in their poverty, and often it plunges them into even greater poverty. The rich in poor countries are often ruthless exploiters, not modernisers.

Capital as such does not lead to development.

8. Blurred visions

The Weberian debate has come somewhat in the background lately, partly because it seems to lead nowhere, and partly because economists have come to dominate the development debate.

The greatest weakness of Weber's thesis is that it seems to necessitate the corollary that a country must be more or less "Protestant" to develop. This might not have seemed so unreasonable then because little or no development had taken place by his time outside Protestant Europe. He, like most others of his age, may have thought that it never would spread much further, or at least not to the same levels as in the West. If he had seen the world today, he would have had to modify or change his theories, as they do not explain modern development in every place it has occurred.

Purely economic explanations of development have not led anywhere either, as can be clearly seen from the obvious lack of development in underdeveloped countries that follow or have followed any of the economic theories on the market.

Development efforts in the poorest countries have shared the fate of development theories and development economics: they have reached a dead end.

9. "Prior conditions"

We shall take a fresh look at the situation in the first countries to develop, prior to and during the early stages of modern development. We shall note how development relates to non-economic and non-ideological factors that had economic consequences. This means that we have to concentrate on north-western Europe from about 1500, where and when the great drive forward began to gain momentum, and up to around 1800. What conditions were created that made modern development possible? Can similar necessary preconditions be replicated? These are crucial questions that must be answered before we can formulate any helpful general explanation of development and suggest guidelines for countries in the pursuit of development.

10. What about the very clever ones?

The scientific and scholarly establishment (especially in the universities) played practically no role in getting modern development or the Industrial Revolution under way.[10]

---

10 The Reformers who created the mass movement that changed Europe were university (or at least university-educated) people, but their general impact was due to their non-academic activities: their popular talks and

More than a hundred years after the Industrial Revolution started, the links between industry and the universities were firmly established, and they are important today. However, it should be emphasised that the intellectual elite took no part in bringing modern development about, although they have done much to accelerate it after it came under way. This is of interest in explaining the causes of development.

The universities in pre-modern days were remote from the mainstream of society, using Latin as the language of instruction and learned debate long after much of the population had become literate in their mother tongues. Scholars took little interest in practical matters or in applying scholarship for practical, "useful" purposes. But development is a practical (and prosaic, workaday) thing, dependent on mass involvement and contributions from the majority of the population. An elite cannot bring it about - nor stop it once it has started.

Not many new inventions were made during the Industrial Revolution. It was first of all the discovery of new *uses* to which old (and some new) tools and inventions could be put that was characteristic of the Industrial Revolution and later development. People, not tools or "economic forces", made all the difference.

The inventions most useful for development were or had been made by *practical* men. It was the wide involvement of common working people that brought about this revolution, not the leadership, guidance or even help of an enlightened or "progressive" elite. Elites have always existed, but before the masses are prepared, no development can take place.

Elite groups can actually be harmful and detrimental to modern development if they take over the leadership of development. This was

---

books, even where scientific work may have been the basis of such work, e.g. the translation of the Bible from Hebrew and Greek into vernacular languages. Luther's books were the world's first "best-sellers".

the case in so-called "progressive" countries, as it is the case in many developing countries today.

11. Getting set for development

What characteristics were necessary for people to acquire in order to get started on the road to development? In other words, how were modern times brought about?

Achieving more than you aim for

We shall turn our attention to what happened in the countries that first developed during the gestation period leading up to modern development. To obtain the proper perspective, we shall survey the time from the Protestant Reformation to the Industrial Revolution, stressing the factors that had economic consequences, factors that may also explain development elsewhere, indeed everywhere.[11]

The specific religious doctrines of the Reformation and Protestantism are *in themselves* not relevant in this context, only what they *implied* in the economic field. Some simple "theology" must therefore be discussed in order to be able to see the points of real importance here.

---

11 Those hooked on Weber's arguments may have to take a first-hand look at the original sources of ideas during this period, both economic, philosophical, religious and educational. Weber's view of the importance of religious beliefs for development is in great need of reinterpretation. This is attempted in general terms in the following pages. It is particularly necessary to know something about the theology from the Reformation to the Industrial Revolution to come to a "revised" view on these matters. However, most readers will find what they need in a general history of the period supplemented by a church history, although a history of religion may do even better as it will contain material also useful for the later discussion of development in other culture areas, e.g. the books by Ninian Smart already mentioned.

We shall concentrate on straightforward and simple questions that are easy to follow even for those least interested in anything that savours of theology.

We shall not try to be "clever" and discover new points nor look for peripheral aspects of Protestantism but go straight to the central concerns and emphases of the Reformers to see what it was in their teaching that had economic implications. Peripheral obscurities (e.g. concerning "predestination") could of course never have brought about the most important and fundamental landmark in the modern world. It is not hard to see the real links between Protestantism and development, but they are not what they are often made out to be, and they are not of a religious nature.

The briefest, simplest, most exact and central definition of what Protestantism is about can easily be given on the basis of the literary output of the Reformers and a mass of later literature.

Reforming more than the faith

The central teaching of Protestantism is that,

- a person is justified before God (or saved, or becomes a Christian) because of God's forgiving grace or mercy;
- a person receives God's mercy (or forgiveness of sins, or becomes a child of God) through faith (which is trust in God's forgiveness of sins and acceptance of God's offer of mercy); and
- the basis for this teaching or belief is the Bible, which is the only authority in matters of Christian faith and conduct.

This is in layman's language what theologians express more succinctly as "Justification by (God's) grace alone, through (man's) faith alone", a doctrine based on "Scripture alone". This is of course the universally accepted statement of the central points of the Protestant Reformation and of the Protestant churches ever since.

People unfamiliar with "church language" may find this obtuse and irrelevant to the present discussion. But it will soon become evident that this formed the mainspring from which modern economic development sprang and encapsulates all the main aspects of it. Still, religion is not the essence of the matter.

We shall try to elucidate the link between this "theology" and economic and technical development step by step.

Take care of the penny ...

The Church in the Middle Ages had stressed that man had to earn salvation and peace with God by doing good works, and such good works consisted, among other things, of giving gifts of charity to the poor (alms), to support church officials, to pay for church services (masses), to contribute to the building of churches, to buy "letters" (indulgences) relieving the faithful of the duty of performing certain religious duties (penances, sacrifices, etc.), to go on pilgrimages to holy places in order to receive blessings from the dead saints associated with such places, and so on. All this cost a lot of money and meant time taken off from work. Much available surplus capital went in this way to religious purposes, in scale only next to, and perhaps sometimes equal to, compulsory contributions to the state. Most people were religious and thought a lot about the welfare of their souls, so in addition to obligatory contributions, many (including political leaders) made great additional and voluntary economic sacrifices in order to obtain "blessings".

Protestants taught that most of these so-called "good works" had no moral or spiritual value, serving only to deceive and exploit people and profiting only the church hierarchy or bureaucracy. That is the meaning of their new teaching of "grace alone" and "faith alone" as sufficient to obtain "salvation". In this way, they freed a lot of capital among their adherents for other purposes. Protestants at the same time preached against all forms of luxury and ostentation, and thus they contributed to the accumulation of capital.

What should people now use money for, when they stopped spending it for religious purposes and were also discouraged from wasting it on adornments and increased comfort?

The state took for a long time over the role of the Church in siphoning off the surplus money from the population. Taxes to pay for matters of state became heavier, and hostilities between the Catholic and Protestant camps, following the split between them, led to increased expenses for military purposes. Religious disputes were fierce and went on for a long time, culminating in the Thirty Years' War (1618-1648). It was only after this that Europe could begin the process of peaceful recovery that gradually led to better times. But even during the most restless centuries, people in Protestant lands were formed in the image of Protestant teaching. This had great economic consequences.

After more peaceful times dawned, capital could be used for more constructive purposes. Since Protestants condemned conspicuous consumption in the form of comfort and luxuries and status symbols, it became necessary for Protestants (and actually for most people living in Protestant lands) to look for new ways to use accumulated capital. It became almost a necessity (for lack of reasonable or acceptable alternatives) to invest surplus money[12] in various "constructive" purposes, in line with their ethos of service to the neighbour and the community.

All this resulted eventually in the production of more and more goods and the multiplication of wealth on a steadily increasing scale and at ever greater speed.

---

12 The peasantry and workers were heavily exploited during all this time, but capital accumulated in the hands of a few who were later able to invest in productive enterprises. Capital was very unfairly distributed, but that is not the relevant point in this context.

Trust your own head!

There was another development that was of equal importance. Before the Reformation, the authority of the Pope and the clergy was tremendous. Their word was final in all religious questions and in fact in nearly all matters relating to life and death.

The Reformers totally rejected this authority of the clergy and the Pope and put the Bible in its stead ("Scripture alone"). Many Catholics would accept this (the Bible as the basis of faith and conduct) if it could also be agreed that the Bible was an obscure book that had to be "interpreted" to be correctly understood, and that the Pope and the clergy were the only qualified interpreters of the Bible. The Reformers totally rejected this view of the Bible, maintaining that it was basically clear and easy to understand in all essentials. Each reader should be able to understand and interpret it according to his or her own intellectual ability. Clergymen would still preach and organise and administer "religion" and so on, but in principle their authority was not above that of any other Christian. In fact, the Reformers taught that every Christian was a priest ("the priesthood of all believers"), and that ordained priests (clergymen) were "ordinary Christians" with a special job.

You are responsible!

This placed strong emphasis on equality in the church (which then comprised practically the whole of society), and it put authority in the church (and eventually in the state) in a very different place from what had been the case before.

Each individual now became responsible for his or her understanding of the Bible and of finding the truth and the way to "salvation". Soon this stimulated people to take more and more responsibility for everything concerning their life and welfare. Equality in all civil relationships became the natural next demand.

Newly-won religious "authority" or "autonomy" led people to question and challenge the legitimacy of all authority, especially "absolute" authority. Gradually they came to demand a say in almost everything in society that related to their lives. In the end, this led to a demand to participate in matters of state, in political life.

Finally it led to democracy, "government of the people, by the people, for the people" (concretely: "no taxation without representation", etc.), to use phrases that were coined in the American fight for freedom and democracy.

Modern economic development and the development of democratic institutions went hand in hand, but not totally in tandem: at various stages, one or the other aspect of modernisation was ahead of its associate, and in most cases the development of democratic institutions lagged behind economic development. The most important point to note in this connection is that democracy and development have the same cause or causes, and that one of them is not the cause of the other.

A bit of reading, 'riting and 'rithmetic: the three R's

The central importance attached to the Bible had other consequences, eventually also economic ones. If everyone had the right and duty to find the truth in the Bible for oneself, a person should also know the Bible. This had several implications:

(1) the translation of the Bible into national languages. This soon paved the way for stronger nationalist sentiments along "linguistic" lines, and this was one of the conditions for the later formation of nation states (from about the same time as the Industrial Revolution started);

(2) more widespread education of people in national languages (and not in Latin as previously).[13] Although the primary purpose of this education in Protestant lands was to enable people to read the Bible, it had far-reaching implications for popular education generally; and it had the same consequences for development then as widespread education in the mother tongue has everywhere: it is an essential aspect of the "enabling" process;

(3) the influence and power of the "learned" classes decreased. When so many people learned to read and write, "learning" was to some extent demystified - although the community of scholars of course tried to retard this process by sticking to Latin as the universal language of higher learning for as long as possible, with the result that the world of scholarship was cut off from modern development trends for decades after the modern world had come into being;

(4) all this led in turn - for all those involved in the process - to mental developments and changes that always follow in the wake of general or very widespread literacy: new ideas take root as people acquire more knowledge, and they learn to think in more rational ways.

---

13 Thorough documentation of the growth of literacy during the centuries preceding the Industrial Revolution is still somewhat scarce for some of Europe. Enlightening is for example R. A. Houston, *Literacy in early Modern Europe. Culture and Education 1500-1800*. Few could read in Europe in 1500. In 1800 literacy was becoming quite general in north-western Europe. Already John Aubrey (1626-1697) wrote towards the end of his life, "Now-a-dayes Bookes are common, and most of the poor people understand letters."

We shall take a closer look at the arguments introduced above, point for point, and show how they relate to economic development.

You change as you learn

In the process of learning to read and write (in) one's mother tongue, a person acquires very many of the skills that are needed in the modernisation or development process. This is not the case when education is given in a language different from the one heard daily and in which a person from childhood learns to talk, think, dream, pray or curse - expressing whatever thoughts or emotions are most basic and intimate to the mind.

All national languages are easy enough to learn to read and write for everyone living in that "language area". The characters used in various "alphabets" are normally (but not always) relatively few and not hard to absorb. Beyond that, in the actual use of any language there are always enough challenges in spelling, vocabulary, grammar and style to stimulate the mind, develop mental alertness and train even the best educated in logical and clear thinking. Here are some examples of how the learning of all aspects of the mother tongue will inevitably influence and "train" the mind:

- When we learn the spelling of words, we learn to memorise and to discover "rules" and a logic in it all. We meet new problems and make spelling mistakes and have to search our brains to remember how to spell a word and thus develop our memory; or we have to "look it up" and learn to work systematically with books in order to check our knowledge, and we go on learning.
- The vocabulary of any language is so rich that people can express whatever they need or want to say fairly easily, but also advanced enough for everyone to go on learning new words and expressions forever, according to one's needs or interests.

In the search for the best and most adequate word or phrase, the imagination and associative skills are developed. Precision may be one of the most useful attainments in the process of learning the exact meaning of words and sentences - and useful for development.

- The basic grammar of the mother tongue is acquired during childhood even without schooling (as is the basic vocabulary). But there are refinements in grammar that will keep anyone who wants to write a letter or an application or compose a more substantial work on his or her toes. In the process, logic and clear thinking are developed and continue to exercise the mind.
- Then there is the question of style: one style will be used in a love letter, another in a note to one's boss or to a "public figure". A person can go on developing his or her style during a lifetime and still feel that there is much to learn and improvements to be made. That is the experience of even the best authors. However, anyone can express most thoughts in a style that is adequate for daily needs if the mother tongue is used. In the pursuit of a good style, one develops not only logic but also aesthetic qualities: a sense of the appropriate and the beautiful and an ability to judge in matters of "taste".
- In ordering one's thoughts systematically in a composition or an essay, one learns to think and argue "progressively" from a beginning towards an end.

In all this, the learner acquires the basic attitudes and skills that are needed in order to contribute usefully also in the development process.

The practical abilities and skills acquired when learning to write the language are also the beginning of practical aspects of development work.

Being "logical" - and practical

The process of learning all aspects of one's mother-tongue proceeds from stage to stage. First the language is acquired by listening. Then the listener learns to speak. Only by more deliberate and systematic efforts can one then learn to read and to write. With each step, mental faculties are developed and mature, and skills are refined.

There is a vast step from being a mere speaker to becoming a fluent reader and writer of a language. It is these latter, literate language skills that most effectively develop logical reasoning, precision, attention to detail, mental alertness, and abilities that involve the most conscious choices of self-expression to achieve one's mental and practical goals. These are also the mental faculties and practical skills most useful for the process of development.

Something beautiful to boot

The aesthetic sense is also enhanced during the process of learning to read and write. The appreciation of good style develops when people learn to read, and especially when the habit of reading is well established (although purely "oral artists" exist in all societies). A good hand adds another aesthetic dimension.

The appearance of letters and written pages can vary greatly in beauty and clarity, depending on the skill and dedication of the writer. This is also a matter of style. There is enough here to challenge the best minds.

The Latinists lagging behind

As long as a dead or foreign language is the means through which people learn basic literacy and receive education generally, the learner acquires the opposite skills of those obtained from an education in the mother tongue: sloppiness and imprecision, because one has to guess at the exact meaning and precise connotation of many words and expressions and cultural, social and historical references that would be readily understood in the mother-tongue; one must grapple with alien concepts in a confused way, falling short of the level of knowledge and understanding that could have been attained if the mother-tongue had been used; one will write ungrammatically and have great difficulties with spelling and precise definitions, etc. In this way, learners forfeit the best chances of acquiring a good style and clear expression as well as precise, logical thinking and deep understanding.

There will be about as many people gaining full benefit from education primarily in a foreign language as there were when Latin was the language of instruction in Europe: very few attain excellence, a few mediocrity, and the vast majority only rather vague ideas of what is taught, and many relapse into illiteracy. (Before the Protestant Reformation, the majority of the clergy - trained in Latin - were in fact illiterate, having forgotten what they had learnt, and they had little idea of what they were supposed to teach. What they retained was some of what they had learned by rote. It was poorly understood and treated almost like magic formulas.[14])

The level of literacy and education generally in countries that use a foreign language as the means of instruction is poor, largely corresponding to their state of development.

A beginning and an end

There is one more point relevant for development that resulted from making the Bible accessible to all.

---

14 The congregations also regarded the rites in church as magical "mysteries". "Hocus pocus" may derive from the Mass (*Hoc est corpus meum*, "This is my body"). Latter-day linguists dispute this derivation, but the Continental variety, "Hocus pocus filiocus" seems to confirm it: the added word probably comes from *Filioque* ("and from the Son"), a Western insertion into the Nicene Creed (also read during Mass).

The Bible tells a simple story of how God created the world and how human history develops under divine guidance till one day God will make an end of it all, and then he will judge the world. The general acceptance of this schema made a big difference to people's perception of reality and attitude to life. Of course this had been taught from the beginning of Christianity, but it was popularised and absorbed by the masses with the use of the mother tongue in sermons and Bible translations and as literacy became more widespread after the Reformation.

People began to think of history (and human life) as a chain of events leading from a starting point (the Creation) towards an end (Judgement Day). What happened in life on earth had implications for eternity. Life could become purposeful and goal-oriented. History came to be conceived of as a "straight line" from a beginning to an end; this is "linear history". The means to determine one's fate also changed fundamentally, from being rather "mechanical" and largely magical to becoming more "rational", depending on understanding and conscious moral choice.[15]

Earlier, history had largely been conceived of as an eternal repetition of things, a cycle. This view of history is circular and not "progressive", and life is generally regarded as something we are "caught up in" rather than as a "gift" full of opportunities for deliberate choices.

The profitability of knowing where you are going

If history is - in the minds of people - linear, it becomes important to advance straight along this "line" towards a culmination, to have an aim or purpose with one's acts and one's life.

The idea of the possibility of progress, of going from one point or stage to a further or higher or better point or stage, is a

15 Cf. Keith Thomas, *Religion and the Decline of Magic.*

result of this linear view of history. It is absolutely basic to development. After the Reformation such ideas became quite general in north-western Europe.

When people acquired a linear view of history, they also began to realise that it makes a big difference how they choose to arrange their affairs, how they live, and what they do and how they do it. Life got a different, more "individualistic" meaning.

The linear view of history leads to certain "new" patterns of conduct: one sets aims for what one does or wants to achieve in life; one's actions become largely goal-oriented, future-oriented. This was a major consequence of the Protestant Reformation, with enormous economic implications.

The same with a difference

Today, history is usually interpreted along "evolutionary" lines, that is, in a linear way but in secular terms. History goes forward, it is progressive: that is how it is taught in all modern schools. With this way of writing and teaching national and world history, the religious and philosophical views underlying such an interpretation are given a "neutral", secular form, in line with a "scientific" outlook.

This forms the life and conduct of people.

The linear view of history can be replicated everywhere, under whatever circumstances (with or without a religious or clear ideological basis, perhaps to some extent also in societies with a basically cyclical or fatalistic orientation). People can be given ideas of the possibility of progress whatever they otherwise believe - except those who prefer to believe that "all is (in) vain", or that the future will be worse than the present and the past, or that nothing we do matters very much.

It should, however, be said again that the linear view of history is of religious origin and cannot be scientifically "proved".

How it pays to be nice

Protestants taught that faith should lead to a certain kind of morality or conduct. There was a shift from a strong emphasis on inner improvement to acts benefiting others. This moral view largely built on biblical injunctions such as, "Love your neighbour as you love yourself" or, popularly expressed, "Do as you would be done by".

The wide popularisation of such ideas gave shape to new forms and institutions of co-operation. This benefited modern economic relations and development.

Protestants also strongly enjoined obedience to authorities - in the family and in society (including the work place and the state). This also was of advantage for modern development (also when it was misused): workers were brought up to be obedient to their employers, and they were taught that poor work and absenteeism were "like stealing".

All this led to relations of trust (at least most workers could be trusted not to "cheat"), reliability (of workers' attendance and attention to one's "duty"), and thus *predictability*, all essential factors especially for modern industry, which depends so strongly on fixed routines, but also for trade and other economic activities. (That this relationship of trust could be - and often was - misused by employers to exploit workers is another matter which became important later in the struggle for workers' rights.)

Family ethics and society

There is one further aspect of Protestant morality that may have been of importance for modern economic development: its attitude to sex and the family.

The Protestant family became the cornerstone of modern society in developed countries, the place where "decent", law-abiding citizens were trained.

Order, obedience and discipline in the family were reflected in similar attitudes and practices in society as a whole.

The importance of the Protestant attitude to sex (no sex before, after or outside marriage) for modern development may be more uncertain, as countries with totally different attitudes to sex are making great strides in development. But it certainly developed self-restraint and the ability to "defer enjoyment", as well as a social order marked by disciplined relations that also benefited work and economic relations.

Self-denial

The Protestant attitude to sex may have been most important economically for the self-control and self-discipline it entailed.

In all developed countries, importance is attached to the strict observance of at least one point of moral life, imparting a shared experience of hardship and frustration during one stage of one's upbringing (or perhaps later). In all cases, the results are similar: a fight with oneself that strengthens self-control, inner discipline, perseverance, a firmness of character (perhaps formed while acquiring the ability to resist or defer satisfaction of natural inclinations) that will be beneficial for economic development, where discipline and perseverance are also needed. It does not seem to make much difference whether this training in discipline, this struggle with one's nature or to overcome obstacles put in one's way, is in the area of sexual restraints (which has both internal and external aspects), or a strict upbringing in the home, or a demanding educational system, or is met in a very competitive work situation, or perhaps in other areas.

We shall come back to this question.

12. Odds and ends

There are a few more points in connection with early Protestantism that may have had an influence on modern development, but the links may be less clear than the points discussed above.

One result of the rise of Protestantism was the emergence in Europe of several forms of Christianity that people had to choose between (few rejected all forms of religion in those days). This proliferation of churches and sects forced people to think about the issues dividing them and to take a stand. This eventually found parallels in the political and secular field, e.g. in the formation of political "parties", a phenomenon that also presupposes somewhat similar mental attitudes and choices as those required when choosing between different forms of religion.

If people are not so opposed to each other that co-operation becomes impossible and development is slowed down, a competitive situation - where people have to make choices but still can work together - seems to have been beneficial for modern development.

Other aspects of early Protestantism worth noting in our context are:

- Protestants were against gambling as it encouraged reliance on irrational chance or luck. Development is also "rational".
- Secular entertainment (which later came to include fiction) was condemned as leading to "escapism" from reality and away from hard work and a down-to-earth attitude to life. "Realistic" attitudes are also good for development.
- By making the sermon the central part of church services (instead of the liturgical mass), an appeal was made to knowledge and understanding (a moderate "rationalism"), and thus a major step was taken away from a magical attitude to life. A "demystified" view of life also benefits development.
- The rejection of a large number of saints thought to take a hand in the affairs of this world developed a certain practically-oriented "rationalism", because it made single-minded, goal-oriented efforts more natural than in an orientation to life determined by uncertainty due to the plethora of forces and supernatural beings that must be considered and placated. Such "singleness of mind" is obviously good for development.

The broad principles of Protestantism that had economic implications led inadvertently to modern development. The Reformers had no idea of modern progress or economic growth, and no aspirations nor interests in that direction. Nobody had any idea that it was possible until it took place.

Economic life can be organised and conducted so as to benefit the majority of people, and profits from economic and productive undertakings need not be made at the expense of others. These ideas gained ground during and after the process of modern economic and technological development had come underway. During the Enlightenment such ideas gained further ground with a secular colouring (but, like the Renaissance, the Enlightenment was much more of an elite phenomenon than the Reformation, and it did not aim at democratic development: it occurred simultaneously with political autocracy, which it often underpinned; and it was strongest in countries that were slow to develop).

The Reformers took no interest in development or economic issues, and they were hostile to the pursuit of wealth. That modern development eventually resulted from changes brought about by and after the Reformation was not intended or expected.

Still, by paying attention to what went on prior to the Industrial Revolution in Europe, we can learn from the process that led to modern development. From the lessons thus learned, we can help to accelerate the development process elsewhere, wherever it is pursued.

13. Who's lost?

When the churches were faced with the new problems created by and arising from the Industrial Revolution, they did not make much of a mark in areas related to social justice or welfare, how to better the working conditions or wages of workers, or how to alleviate the situation of poor and suffering families, and so on. Instead, they continued stressing obedience to authorities, doing as one is told (one's "Christian duty"), working with dedication for others (especially the employers), etc. Little consideration was given to misuse of power and exploitation of people. In spite of (often uncharitably performed) deeds of "charity", they were generally lost in the new situation that gave people new problems but also political and social responsibilities and a share in power unheard of before.

This led to a decline in the influence and relevance of the churches, and they have never recovered from a state of incomprehension or properly come to terms with modern society. As they try to accommodate and "modernise", they seem only to become increasingly irrelevant. Other forces that seem better suited to meet the felt needs of modern man are taking the place of the churches in the minds and lives of more and more people.

The fact that churches have never been pioneers when it comes to democratic or progressive ideas is here mentioned in order to stress that it was not the religious aspects of Protestantism that gave the boost to the forces leading to modern society but other aspects discussed above.

14. Mammon isn't God after all; or is it/he/she?

Secular influences that helped to shape Europe immediately before the Industrial Revolution also emanated from the so-called Enlightenment. This movement resulted from the advance and secularisation of education and knowledge. It contributed to further secularise mental attitudes, and it stimulated intellectual pursuits along more "scientific" lines. The Enlightenment did not "override" the religious influence in Europe. In a way it fused with it, because simultaneously with it there popped up many religious movements ("revivals") that put new life into religion for the masses. But from then on, religion did not have an unchallenged monopoly in the minds of Europeans. More people now began to take a deeper interest in a number of things: science, mathematics, history, geography, and so on. Philosophy also became more - and mainly - secular.

Although largely an elite movement, the main ideas of the Enlightenment spread widely because many of its proponents were great popularisers (in this they resembled the Reformers), and some national leaders influenced by the ideals of the Enlightenment did much for popular education (thus for example Joseph II of Austria). Where many people could read, "enlightened" ideas thus stimulated the modernising of Europe. Where fewer could read, it led rather to confusion. It may be worth mentioning that the continental countries where the Enlightenment movement was strongest were not among the first to develop. It seems that it led to expectations that outstripped abilities to modernise, and as a result, destructive upheavals detrimental to development (revolutions and subsequent dictatorships) were more common immediate consequences of the Enlightenment than development and democracy.

We and They

With the increased use of national languages, a new feeling of togetherness and self-assurance arose among speakers of a common language. This national sentiment finally resulted in demands for nation-states: states enclosed by borders along linguistic lines. This process gave shape to the nation-states of Europe. The idea of a state where people *feel* like members of one "nation" is in this context the important thing. Even people not born as members of the nation where they live have at all times been able to identify and merge with the majority, thus eventually becoming full ("natural") members of this "nation" (a "nation" which is in reality always an "artificial" and "imagined" construct; but that is not the point that matters most in this context[16]). For economic

---

16 Cf. Benedict Anderson, *Imagined Communities. Reflections on the Origin and Spread of Nationalism*, and Peter Worsley, *The Three Worlds.*

development, the unity - in the sense of the ability to communicate and interact easily - of large groups of linguistically "homogeneous" people is important as a basis for co-operation. A common culture, including a common religion, was long regarded as more important than a common language in the definition of a nation. However, the essential element in the creation of a national spirit has become clearer today: it is a common language. No modern society can function properly without a common, generally understood means of communication.

15. Any shortcuts to development?

When the French Revolution started in 1789, about the same time as the Industrial Revolution was taking off in England, the French people were not prepared for development. Elite figures tried to advance the country by stirring up the mob, until it all ended in a blood bath. A strongman, Napoleon, had to take dictatorial powers to restore order. Nothing of this contributed to the development of the country. Development is not an elite task. When the masses are unprepared, no development is possible. Revolutions are no shortcuts to development. This has been proved again and again by revolutionary movements that have followed upon the French "prototype".

16. You do what you are

When the Industrial Revolution began in Britain, there was a work force largely prepared for the necessary tasks at hand (and more were being prepared as part of the process). These people could gradually influence society sufficiently to create the political and social conditions required for modern life and society and for further development.

After the Industrial Revolution, governmental institutions (e.g. schools) have now taken over practically all the functions beneficial to development largely performed by churches in earlier centuries. Religion (or a special kind of religion) is not required for a country to develop, and the conditions for development can be recreated and replicated everywhere, under whatever ideological umbrella. However, one should not overlook the possibility of making a Frankenstein-monster out of development: any society without a moral foundation (which mostly has a religious basis) can (and most probably will) turn out to be inhuman, and a high level of purely technical "development" could go along with an inhuman society (particularly if this partial development is achieved by means of a specially trained work force and not by the society at large).

The essential conclusions of what has been written above are, however, that conditions for development have to be *created* for modern development to take place, and that *it is possible* to create such conditions.

CHAPTER 6

HOW DEVELOPMENT HAS SPREAD

1. WASPs and other WPs

Modern socio-economic development[1] started in north-western Europe, more specifically with the Industrial Revolution in England, at the end of the 18th century, and this first "revolutionary" phase lasted till around 1830. No exact dates can of course be given, but disagreements about precise dating are of no consequence here.

From England, similar developments spread to the European continent but were for long largely limited to the north-western (Protestant) fringe of that continent.

The development process went on more or less simultaneously in North America, and it was soon going the same way in Australia and New Zealand, settled mostly by Europeans from developed or rapidly developing countries.

The social, economic, natural and political conditions of England at the time, which have often been drawn into the debate to explain why modern development started there, were not so closely replicated elsewhere that these conditions can be said to be necessary conditions for development. But the basic skills and outlook of the people inhabiting

1 The history of this process has often been told. See for example Eric Hobsbawm's books *Age of Revolution*, *Age of Empire* and *Industry and Empire*.

these areas were (and are) so similar that it is natural to explain development there and elsewhere in terms of the similar conditioning and background of the people in these developed areas, as outlined in chapter 5.

South Africa also developed, a process brought about by mainly Dutch and British (and also many German and other) immigrants who had the same background in upbringing and training as those who brought about development in Europe.

South Africa may be the only example of a country that has developed under the drive of a (very large) minority in a country; but broad mass participation was still a precondition. In many ways the situation in South Africa was atypical of developed countries, and its (previous) apartheid policies should of course not be replicated.

2. Only for the WASPish?

When the basis is there, rapid development is possible everywhere, under the most dissimilar conditions. People who are able to bring about development in one place are able to deal with and change essential conditions ("tame" the elements and modify political structures) opposed to modern development.

Much has been written about the violence and exploitation that accompanied development leading to modern society (slavery in America, racial segregation and unequal pay for work in South Africa, workers exploited in inhuman ways in Europe).

But in spite of the just condemnation of such practices, their occurrence does not explain development. Brazil with its numerous slaves did not develop like North America. France was not less ruthless in its treatment of slaves or less zealous in the slave trade than England; but France was less successful in developing, and in the end also less successful as slave traders. Such examples are legion. Spain exploited South America and did not develop. The conditions for development were not present in the Spanish population at the time. Many African governments exploit their peoples more than the white government of South Africa, but this has not led to development.

In fact, ruthless exploitation of the work force is more likely to slow down rather than to speed up development.

What needs explaining in this context is why and how England became more successful than others; and the explanation of that is the explanation of development generally.

3. How far?

From its origins in the parts of Europe that first developed as well as from other areas populated mainly by people from these areas (the Protestant areas of the world), development has spread to other countries and regions with very different orientations and more or less (dis)similar natural conditions. Chronology is in what follows not stressed so much as the types of societies where modern development has taken place.

Facilitating factors?

As great ancient civilisations grew up under conditions and in climates different from those in developed countries, much importance should not be attached to climate as a factor in development. The climate in North America, Australia and South Africa did not change when these areas started to develop, which happened at a time when they came to be inhabited by immigrants with a different conditioning. Farmers and others from developed countries have been able to develop hitherto underdeveloped tropical areas.

The only facilitating factors nature may provide are a wealth of natural resources; but only people with the right qualifications (conditioning) can make proper use of them for development; such people can develop their country even if the natural resources are scarce. (Japan is rather poor in natural resources.)

Modern development can take place everywhere, under any conditions whatsoever.

4. More for whites

Most of Europe is today counted as developed.[2] We can distinguish between three general areas or divisions of Europe for our present purpose: the Protestant north-western fringe; the Catholic south; and the Orthodox and till recently more or less socialist east.[3] But the lines of demarcation should not be drawn too rigidly, either with respect to geography, religion or culture. The first - Protestant - areas have already been dealt with.

P for Protestant - no condition

Southern Europe has a less harsh climate than the northern areas, and over the centuries it has excelled in many areas of modern civilisation: in art, architecture, music, literature, scholarship, inventiveness, the art of living. In the past, the southern countries outshone the north in almost every respect, and a number of well-known geniuses from the south of Europe set their mark on history. But here we are only concerned with modern socio-economic development.

Southern (Catholic) Europe has always been more class-ridden (held back by class differences) than most parts of the (now more developed) north. The class structure of British society and other developed countries has been less of an obstacle to development than the (partly ecclesiastically based) class distinctions of the south, at least until recently.

Once people were absorbed in the social, political or church hierarchies in southern European societies, power was in their hands, and they were not inclined to share it democratically; the common

2 Cf. David Thomson, *Europe Since Napoleon*.

3 Although these regions are designated here by their differences in religion, the important elements in our context are *cultural*. However, it is difficult to find other ways of describing these areas in broad terms.

(or lay) people were kept powerless. Learning was for long practically monopolised by the Church and the upper classes, and they wanted to keep it that way. Education of the laity was not regarded as profitable or desirable.

Mass education on a large scale did not take place in Catholic countries in any way comparable to what was the case in Protestant countries up to fairly recently, and for reasons that reflect different social and ideological values. In Catholic countries, the life of the people was extensively controlled by the clergy and the upper classes. Education was for very long almost exclusively in Latin, a language the laity did not understand. Knowledge (including religion) was largely mystified and "controlled", and this contributed to creating a great chasm between the clergy and other educated classes on one hand and the common people on the other.

New forces

This situation has gradually improved tremendously in Catholic countries, but hardly under the stimulus of the Catholic Church. Well into the 20th century, the Catholic leadership declared its opposition to "modernism", which included economic development and the necessary preconditions for such development. Under such adverse circumstances, people who wanted economic progress sought ideological and practical support from non-Catholic sources and systems, and mostly from leftist movements (Marxism or other socialist/communist doctrines and paradigms).[4]

---

4 Socialist "heroes", such as Fidel Castro and Che Guevara (and Antonio Gramsci), flourished in Catholic countries, as did many movements clamouring for "liberation" (in Latin America, Angola, Mozambique, etc.); and "liberation theology" is largely a Latin American (Catholic) phenomenon.

Socialist movements were for long strong in southern Europe and Latin America. Under pressure from more progressive movements and groups, even the Catholic Church has turned round and now supports popular education in national languages, at least some aspects of the welfare state and other aspects of "modernism". Still, Catholicism as such has hardly been a driving force in modern development.

Because of great opposition between the establishment and more progressive forces, violent revolutions have often taken place in Catholic countries, a phenomenon hardly known in Protestant countries, as this has not been needed for a Protestant country to progress: the Protestant establishment has been in favour of, and a contributory cause of modern development. Opposition between the Protestant churches and progress has not been strongly felt.

Under the weight of "progressive" forces (and probably the example of Protestant countries), the conditions for development were created also in southern (Catholic) Europe, and gradually the south of Europe is catching up with northern Europe, although some areas are still very poor. Some Catholic regions may perhaps be overtaking parts of the Protestant ones in development.

Can the Marxist faith move mountains?

Eastern Europe (including the former Soviet Union) developed for decades under the banner of socialism (communism, Marxism), although some of these countries became socialist only at the end of World War II.

The difference in development between the West and some parts of eastern Europe is still so vast that many hesitate to count all of eastern Europe as developed. But mostly analysts consider eastern Europe as part of the developed world.

Recent events in eastern Europe and the former Soviet Union have shown that Marxism or communism was not a firm foundation for development. Marx does not point in the right direction for countries looking for paths to progress.

Parts of eastern Europe are Protestant (the former East Germany, parts of the Baltic republics, etc.) or Catholic (Poland and large parts of other countries), but Russia and parts of other eastern European countries are Orthodox.

There are Muslim areas in south-eastern and eastern Europe, but these groups shall not be discussed in this context.

"No treasure on earth"

The Orthodox churches, the most mystical, meditative and speculative branches of the Christian Church, consider the world so evil that to withdraw from the affairs of this world is a spiritual ideal. They are not strongly concerned with mundane matters. Naturally, they do not take a deep interest in the development debate or in development activities. With their ideal of rejection of and withdrawal from the world, they do not implant much initiative or drive for development in their followers or people influenced by their ideals.[5] They do not create a social or cultural climate favourable for development.

This indifference to "progress" is indirectly an obstacle to development, as development requires a population that is active, interested in secular or worldly matters, individualistic in its pursuit of better social conditions and higher productivity, hungry for knowledge and eager for change.

Aggressive for earthly treasure

Russia had many progressive individuals before the Revolution in 1917; but development takes place only with the support and participation

5 Orthodox people may of course have absorbed "progressive" ideas and attitudes from other sources, which is in fact very often the case.

of the majority of the people in a country. Progressive and enlightened individuals cannot alone bring about development.

Development in Russia after 1917 in many respects meant doing or continuing what had been started or planned by the Tsarist government before the communists came to power. Still, the 1917 Revolution made a difference. Russia was dragged out of its lethargy, and the mass of the people was forced into the development process, for example by means of large-scale educational programmes. The Marxist ideology proclaimed the possibility (indeed the historical inevitability) of progress. The Revolution created a vacuum in strongly religious Russia - a vacuum where change could take place, and it created so many changes that people had to re-orient themselves in society. To be sure, some held on to past values, but others identified with the quest for a better society. However, on the whole, in spite of positive aspects, many of the communist "innovations" had a negative effect and held Russia back in the long run.

5. Gentlemen in blind alleys - and myopic elites

In countries where an elite or vanguard has led the people, progress may have reached a certain level of development "under the whip", but then it has stopped up. Without the contribution of creative work, ideas and initiatives from the masses in a society, much of the mental and physical energy of a people is wasted and lost. Although some degree of co-ordination (central planning) is needed, progress is rapid only where personal contributions from the masses can accrue to the benefit of society - and that is not the case where people are kept in a strait-jacket.

Outsmarting oneself

One socialist "miscalculation" contributed to the escape of socialist countries out of the socialist vice: socialists have been convinced that people can be trained and conditioned (like Pavlovian dogs) to think and behave according to the will and indoctrination of a "teacher", so that people will accept and do what they are told if this influence is pervasive and of long duration, and especially if it starts early in life.

This is patently not true; but the belief had one important consequence: socialist governments stressed popular education to a very high degree.[6]

People do not only passively absorb what they learn. During the learning process, they learn to reason and draw conclusions and make up their own minds. This led people to challenge, as well as to support, socialist interpretations of society and of development. It did not lead to a single set of collective socialist thinking but in many cases to greater individualism, the questioning of authority, new aspirations that transcended socialist ideals, and a quest for political freedom, power sharing and free choice beyond what a socialist country could provide. It made it possible for people to see (and long for) alternative solutions to social and economic problems, even if these were not officially taught but attacked; and it gave many the desire to be able to choose freely.

As socialist countries matured, they produced more and more people who wanted to break out of the socialist mould. An unfortunate (indirect) influence of Soviet myth-making on "dissidents" was (unintentionally) to create exaggerated expectations of "capitalism" and "the market economy" - the opposite of what they had (the "good" versus the "bad"). Unrealistic dreams and hopes have made it difficult for people in these parts to adapt to "modern times".

When people are ready to become full participants in modern socio-economic development, they will transcend the heritage of socialism (communism, Marxism) and eventually achieve further economic development more or less at the same pace as they progress towards genuine

---

6 Statistical "information" in socialist countries was a total fraud. Figures for literacy were utterly inflated; but evidently a very large number of people did learn to read and write, and some even to think independently.

democracy. This is because the ability to arrange one's socio-political and one's economic affairs develop more or less in tandem in a nation.

An unexpected start

Socialism (communism, Marxism) sometimes helped to jolt a backward and indolent people out of their sleep and to start the development process where it seemed to be slow in taking off.

However, the extent to which socialist doctrines and practices could lead to development was very limited. Several former socialist countries in eastern Europe (for example what was East Germany) could undoubtedly have reached far beyond their present state of development if they had not been led by socialist governments at all.

It should be pointed out that by "socialism" is here meant the social systems of the former states of eastern Europe and some of eastern Asia, not the social democracies of western Europe, where market forces are only partly regulated by state interventions, so as to secure a reasonable and fair distribution of wealth to all citizens and to prevent too large fortunes from accumulating in a few hands, the formation of capitalistic monopolies, and an unreasonable exploitation of workers. The ideals of social justice behind such practices are in reality very different from what was taking place in purely socialist (i.e., communist) countries.

Social democracies in many ways combine the virtues of capitalist and socialist systems. As both capitalist and socialist societies mature, they tend to take on more and more of the features of social democracies, where the wealth of a nation is shared by the majority of its members without quashing their initiatives.

6. Catching at a straw

Many developing countries opted for a socialist path to development (mostly on the Soviet but some on the Chinese model). But as a development model it did not and could never take them very far.

Socialist countries deluded themselves about human nature and the development process, as well as the nature of "capitalism" and Western society. A free and just society, which Marx dreamt of, is incompatible with Marxist social, economic and political theories. Marxism has, everywhere it has been practised or attempted, led to loss of freedom, to social injustice and to economic stagnation and ruin (and staggering corruption).

The reason for this (that Marxism leads to the opposite of its stated aims) is, inter alia, that Marx thought that an enlightened vanguard (of workers and intellectuals) could, through revolution and class struggle, achieve what only an enlightened mass of people can achieve in free and voluntary co-operation, under democratic conditions.

7. Breaking the magic spell

The other major area where modern development has taken off is in parts of east and south-east Asia, the so-called Confucian sphere: Japan, Taiwan, Hong Kong, South Korea and Singapore.

There are promising signs in some adjacent areas as well (including China and Vietnam), but it is less clear to what extent genuine overall development is taking place there yet.

"The Master"

Common to this area is the influence of the teaching and ethics of Confucius. Several aspects of Confucianism are important for development, and especially the following:

(a) Confucianism stresses education, and wherever it has been influential, an educated class of scholars and officials has been trained in the Confucian spirit. This ideal, and high respect for education generally, spread gradually to a wider public, although education in most countries influenced by Confucianism remained largely an elite phenomenon.[7] Thus it did not lead to development until it was fertilised by other ideas in recent times, when the masses were educated and got more involved in shaping social life.

(b) Confucianism values order in the home, the community and the state. This has contributed to "solidarity" (discipline and co-operation) in all areas of social and national life and helped to inculcate strict "rules", respect for the law, obedience and predictability. This facilitated but did not in itself lead to modern development.

(c) Confucianism encourages hard work and stresses the obligation to do one's duty.[8] This became very valuable for economic life and development when other factors triggered modern development.

(d) With the great respect for history ("tradition" and the past) in this culture area, it was not a big step for people with a Confucian orientation to accept a linear and progressive view of history,[9] without which modern development is very problematic and must seem rather pointless.

Although Confucianism as an ethical system (a code of conduct rather than a religion) remained largely an elite phenomenon, its influence has been extensive and very profound. People may not describe themselves as "Confucians" in all of the vast "Confucian area" (most of them have another religion, e.g. Taoism, Shintoism, or Buddhism), but few there have escaped the Confucian influence and spirit. It spread with the travels of Chinese people and Chinese culture to Japan and

---

7 Confucius himself was for mass education, but this ideal was not easy to fulfil and it was hardly attempted. However, his general ideas became a potent influence among the broad masses.

8 For this and other reasons Confucianism, while stressing conformity, engendered some individualism.

9 Confucius was eager for *reform*, which was in fact his strongest preoccupation and concern. The idea of progress is inherent in the belief that reforms are possible.

Korea, in addition to the areas where the Chinese constitute the majority of the population, and less strongly also wider afield. (Hong Kong and Taiwan are of course Chinese, and 75% of the population of Singapore is Chinese.)

Although Confucianism nowhere of itself brought about modern economic development, it laid a foundation which helped to speed up development when the necessary additional impetus for rapid development came from outside.

And Shinto

In Japan, the nationalist spirit, stimulated by Shintoism,[10] was probably a strong factor in the country's desire to develop and not fall behind any country in the world. The major motivation for the Meiji Restoration of 1868 was nationalistic: Japan did not want to be a secondary power threatened by a more powerful West (and suffer the fate that had befallen China). In addition came the Confucian ideals: pursuit of knowledge, discipline, order, obedience, hard work, persistent effort and respect for the past (history and tradition). It was the combination of these influences with Western ideas and skills that made it possible for Japan to succeed where others failed. However, it was the example and especially the threat posed by the rising West that triggered the determined pursuit of modern development in Japan, and it was the success of the West that motivated its drive towards modernisation along Western lines.

Wisely, the Japanese at first tried to learn all they could from the West. They sent a lot of students to the West to learn, and they opened the country for Western influences and products. Education

---

10 Shintoism is peculiar to Japan. Perhaps therefore they came early to think of themselves as "special people", and the national consciousness of the Japanese had thus a fertile ground to grow in.

was modernised and is of a very high order. It is the kind of education that promotes development.

The influences and changes that prepared the Japanese for development made rapid progress possible. Today they hold of course a formidable position in the developed world.

There is no need for any developing country to re-invent the wheel. Japan, like Russia, tried at first to learn as much as possible from what had already been achieved in more advanced countries. This was particularly the case during the initial stages of modernisation and development.

When the Japanese had learned as much as they could from the West, and thus saved a lot of time in the development race, they are now well qualified to forge ahead on their own and take the lead in achieving many further advances.

Other developing countries trying to imitate the West have mostly failed. Development is not primarily a question of imitation: something else is needed for successful imitation to lead to the desired result.

Development requires certain initial (pre)conditions that are not present everywhere. Unless these conditions are created, nothing can make underdeveloped countries develop. In Japan, these preconditions were created before the country took off into modern development.

Beware of Little Tigers

Taiwan and Hong Kong have developed largely along the same lines as Japan, and so has Singapore and South Korea.

China may have had to get rid of burdensome imperial traditions in order to move forward, and it found the help it needed in Marxist socialism (suitable for destruction - less so for construction) to rid itself of this yoke. But socialism proved a troublesome bedfellow for this giant, and it has not yet brought much development. As China is now abandoning strict socialism, it is doing better in every way.

China will no doubt soon become a major force in the modern world: most of the conditions for take-off into development seem to be there. When the reactionary socialist leaders are out of the way, the most serious obstacles to development will have been removed, and China's way ahead seems clear.

8. Israel in the European Song Contest?

One other small Asian country is also counted among developed nations: Israel. Judaism is both nationalistic and individualistic. It stresses the importance of knowledge, obedience, doing one's duty, and family loyalty, and it presents a linear view of history. It fulfilled many of the conditions for modern development from of old. However, Judaism alone did not make Israel a modern state. Other factors were needed before that could take place.

The difference between western and eastern Jews (the latter less "modern" than the former) shows what formative influences the West has had on Jewish attitudes and other qualities that are basic to modern development.

Experiences in a world where they have had to succeed or perish through fierce competition in many ways prepared the Jewish people for modern development. (They might possibly have been the first nation to develop along modern lines if they had been able to keep their own country all along and been more numerous than they are. Many progressive attitudes and achievements in the past point in that direction. Their chequered history has prevented this, although many of their difficulties have also been spurs to "make it" in a competitive world.)

The drive to succeed that often characterises minority groups in any society is also illustrated by Jewish history in the diaspora, and perhaps it is also an incentive in the small country of Israel surrounded by hostile or unreliable neighbours.

9. Seek and ye may find

A couple of the countries in Latin America (Argentina, Chile and Uruguay and perhaps one or two more - Mexico is sometimes mentioned) are by some counted among countries that seem to have started the process that may lead to modern development. Their mixed populations with many immigrants from the developed West, as well as greater openness towards the West than most other Latin American countries, can perhaps explain the greater strides in development there than in the rest of Latin America.

The possible influence of "liberation theology" (a mixture of liberal Catholicism and radical socialist ideas) should not be overlooked as a possible help for these countries to make a break with more conservative forces.[11] The attempts of Latin American countries to break "dependency" relations with the rich indicate a spirit of independence that may be a sign of modernisation.[12]

In many respects, Latin America seems to be experiencing many of the same problems in their push towards development as Catholic countries in Europe experienced not so long ago.

10. Knocking on closed doors

Some countries that have suddenly obtained great wealth, especially through oil extraction, have acquired many of the paraphernalia of the developed world but otherwise not made noticeable advances towards a state that can be called developed.

---

11 Cf. Gustavo Gutiérrez, *A Theology of Liberation*, José Porfirio Miranda, *Marx and the Bible* and Juan Luis Segundo, *A Theology for the Artisans of a New Humanity*. Camillo Torres, a priest, claimed that "the Catholic who is not a revolutionary is living in mortal sin".

12 Cf. André Gunder Frank, *Capitalism and Underdevelopment in Latin America.*

Money cannot by itself bring development. Unless the people of a country are prepared and conditioned for development, that is, to bring about development through their own efforts, no amount of money can make any difference to that country's state of development. If substantial investments are made in the right kind of education, a preparation of the people for development would have been made.

Islam seems not to be giving any impetus towards modern development at present. Its aggressive expansionism and thirst for knowledge that characterised certain stages of its early history did not persist. It has become more backward-looking than progressive,[13] even stressing the importance of teaching their religion and other subjects in classical Arabic rather than in the speech of the people. This is detrimental to development (and imparts of course also rather vague and unclear ideas about details of the faith). Perhaps Islam's emphasis on submission and a fatalistic acceptance of whatever happens as the will of God serves to subdue individual ambitions and personal pursuits and initiatives. Islam was once progressive (for the times) and might perhaps become so again (but an atavistic grovelling for a dead past is not the way to enduring revitalisation).

The somewhat ambiguous signs of progress in a mostly Muslim country like Indonesia may perhaps be the result of Confucian and Western influences combined with a rather weak, superficial attachment to doctrinaire Islam. Possibly the Westernisation and secularisation of Turkey may one day bear some fruit in the form of development.

The main thrust and aspiration of mainstream Islam is not modern economic development but rather faith and morality (right conduct). However, many changes are taking place in the Muslim world, and some of them may perhaps be preparing the ground for modern economic development.

---

13 This is also a characteristic of Islamic fundamentalism.

11. Similarities and differences

The view of history as linear, progressive and time-bound characterises Christianity (and popularised by Protestantism), Judaism, Islam to some extent, socialism and partly Confucianism (with its respect for history).

This view is largely absent from (or at least not explicit in) Indian religions and philosophies (Hinduism and Buddhism and their derivatives), from African and other "traditional" religions, and from most mystical religions. (A mystical view of the world was common also in Catholic and Orthodox Christian cultures when religious knowledge was largely monopolised by the clergy and other religious specialists. This is, however, changing, largely due to outside pressures.)

The chief aims of education in non-progressive systems were and are the continuation of "tradition" and customs (which is actually the essence of their interest in history[14]), the imparting of basic religious, ethical or ritual knowledge, the memorisation of sacred texts and set prayers, perhaps the learning of magic formulas, etc. Only recently has this state of affairs begun to change under the influence of modern development.

Many non-progressive cultures idealise knowledge preserved in texts in a special "sacred" language (Sanskrit, Latin, Classical Greek, Classical Arabic, Geez, etc.). This "mystifies" knowledge and (purposely) hinders most people from benefiting from whatever values might have been transmitted to the masses by these religious, ethical

---

14 In the writing of history in such "traditional" societies, there are usually numerous references to similar events in the past: what happens now, or has happened recently, has happened before. Perhaps the prototype for the present is found in some sacred book. Thus even the teaching of history (which for most people in developed countries is the record of unique events) becomes "proof" of an eternal cycle or repetition of events.

and philosophical systems; this would not be the case if they had been in modern languages.

The emphasis on external and internal discipline noticeable in all progressive cultures seems to be weaker in less developed countries and cultures, although external pressures ("shaming", etc.) and certain forms of self-control, such as yoga (which is not of the slightest benefit to development whatsoever) may be strong in some "conservative" and backward cultures.

12. "Folk" may be wise but they are not progressive

Folk wisdom, as exemplified in folk-tales and proverbs, etc., is not progressive, whatever romantic souls may find in it,[15] and it has contributed nothing to creating a modern outlook or modern development.

In fact, folk wisdom is the supreme example of the "zero-sum" view of development, according to which one man's gain always means another man's loss.[16]

---

15 Cf. Jack Zipes, *Breaking the Magic Spell.*

16 Cf. W. J. Ong, *Orality and Literacy.*

Chapter 7

ARE THERE DIFFERENT PATHS TO DEVELOPMENT?

Many attempts have been made to discover and chart the path or paths that lead to modern development. Some such attempts are summarised below.

1. The great man's limitations

Development, it has been maintained, is the outcome of the genius, the leadership, the achievements of some great, strong, progressive individuals who have shown the way and paved the path. When times are ripe or the situation mature, the masses will follow the lead given by these pathfinders, heroes, "historic personalities", or whatever.

Not all in the mind

Geniuses and vanguards create an elite culture, and rather than leading the masses along, they widen the gap between the elite and other people. As long as such elitist ideas remain elitist, they do not promote development. This was the case among the "best" in ancient Greece and Rome, the priesthood of the Middle Ages, the great figures of the Renaissance and Humanism, the Enlightenment, the French Revolution, the ideological vanguards in communist countries, and the educated classes in developing countries today.

Sometimes progressive ideas have spread from "above" and been absorbed by the masses. This happened in north-western Europe with

Protestant ideas, in the Confucian areas of East Asia and in other parts of the world. In such cases, these ideas and their originators have contributed to the transformation of societies; but this is not so when they have remained within an elite culture.

"Democracy" on behalf of the people

As for Marxist ideas, when they penetrated to the masses in communist countries, the ideas still remained elitist because they were rejected and opposed by large sections of the populace, and only the ideological "priesthood" had the "right" interpretation (communist parties even had their "chief ideologists" - their infallible "popes").

Because people have always had (and retained even in communist countries) an ability to think independently, communism was of course recognised by many people also in Marxist states as an obstacle rather than as an incentive to modern development, in spite of the successes scored by communist countries in some areas.

Destroying oneself while fighting "the enemy"

The "class struggle" as Marxists defined it removed large sections of the people (and perhaps the most energetic and creative ones) from productive life. Nothing set Marxist states back as much as this.

The effect on economic life of making entrepreneurs, industrialists and progressive individuals the evil forces that must be defeated and eradicated by the "broad masses", headed by "workers" or "the proletariat", in the name of progress, was disastrous. By this idea, Marx caused untold harm and suffering and economic stagnation in countries that believed (in) him.

2. Is it all a matter of luck?

Another theory of development tries to identify the greatest possible number of forces at play in the development process. It is believed that a lucky combination of these - unplanned and fortuitous or planned and calculated - will produce development when the right time comes. In one version of this view, it is futile to plan for development, as the result will never be what one planned for. But some think that one can influence events so as to produce the lucky combination of factors. It is not strange (considering the meagre outcome of their efforts) that many development workers and development theorists despair of ever finding the lucky combination.

Do we only see what we want to see?

Many students of development have therefore suggested that development may be triggered by a wide range of impulses, mostly beyond conscious control, but many also "induced" consciously.

Among proposed progressive "impulses" or factors to get development started are: Protestantism, the Protestant ethic, the capitalist spirit, Confucianism, certain religious systems (or religion in general, but others think that religion is an obstacle to development), certain philosophical ideas (e.g. materialism or Marxism), ideas rather than techniques and skills - or the opposite, high technology, intermediate or "appropriate" technology ("small is beautiful"), technical assistance, trade, economic theories, economic planning, market forces, an entrepreneurial spirit, free opportunities for entrepreneurs, liberalism, conservatism, socialism, capitalism, state intervention, private enterprise, race, nationalism, internationalism, leadership of the proletariat, leadership of capitalists, institution building, bureaucratic control, child-rearing practices, the stability of the family, population size and density, peace, conflict, inventions made under the exigencies of war, peaceful coexistence between states, state rivalry, the amount of accumulated capital - privately or by the state, savings, investment, discipline, coercion, incentives, supervision and authoritarian direction, land ownership patterns ("land reform"), the creation of a middle class, the creation of a working class, the creation of an elite (who may lead, and whose progressive ideas may "trickle down" to the masses), an affluent class (whose wealth may "trickle down"), education or "capacity building"/"enabling processes" (elitist or popular, general or professional), the promotion of "key areas", starting development on all fronts simultaneously, urbanisation, industrialisation ("bigger and better"), rural development, agriculture before industry, industry before agriculture, subsistence farming, import substitution, production for export ("export expansion"), exploitation of natural resources, export of raw materials, export of finished products, a high level of spending, a low level of spending, ecological influences (climate, resources, access to the sea), and so on and so forth.

This amounts to an admission that one has searched for causes and found no ultimate cause or causes of development. Instead of judicious analysis built on experience, a haphazard jumble of ideas or guesses is put forward based on superficial observations of what is taking place in societies that have already developed. It is like saying that since such phenomena have been observed there, any or all of them may have led to - and can therefore again lead to - development somewhere at some time.

Nothing is explained in this way. The phenomena mentioned above may be results rather than causes of development. They do not explain development, nor do they help people engaged in development efforts to speed up or bring about development. "Development work" initiated on the basis of such views can lead to no real development.

We cannot force the issue

The only cases where external inputs (money, or help with training, or "experts") have proved beneficial in accelerating and promoting development are when and where the conditions for development have been created or have already been present. Then some such assistance can speed up a process (guided and carried out on the whole by the citizens themselves) that was about to start or already under way anyway, and such a process would have led to the same result without aid - although it would then probably have taken some more time.

External aid may have similar effects in eastern Europe and perhaps China as the Marshall Plan had for Europe after World War II, because the attitudes and skills needed for development seem to be there - as they have to be in order for development aid to have any beneficial effect. Aid to stagnant underdeveloped countries does not have this effect, because the conditions for development are not present. The right foundation must first be laid, the right start made before development aid can do any good, although some forms of aid can perhaps help to lay the proper foundation. We shall come back to this question.

3. Many models?

Another view of development is that there are three development models, or ways to development, that have proved successful to various degrees, and led to development in different areas.[1] In this view, the three models are:

- the capitalist ("Western") model;
- the socialist ("Soviet" or "Maoist") model; and
- the state-controlled capitalist ("East Asia or Japanese") model.

According to this view, there are conceivably many different paths to development, or development models, but of the many theoretical possibilities, only the three mentioned above have succeeded at least to some extent, that is, led to (some) real development.

---

1 Cf. Brigitte Berger, *Societies in Change.*

(A) The Capitalist Model

Western development was and is largely entrepreneurial, with capital in private hands, and the state's task in the area of development was and is mainly to facilitate the smooth running of industry, trade, agriculture and social services by supporting private enterprise, but also by lending a helping hand when needed (there are various degrees of "intervention" from the state in all Western societies). In general, economic life is seen as functioning best when it finds its own ways (regulated by "market forces"), with a minimum of independent economic initiatives by the state.

However, regulation of economic life occurs in all these "liberal" societies. Totally "free" (laisser-faire) policies and practices do not exist. There are laws against monopolies; more or less progressive taxation to some extent regulate the distribution of wealth and put a limit to the greatest fortunes in private hands, and so on. However, the difference between the "freest" (most "liberal") capitalist societies - with low taxes on high incomes and few state-supported or state-run services, and the social democracies - with higher taxes and steeper tax progression and more state-run social services ("the welfare state"), is big.

The totally "free" society, where "man eats man", or where the capitalists can exploit the workers without any constraints, is a myth and figment of the (mostly Marxist) mind. What comes closest to such a free-for-all, "man-eat-man" society is the situation in some of the least developed countries in the world that have chosen the "capitalist" road in theory but which are in fact not capitalist at all but just one big confused, non-developing mess, and where the leaders want freedom to rob and exploit the whole population in the name of progress and "Western", "capitalist" development. In reality no development is taking place there but the opposite. The same situation has come to prevail is some former socialist countries where people seem to think that this is in fact "Western capitalism", just as they were indoctrinated in the heyday of communism. This is a caricature of "capitalism" and developed capitalist societies. These latter are, in fact, well-regulated states, run according to rules and regulations, "the law" democratically enacted, and where the majority of the people have a fairly good chance to make the best use of their talents in ways that satisfy them, where workers are paid quite well for their work, and where people as a whole make a contribution to the common weal.

(B) The Socialist Model

In the earlier socialist (communist, Marxist) societies of the Soviet Union and communist eastern Europe and some other countries (China, etc.), the state used to play a much bigger role than in the freer societies of the West. Economic life was subjected to comprehensive and oppressive central planning and regulation (a "command economy"). It seems that this policy gave a thrust forward to some stagnant societies (e.g. those under Soviet control early in the 20th century and later), but it may at best only have accelerated developments that had already started before. What was typically "communist" (central planning and control, state ownership of all means of production, etc.) retarded development.

After some years of real or apparent progress, this policy led to stagnation, a fact that is now, rather late in the day, realised by all.

Of course a multitude of brains will do better for the development of a country than a few ideologues and technocrats who cannot possibly foresee and satisfy all the needs of a whole population and keep control over all factors of production.

The results of the socialist (Soviet or Maoist) model of development were disappointing in practically all fields that affect people's material welfare, except perhaps in the areas of popular education and health care.[2] Space rockets and nuclear bombs have nothing to do with real development and general welfare; even underdeveloped countries can train an elite to demonstrate spectacular achievements in some such areas if they are well (and wastefully) funded. Real development involves and benefits the majority of the people in a nation, whereas high investment in status symbols (including spectacular scientific feats) diverts wealth from and impoverishes the common people in order to satisfy the vanity of a few leaders and scientists.

Heavy industry is the area where socialist countries took greatest pride, but anyone with knowledge of and experience with machinery produced in these countries will have noted their poor quality compared with Western products.

Consumer industries and agriculture were poor in communist countries and shortages and queuing the order of the day. Service industries competed with consumer industries for the back seat among the failures of socialist societies.

The distance between ideal and reality in the Soviet Union, eastern Europe and other socialist states was vast. Nobody who knows both socialist and capitalist countries at first hand can doubt that all "classes", and especially the "workers", got a raw deal in socialist or communist countries. The only societies that might be worse off are the non-developing countries that have succeeded only in creating a mess of their social, economic and political life. Even among these, those that opted for socialism were able to push their countries deepest into the mire.

What was true for the Soviet Union and eastern Europe applies on the whole also to China and other communist states.

---

2 Even in these areas reservations must be made, as "facts" were pure fabrications, and new knowledge is now coming to light little by little to correct official statistics of former governments.

(C) The State-controlled Capitalist (East Asia) Model

The third successful model, in this view, originated in Japan but has spread to some surrounding countries: Taiwan, Hong Kong, South Korea and Singapore (known as the "Four Little Tigers"), and also to other areas of Asia, but not everywhere with the same speed.

Common to these countries is a strong Chinese and Confucian influence. Unlike what was for long the case in China (where Confucianism started and has been strongest), the possibility for private enterprise is also good in these countries. Individualism is not as prominent as in the West, but free, competitive enterprise is possible to various degrees in all of them.

However, the role of the state is much more significant in many economic activities there than in the West. This last point could give the impression that there is greater similarity in economic affairs and development between socialist countries and East Asia than between East Asia and the West; but this is not the case.

In these developed Asian nations, the state helps private enterprise or corporations with loans and other incentives, and it has introduced legislation that benefits national development. Where it seems to be necessary or beneficial, the state has become a direct partner in economic institutions and undertakings to promote development.

This is in a way another version of Western societies with a mixed economy, where the state may own certain industries or be responsible for certain services, and so on, whereas other enterprises are in private hands: the mix in mixed economies is never constant, and the pattern of mixing or distributing tasks or ownership of means of production varies from country to country. The degree of state intervention may differ, but the principles are not really at variance with each other.

4. The agony of the choice

It seems as if corporate attitudes and ways of ordering one's life (implying rather strong suppression of individualism) are prominent features of most developing countries. They may therefore find what they perceive as the East Asia model of development more attractive than both the Western and the socialist models. On the other hand, many leaders in underdeveloped countries have been attracted by the authoritarianism of socialist states, which seems to suit their temperament.

Civilisation and its malcontents

Many people in the East, the West and the South have sought hard to find a more humane model of development than the one prevailing in the West, while they still want to reach the same level as the West in economic or material terms.

Thus, African Americans have been exploring the possibility of creating an alternative society and culture within the United States; but this has been hard to realise. As more and more of them succeed in "doing well", they realise that this is achieved by identifying with the wider society, becoming an active part of it, and not by standing by the roadside asking for a free ride, or by antagonism or by building an "anti-culture". From "inside" society, they can probably also work more effectively for a society more to their liking than if they remain on the sidelines.

The creation of another, separate, "alternative" society within one's own country does not usually give rise to a better society. Instead, it seems in many cases to be obtainable only at the cost of greater poverty, frustration and marginalisation. However, a few minority groups have been able to create an "upper class" culture of their own. As their self-confidence and self-reliance increase, African Americans may be able to preserve and develop their own cherished culture without clashing with the rest of society. In this way, several cultures in unison could enrich and fertilise each other. This would of course be a good thing. But opting out of society does not enrich anyone.

It is likely that developing countries that want to create a separate economic order, apart from the developed world, will find the going much tougher than if they "join" the international community and play the economic game according to established (which means the best, not the worst) procedures or "rules" (which are, however, being modified all the time).

Going it alone

Minority groups everywhere seem to have had to make great sacrifices to achieve security, sometimes at the cost of a loss of acceptance and a feeling of belonging. This is the price to be paid for success while still keeping one's separate identity. By interlinking among themselves, they have often done astonishingly well. However, they have not helped (much) to develop the societies in which they live beyond their own narrow circles, although they may have made deep imprints on the economy (e.g. through trade and "business") and in other ways. Strong attachment to one's culture keeps these communities together. Only a feeling of superiority in cultural (in some cases also racial) terms and a weak desire to integrate fully can unite and stimulate such groups to succeed in "alien" surroundings. This may have been the case with Indians in East Africa, Lebanese in West Africa, Boers and other whites in South Africa, and Jews past and present.

Birds of a feather

In general, societies that are well integrated do best in overall economic development, although integration is only one of the conditions that must be fulfilled for development to take place.

In Europe, strong national feelings, "patriotism", grew parallel with modern economic development, and as a result almost all the countries that did well were (and are) nation-states. The same applies to countries that have done well elsewhere. Even communist Russia and other communist countries in fact left the ideal of internationalism long before they collapsed (although they continued to pay lip-service to it as a euphemism for imperialism). In practice, for example Russia opted for strong nationalism and the glorification of mother Russia and the Russian past (cf. their term "the great patriotic war" for World War II).

5. Much of a muchness?

Something has to be added to the above analysis. The degree of state intervention is seen as an essential difference between the three development models outlined, justifying the view that development can be achieved by following different, diverging development models, or paths to development.

But another - and probably the more correct - way of looking at it is to regard the degree of state intervention as irrelevant for the development process as such. Other factors determine the achievement of development aspirations.

The state cannot bring about development; neither can it delay the process indefinitely, although it can put obstacles in the way for its citizens for some time. On the other hand, it can also serve as a facilitator in the development process.

Many countries both among those with freedom of operation for private capital and among those with strict state controls (state capitalism or socialism) have failed to develop. These things are in themselves not decisive for development.

Where the people of a country have been "conditioned" for development and acquired the ability to develop, any kind or degree of state role or intervention can serve development, or be an obstacle to development, although "total control" has always had negative effects.

Similar comments can be made concerning other differences between developed societies, differences that in the view of some indicate basic divergences. These variations do not justify the view that there are different and conflicting paths to development.

Are we "converging"?

One theory holds that all advanced societies tend to "converge" and develop similarities in more and more areas of social, political and economic life.

There are limits to the economical ways in which to make clothes, cars, foods, arms and so on. It is therefore natural that industrial countries exhibit many similarities in finished products. Such external similarities may influence lifestyles and social life generally and perhaps also culture and political institutions.

Development may lead not only to more and more similar products but also to gradually more similar political systems, with more and more democracy (as the most likely outcome), although more social and other services - that is, state interventions - may also be expected from governments as countries develop. Educational systems and uses of the mass media may also "converge", at least in general content and style, although stated aims and levels of education vary considerably among developed nations. All this may combine and lead to greater universal conformity and "convergence" generally. This development may not only go one way ("forward"). Thus, the educational systems of the Western world are deteriorating dramatically as the development process seems to be grinding to a halt in (many of) these countries.

"Divergence" is, however, also possible in an increasingly competitive climate. There are forces associated with development that enhance differences between nations and accentuate their "individuality". A prime factor in this process derives from the use of national languages. No country has been able to progress without the general use of its own national language. If great prominence is given to the mother tongue in the educational system, this serves to enhance, deepen and perpetuate the uniqueness of national cultures. This is of benefit for the development of any state.

How can anyone who grows up despising the most intimate thing in life, the mother tongue, ever develop? It is impossible. Development starts with self-respect, self-confidence and respect for one's own culture.

The real point

The question of convergence or divergence as a consequence of development may be interesting to pursue in itself; but in a study of how development comes about it is rather irrelevant.

What is more to the point is to try to find out if there are common features in relation to development in all societies that have developed, and also to find out if these common features are sufficient to explain the origins of progress and take-off into development. That is what we shall attempt to do in the next chapter.

There is more to life than "things"

The question of the distribution of wealth, of social justice, of human rights and values and the quality of life and so on are probably more important (at least to many people) than the question of development per se, although economic development has generally led to improvements also in these areas. However, the concern of this study is not to discuss humanitarian issues but only to investigate how development comes about and how it is sustained.

CHAPTER 8

COMMON FEATURES OF THE DEVELOPMENT PROCESS

There are common features of the development process wherever it has led to real, successful, lasting development. Inessential variations in form or appearance do of course occur, but as these are not fundamental elements of development, they do not determine whether development is under way or has taken place or not. References to the common, essential features of the development process have of course been given already, when development was discussed in historical and geographical contexts. Here we shall try to systematise and summarise and thus come to an overall view of the issue.

The purpose of this chapter is, then, to draw conclusions from previous chapters in such a way that "lessons" can be learnt about how development takes place, and so that we can discover what way to go, and thus indicate guidelines for countries in search of or in the process of development. By inference, it should also be possible to see why the development process is reversed in some parts of the world and decay sets in.

Essential ingredients

The enumeration of as many different causes of development as possible only leads to confusion: one cannot see the wood for the trees. The important task is to discern essentials in a mass of details.

The points mentioned below do concentrate on essentials; and so as neither to complicate the issue unnecessarily nor to over-simplify or over-generalise, important details are discussed under six major headings. Even if the six "points" may seem few in number and easy to implement, it takes generations to absorb them fully and to put them into practice in and by a society. It involves the whole process of internalisation of ideas, values and skills in the socialisation of individuals, starting from childhood and lasting all through life. Only in this way can these "conditions" become part of the common ethos, value system, psychological make-up, and customs of a nation and the "habits" of the majority of its members. Probably only children brought up by parents who have themselves internalised these values and habits can become fully modern people.

I takes a long time to change values and behaviour, to implant new views, attitudes and skills so that they penetrate into the subconsciousness of people, but without such an educational and socialisation process, development is impossible. No country has ever developed overnight, and there is no evidence that the process has become much easier over the years, but perhaps it is possible to speed it up due to the many more examples of successful development to learn from. When the principles are correctly understood and applied, the right foundation laid and the process followed through, every country in the world can develop.

Being and becoming

It is fairly easy to characterise a developed country by pointing out the essential features of how it functions. But how did this development start and come about?

Countries do not develop just because their people want or plan to develop. Many have tried and not succeeded. Those that first succeeded seem to have developed almost without knowing or fully understanding why or how they succeeded. This applies particularly to Western societies. More deliberate planning was the basis of development in East Asia. Successful countries like of course to think that they have been in full control and succeeded by virtue of great qualities like hard work, discipline, high intelligence, good planning, wise government, and so on; but others who have these qualities have failed. It is important to understand the reasons of both successes and failures.

Our task is therefore to explain why some have succeeded where others have failed. Disregarding superficial variations that make no real difference to development, and also leaving aside non-essential characteristics of developed nations, we find the following common features of all developed countries.

1. Educational characteristics

A right start

The first point we need to pay attention to is the educational system or process, starting with the upbringing of children in the home and going on till the highest levels of education.

The unique quality or feature of education in all developed countries is that it starts with the known and concrete in the immediate surroundings of the learner and proceeds gradually to explore the more remote and abstract, without losing contact with the factual and observable (the "scientific" basis).

This differs from all educational systems that either

- try to imitate slavishly the educational system in another ("model") country, or
- stress abstractions and ideas like universal truths and international values (e.g. some kinds of elite or "traditional" education) rather than the near and concrete, or
- glorify old, "classical" knowledge and wisdom (dead languages, a golden past, etc.) rather than the present.

Don't miss the nearest thing of all

What is the near, the known and the concrete to the learner? The main point is so simple that it is usually overlooked by many developing countries.

The nearest thing is the mother tongue. Everyone can master it, and nobody can master it to perfection. It trains the learner in most of the skills a person needs in order to become a partner in development - but only if this language is the most important subject to learn from earliest childhood (even before school age) and throughout the whole educational process.

Those who have not gone through this kind of educational process can only with great difficulty become full partners in development. There may be a few brilliant people here and there who may be exceptions to the rule, but these are never numerous enough to make any difference to the development of a country.

A few outstanding people in developing countries where a different educational system is in force can make a mark, just as there were a few noteworthy people in Europe when Latin was the medium of instruction, but they rarely make much of a contribution to development, not more than scholars in pre-modern Europe made any contribution to modern economic development.

The easiest, simplest and best

In learning the mother tongue properly, in and out of school, the learner is trained in many skills: precision of thinking and execution while learning correct spelling and grammar, the proper use of words and expressions, fluent sentence building, to divide material into logical paragraphs, to acquire a good style, and so on.

This training benefits all other subjects, and where this training is lacking, the understanding of all other subjects suffers, precision is deficient, sloppiness and what is "almost right" are tolerated and become "normal".

If imprecision and carelessness are tolerated and accepted in learning the primary language of instruction (as is the case when a foreign language is the means of instruction), all processes related to development will suffer from the same attitude of carelessness and acceptance of what is only "almost right" - but not quite right (which means: wrong). That is not compatible with modern development; it makes in fact such development impossible.

Long and basic education in the mother tongue makes a tremendous difference to understanding and thinking, habit formation and practical work. (The skills acquired in thus learning the mother tongue may be strengthened if a foreign language - as a subject, not as the means of instruction - is added later, but not if this is done instead of learning the mother tongue properly.)

No substitute

Education in the mother tongue cannot be replaced by any other form of education and training without great loss to the learner, a loss that affects development negatively.

Without prime place for the mother tongue in the educational system, no people or nation has ever developed. Not a single developed country uses a foreign language as the normal means of educating its people, nor of everyday communication.

This is basic. This is the most important point of all to notice and draw the right conclusions from. It is, however, the most overlooked point in very many developing countries, first of all in Africa.

Don't jump over the horizon too soon!

The principle of starting with the known and proceeding to the unknown, going from the near to the more remote, from the concrete to the abstract, is followed by all developed countries in their educational systems.

Thus, geography starts with the home surroundings and the home country and then leads further afield. History starts with the history of one's own country and only then goes on to other countries. Science starts with observation of what is at hand and only later leads to more abstract concepts.

Underdeveloped countries often start with a foreign language. Students may learn more about other (developed) countries (where the textbooks they use may have been written) than about their own. They often start afar and perhaps never reach quite "home" in their studies. This is not education for development.

Don't look back like Lot's wife!

Nor does it promote development to glorify the past at the expense of the present. Europe used to exalt classical languages and learning till modern development was well under way, and therefore the academic establishment at first contributed nothing to modern development.

Modern development was rather promoted by "lay" education in the local language about the near and familiar - and with items of new knowledge added gradually.

Until China and Japan sought to develop along modern lines, they valued "classical" learning (in schools emphasising their great writers of ages gone by) more than "the near things". So did India (and perhaps still does). Muslim countries tend to do the same, as does also Christian Ethiopia.

Only countries with a strong orientation towards a better future have been able to develop. That is the case in Japan, Taiwan, Hong Kong, and Singapore, and increasingly so also in China and some other countries.

Education for what?

The educational system lays the foundation for all communication of value for development. It opens markets for mass publication, which forms reading habits (people in developed countries read quite a lot, whereas people in underdeveloped countries read much less except to pass exams); it makes it possible to use the mass media effectively to increase popular participation in social and political life; it facilitates the understanding of instructions for the use of the products of development, including information about food and food making, health care, child care, child rearing, etc.; it enhances the opportunities for skills training and popular participation in all areas of life (thus transcending traditional divisions into castes, guilds, or classes), and so on.

Everything of relevance for development follows from an educational system giving instruction by means of the mother tongue. Nothing can replace it as a "force" promoting development.

You change while you forget

It is important to understand that what counts and makes a real difference in the educational process in relation to development is not what one learns in school but the learning process itself.

About 90% (ninety per cent) of what is taught or learnt in school is soon forgotten. What is the value of keeping up an educational system that seems to have so poor lasting results? The answer is: the forming of the learner is the result that counts.

Through the process of learning (paying attention, doing one's duty, being precise in how the work is done), the learner becomes a different person.

The learning process forms the learner, and it is this learning and forming process that has lasting and permanent results and effects: nobody who has gone through years of learning has quite the same personality traits at the end of that process as when it started, and learning in the mother tongue makes the deepest and most enduring imprints.

Besides, one mass of valuable knowledge and information remains: a rather firm grasp of the mother tongue itself in all its aspects, written and oral. By having applied the mother tongue to the understanding and learning of a variety of subjects, one can go on applying the mother tongue to increase one's grasp of other matters. It makes it possible to perform a variety of roles in life efficiently.

One needs to be able to use the mother tongue in a variety of ways and situations in order to learn the processes needed for development and to become a full and active partner in development. It is not enough to "know" the mother tongue from the home and one's surroundings: disciplined and systematic learning over many years is required.

Only by using the mother tongue to understand a variety of subjects during several years does one become versatile enough in the mother tongue for it to become a tool - the most important of all tools - for development.

As all learners soon forget nearly all that is taught in school, what is taught is less important than how things are learned, the learning process itself.

The learning process shapes character and forms habits - working habits, habits of thinking, attitudes, values, and so on. It is therefore very important to be exposed to precise formal training during the educational process. It is not the same as to "develop" (rather than to form and transform) one's personality, or to "express oneself" (one almost gets another self), or to be trained in a skill or skills (many in developing countries have sufficient skills without promoting development; we shall look at the reason for this later).

Education for development is learning to do a lot of things correctly with one's brain, body, ears, mouth, eyes and hands. When this is achieved in a co-ordinated manner, it does not matter all that much if most of the content of the lessons is forgotten. To develop understanding and the ability to think and express oneself is only one aspect of this learning process, and perhaps not the most important one. To form the mind and character and to establish firm habits of doing things, to learn precision and to work to schedule and to do "one's duty" on time are the most important aspects and results of an education that furthers development.

To develop imaginative skills and creativity may be significant for a happy life and for entrepreneurship but may be less important in mass education aiming at making each learner a partner in development. However, stimulation of curiosity and inventiveness are important to train workers given tasks requiring personal initiative and imaginative approaches, of entrepreneurs, and of "leaders in development". Practical creativity is perhaps the most valuable aspect of inventiveness and an enterprising spirit in relation to development.

The confused and dithering character of modern Western education at present[1] is probably one of the main reasons why the West is less competitive in development than it used to be. Westerners' refusal to adapt their working morale and their living standards to the demands of a more competitive world outside the West is another reason for reduced Western competitiveness.

Outsmarting the smart alecs

No elite (vanguard, pioneers, leaders, intelligentsia) can develop a country. The mass of the people has to make an essential contribution, and they can be enabled to do so through solid mass education of the right kind.

A more or less uniform educational system that practically all can participate in and benefit from contributes to the social cohesiveness that makes it possible for national development to be of one piece, to have unity. It makes it easier for people to work together for common goals. And it makes it easier for national leaders to co-ordinate and "direct" the development of the nation after the population has been "equipped" for development. Such goals can be achieved only by

---

1 Educational psychology is a popular instrument in the service of a system that tries to teach young people who do not want to learn what they do not want to learn. Of course it does not achieve the same as the "disciplined" kind of education that took the West where it is today (or was till yesterday). No wonder that the West is going the same way as its educational system.

an educational system which uses the mother tongue as its means of instruction in all subjects.

Without a broad base in an educated populace, no leadership or economic or political system can bring about development. The training in skills of select groups with the aim of creating a technical elite is no substitute for mass education. In fact, the present policy of many developing countries - to train lots of technicians rather than giving priority and full support to general education of the masses - has not helped the development of these countries in the least; on the contrary: these "elites" have become a burden on the economy without contributing much to, and often retarding, the development of their countries. Furthermore, these countries do not show any great ability in making the best use of such "skilled" people.

Looking for scapegoats

The complaint about a "brain drain" from the Third World is one of the many "excuses" underdeveloped countries make to explain away the fact that they have not been able to develop. However, even available brains are rarely properly utilised.

Other "excuses" for failure are: unfair trade terms; colonialism; neo-colonialism; exploitation; the creation of relations of dependency through loans, aid and unfavourable trade agreements and other economic transactions;[2] conscious underdevelopment of developing countries by developed ones;[3] political interference; military adventurism, and so on. But these are not the real reasons for underdevelopment.

North-western Europe was also underdeveloped and exploited when it began to take off into development. America was a colony when it started to develop, and slavery contributed little to the process, as the

2 Cf. André Gunder Frank, *Capitalism and Underdevelopment in Latin America.*

3 Cf. Walter Rodney, *How Europe Underdeveloped Africa.*

northern States with the smallest number of slaves developed before the southern States, where most of the slaves were - and the West Indies and Brazil, that were crowded with slaves, failed to develop. Slavery is in fact a poor foundation for development; no "slave society" (where all significant "productive" tasks have been performed by slaves) has ever developed. Even the United States had to abolish slavery in order to shoot ahead, and productive work was never left exclusively to slaves.

Only an educated population can develop a country.

2. Essential mass participation

A country develops only when there is mass participation in the development process.

Not primarily a question of organising the masses

It is popular in development work to talk of community participation (or involvement), that is, to get people (the masses) to take part in community projects, for example the building of a road, or a clinic, or a school, the digging of a well, and so on. This is of course good and often necessary in order to get some small projects carried out. But it is not what is here meant by mass participation in development.

Unless people are enabled or equipped to be full partners in development in all respects, occasional or regular efforts by a community to undertake "community work" make no real difference to the development of a country. The enabling process leading to development starts with motivation, child rearing and education and leads to practical involvement of a whole society in the total development process.

More than know-how

The emphasis on this aspect of development is made in view of the belief quite common in developing countries that the training of an elite can bring about development, whether this means training in politics, administration or skills, or the training of trainers. These countries are now crowded with engineers and skilled professionals, and still they experience "negative growth", going backwards rather than forwards, while still crying for increased "technology transfers". A helpful step in the right direction would be to make good use of trained people and knowledge already acquired - but it is in the very nature of being underdeveloped that a country is not even able to make the right use for development of people and skills they already have.

No amount of skills training can by itself bring a country forward on the road towards development. One could usefully keep this lesson in mind: Thou shalt not kow-tow to know-how! Development requires a popular base of the right kind.

The whole populace must be trained for development if development is to take place. This must be done by all means available, especially the schools, but also by adjusting social institutions so that people receive the most appropriate training and suitable employment. Then even professionals can be fully and properly utilised.

To repeat: it is less important what one is taught (which is mostly forgotten anyway) than how one is taught (the learning process), in what language one is taught (the mother tongue), and that the whole population receives at least primary education.

What you are and what you know and what you do

When people receive the proper training for development, they learn to think in a modern way, to make goal-oriented choices, to evaluate tasks and perform work along progressive lines, and so on.

This has a dual influence and result: people who have been trained so that they can contribute to the development process also become able to make choices and decisions about how society should function so as to support economic development and human welfare generally.

In other words, the population in an economically developed country has also become politically conscious and can influence national politics. The qualifications needed for development and for political participation are the same.

That is, development and democracy go hand in hand, but one is not the cause of the other.

A developed country does not need an "elite" or "elites" in order to develop. A "vanguard" in development tends to distort development and become a burden for a developing society.

In a developed country, people themselves can take control of their political life and institutions. The very smart guys alone have never been great assets to the economy or the political life of any nation, whatever other contributions they make. But where the masses are enabled to make real contributions to development, the highly skilled can of course also be of the greatest value - and only then can they be really useful.

"Elites" can enrich life but they are not progressive

After the repeated emphasis on mass participation - against elite leadership or elitist domination of economic or political life - as a precondition for development, something more should be said about "elites".

Elites in economic and political life are an obstacle to development if they are in control of it. In highly developed countries, such "elites" are not dominant because these countries are not dependent on them in order to function well and to progress. In developing countries they are normally among those who suck their countries dry. There may be progressive individuals among the elite, but as a group they are not progressive.

Economic development is not an elite phenomenon, it is a mass movement, requiring mass participation, and both the clever ones and the less clever ones are needed: all must do their bit.

Southern Europe - slower to catch on to development than the north - has had greater artists and other "elite" persons of a cultural and social kind than northern Europe, and people there have also long known how to live more interesting lives than northerners. But this is not the same as being in the forefront of economic development.

However, it needs to be stressed again that development is not the end or peak of all human endeavour and aspirations. On the contrary: many people in developed nations are continuously seeking values not always easily found there and that may in fact be more easily found in poorer countries: spirituality, simplicity, spontaneity, joie de vivre, humaneness, warm personal relations and so on.

Fringe benefits of development: the real thing

In view of what has just been said, we should, however, add one thing: in developed countries, the creation of literature, music, art, schools, museums, parks and so on tends to increase as a result of development.

Elites are contributing to the enrichment of life in all developed countries. The search for better human and social relations and spiritual values is going on there all the time, partly as an outcome of development. With more leisure, many people start looking for values that transcend material things, although materialism also increases.

Elites and elite products contribute greatly to make life more worth living in all developed countries, and without them, life would be very poor. They are not only needed but may even be increasingly appreciated the more a country develops.

This said, a return must be made to the earlier point: development is not an elite product. Elites cannot bring about development, but they can be participants in the process. If elites are in power, they tend to slow down the development process. Elites do, however, take first place in other areas of a nation's life.

Development is the result of mass participation, and it takes place when the masses are enabled to contribute to their own development. They can do this to the same extent as they can influence public affairs through creating and controlling democratic institutions. They are able to gain power and control political life through the same slow and gradual process as they can develop their nation.

If "reforms from above" are successful and contribute to development, they are always the result of pressures from below, from people who are ready and in fact able to control the "top". Without this base, "reforms from above" invariably fail and normally cause chaos and slow down development.

Putting the cart before the horse

Mobilising the masses for development before they are prepared, enabled and equipped for it only leads to confusion, as for instance the "Great Leap Forward" - which was a great leap backward - in China.

"Community participation" organised from above may be good for minor local development tasks, but this does not lead to overall development. Something much more fundamental and sustained is needed for development to take place. If it is meant to be a shortcut to development, community participation is rather like putting the cart before the horse, an attempt to turn an effect into a cause.

'Revolution!"

Something similar has been attempted in political life. When progressive elites want rapid political, social and economic changes before the population is ready and equipped for it or enabled to be full partners in development, they usually appeal to the masses to help them overthrow the existing order. This often leads to mob rule, chaos and destruction, as mob leaders rarely (if ever) are able to control the forces set in motion, unless they become ruthless tyrants.

From the time of the French Revolution, many have tried this method. It has always led to regression and stopped development processes under way, or delayed the start of these processes.

Revolution is the tactic of people who think they can bring about development before the ground is prepared.

There has been only one development path that has resulted in the emergence of developed nations. All the seeming alternatives (the "different roads to development") are illusory, because elements that have nothing to do with development are thought to relate to this process.

There might possibly be other ways to development, but so far they have not been found.

3. Nationalism and the nation state

Too much of a good thing?

Nationalism can be interpreted as ethnocentrism, self-centredness, racism (and in some cases it has developed into the most horrible forms of racism, as in Nazi Germany, Fascist Italy, apartheid South Africa, and so on), tribalism, or other forms of narrow-mindedness.

"Ideologically" or "intellectually", nationalism seems to be on a much lower level than internationalism. The latter has been the ideology of many empire builders at all times, of communists and proponents of a World Government. (This latter may have been one ideal behind the United Nations; however, the United Nations' inability to stimulate economic development in the Third World may serve as a strong argument against it.)

Something can be said for accepting to be what you are

Leaving the theoretical arguments for or against nationalism or internationalism aside, it should be pointed out that development has only taken place in countries with a fairly strong national consciousness.

The nation-state seems to be the ideal unit for development. The following points may help to explain why this is so.

- For a country to develop, it needs a unitary means of communication (a common language) and a unitary "spirit" for easy, efficient co-operation.
- When people share a "heritage" that binds them together, making them "one", they seem best able to work together, make common efforts, strive towards common goals, and live peacefully together.

What is "nationalism" anyway?

It is not easy to state what the national "common feeling" or unitary spirit is, and it has changed over time.

- At one stage, a "common culture" was thought to be essential; however, the concept of culture has undergone changes, and the views of what is essential in a culture have changed.
- Earlier, a common religion was considered a strong unifying factor, and different religions as divisive. Where people are "fanatical" about religion, this is still partly true, but fanatical forms of "fundamentalism" are also divisive within the same general religious community. In developed countries, religion is now much less important for national unity than it used to be.
- Race is today becoming less and less important for national unity, in spite of the racial (ethnic) conflicts that flare up here and there. Even states or nations that consider themselves as being "of one blood" are in fact always mixed, and nations are "made up" or "built" to a much larger extent than is commonly thought. Race should be of no importance at all in creating unified nations.

- A common historical "memory" may still be important. Where people identify with main events in their country's history, national cohesion is cemented, and this cohesion can be strengthened through the educational system and other means of social integration. However, as people living today did not take part in events before their lifetime, and as events in any case take place locally and not in the whole nation, a "common history" is a psychological phenomenon. Immigrants can share in this "experience" by identifying with what the adopted country stands for. (What other reason could for instance the United States have for demanding a knowledge of the country's history before granting citizenship to immigrants?)
- Today, a common ("native") language as the general means of communication and education is the most important factor for a people living together to feel and act as one, to be a nation in practice. The general trend of state formation in developed countries has since c. 1800 been that people who speak one language join together within national state boundaries. These states have been able to develop the fastest. It thus seems likely that there is a close link between these two phenomena: nationalism/nation states and development.

The most important factor is not the only one

A common language is in itself not a sufficient cause of development, as seen by the fact that also underdeveloped countries may have a common language but without developing; however, it is a strong contributory factor if combined with other elements. It makes a tremendous difference to the education process and to people's consciousness of unity.

People who become fully bilingual can identify with speakers of a national" language they have adopted and acquire a feeling of belonging to that nation. This has been so for immigrants to the United States, and also for inhabitants of states built up of several nationalities or "tribes". Such an integration process must be harmonious and voluntary, if people are to accept as "theirs" features of a "common" history, and customs and ideals that serve to unite them. In both "plural" societies (with several "nationalities") and "pluralistic" ones (with several religious and political parties, value systems, etc.), what unites people must be felt as more important than what divides them in order to develop a national "spirit".

It is a prerequisite for harmonious nation-building and a contributory factor in development that a national language is used continuously in one's surroundings as the "natural" medium of expression and education, and that any citizen can thus easily absorb it and become completely fluent in it. This has been happening in for example the United States, Latin America and Tanzania. It has not taken place in any country that has "adopted" a foreign language without strong natural roots in the population. Where English or French is chosen as the national language in a developing country, it slows down the process of "nation building" and is detrimental to the educational process and to development.

No nation has ever developed in this way, and if precedents are anything to go by, no nation ever will.

Abuses are no objection to proper uses of nationalism

"Reasonable" nationalism can be nurtured and developed, and it can mature to the benefit of a country.

Different "nationalities" or "tribes" can be united in a wider feeling of belonging together within the same state borders. If this is attempted through repression rather than by transcending tribal feelings, conflicts rather than unity are fostered, and this is detrimental to development.

A nationalism that is exclusive creates hostility and harms intrastate and interstate relations, but "reasonable" nationalism (patriotism) need not take this turn: people can learn to feel as one and develop a fellow feeling without being negative to others. Such a nationalism is inclusive and can normally easily incorporate new members who will "merge" rather than create a nation within a nation.

Competitiveness within a country and a wish to excel can benefit development without creating feelings of antagonism. International sports events develop a spirit where competitiveness may foster friendship. The same can happen in economic relations between nations, and this can help countries to speed up the development process. Healthy competition is no obstacle to development but a spur.

Nation states can serve a useful purpose

A nation state seems to be a natural unit for co-operation, for maximum exertion, for common political, social and economic organisation, and for development.

There are some very large states where organisation and management may suffer from too large a size, and in such countries, extensive local self-administration may work better than strong centralisation. The federal principle or system has worked well in some such countries.

On the other hand, there are nationalities ("tribes") that are so small that they will benefit from combining with others to form larger states. In such cases, (some degree of) self-rule (autonomy) in "internal" affairs may be advisable, at least as a temporary measure till stronger ties are forged with other nationalities in the same state. Effective "mixing" can occur through extensive voluntary movements of people within the state, in search of employment, for purposes of trade, through intermarriage, etc. Learning and using a common language can stimulate unity across "tribal" divides. Also here, voluntary federal arrangements may be found suitable.

Can others learn from the nation state?

On the pattern of existing "successful" nation states, reasonably large states can with advantage be formed or "built" in developing areas fragmented between a great number of small "tribes". The process of "nation building" is an important task for all such countries as a preparation for take-off into development. Elements of such nation-building are: the creation of symbols and expressions of unity, such as a common language, a "common history", uniform cultural manifestations and customs, and a uniform educational system, in addition to a central government, a common monetary unit, a common flag and national anthem, armed forces under a central command, a common foreign policy, and other "normal" symbols and expressions of unity.

However, unwise and harsh policies to unite a tribally divided country can be a cause of friction, disunity, and continued backwardness.

When different nationalities are combined in a state, it would be best to create "natural units" to facilitate the process of nation building. Overcentralisation and very strict state controls are no solution but will probably prove detrimental to the forming of harmonious unitary states. A federation built on mutual respect and support may work better than enforced unity.

Making good use of a patriotic, "nationalist" spirit

Nationalism can be used to whip up hostile feelings towards others and thus be a force for destruction. On the other hand, nationalism can be a positive force for co-operation and belongingness. It is compatible with a desire to compete to reach the highest levels of excellence among one's own fellow citizens as well as in relation to other nations. The highest possible degree of achievement can be an aim for a person or a state without therefore trying to get others down or to succeed at the expense of others. This "positive" form of nationalism can benefit development; its absence from a country seems to make rapid and high levels of development very difficult if not impossible.

4. Mastering oneself: self-discipline

Doing what does not come naturally

There is a spirit of self-discipline and self-control among people of all developed countries that leads to a high level of exertion and efficiency, but also to frustration. This kind of discipline takes different forms and has different causes in different cultures, but it is never absent from any developed country. This training in discipline starts in early childhood in (most) such societies.

Is the family out of date?

The first point worth noting is therefore that in developed countries the family has (until very recently) been seen as a central, close unit where primary socialisation has taken place, and this socialisation in the course of child-rearing has been given high value and priority. It has closely followed established cultural patterns and norms.[4]

During earlier centuries in the most developed parts of Europe, religious norms were prominent. Because of some idiosyncratic ideas among those who had gained wealth and pretended or aspired to belong to an upper layer of society, a certain "bourgeois" form of behaviour and associated norms developed. The "bourgeois" way of life is only a superficial and irrelevant manifestation of an ethic that (in Europe) originally stemmed from a popular, watered-down religious inheritance. A "bourgeois" ethic has as such no value for development, except that strict norms of any kind may form disciplined personalities.

After modern development had reached a fairly advanced level in Europe, much of the "bourgeois" ethic was replaced by secular norms

---

4 The family as a fundamental institution is in the process of collapsing in the West. So is the economy. There may be a causal connection if the old maxim is true that society is a reflection of the family.

(of "decency" and "propriety") that differed little from the older ethic until very recently (perhaps till around 1968). Now these norms are much relaxed and may be in the process of being forgotten in the West. However, the old norms have not been completely abandoned, although the ostentation of the proponents of the "new ethic" or new morality may give the impression that it has.

The new ethic stresses values of more unrestrained freedom, almost limitless enjoyment, and a low level of involvement in many of the traditional "values". All this may have relaxed discipline and contributed to the economic decline of the West. The weakening of family ties may be both a cause and a result of this development. This also has contributed to and accelerated the tendency towards weak discipline and thus to economic laxity.

The relaxation of earlier norms has not been replaced by a generally accepted "new ethic" in the West but by widespread normlessness.

The socialist ethic initially stressed full freedom of individual choice in familial relations; but gradually all socialist or communist countries had to make laws to protect the family, as very loose family ties resulted in the near-dissolution of other social ties and cohesive forces, including those relating to work and development. Together with other aspects of the "socialist ethic", laws protecting the family and giving children a more stable home atmosphere suitable for "progressive" socialisation helped socialist (communist) countries to reach the stage of development they eventually reached. However, the attempt at controlling people and forcing them to adopt an ethic that did not evolve relatively naturally, freely and voluntarily led to only reluctant co-operation between the populace and the authorities. This prevented these societies from reaching their highest potential of development. Social "containment" is not the same as self-discipline.

In the "Confucian" areas of East Asia, the family is rated highly, and family cohesion is strong. Children are cared for and trained (socialised) for adult life in loving and concerned ways, usually largely in the care of the mother. This has most likely contributed to the speed with which development has been able to take off there.

Child-rearing

Earlier in Europe, children were brought up strictly, and they were soon taught adult norms and duties. Children were early taught to "take responsibility".

Particularly in the area of sex, European parents tended to instil views and behaviour patterns that led to much frustration in the European population, but also to self-control and self-discipline. (This may, by the way, also partly account for the widespread aggressiveness in modern European history, manifested in such phenomena as conquests, wars, colonisation, racism, fascism, ethnocentrism, etc. This tendency was exacerbated by the "exclusiveness" of the religious indoctrination of the strictest forms of Christian triumphalism or fundamentalism.)

With the weakening of religious influence in the West, some of these attitudes may be changing. However, as no constructive new values and norms seem to be replacing the old ones, society may be in dissolution and development in regress. As people are unwilling to give up accustomed privileges, forms of fascism may replace old-fashioned religious bigotry.

In developed East Asia, child-rearing is as "careful" as in the West (or as it was in the West when the West rose to and held a position of leadership in the world), but with a difference. In the East, young children are given much more freedom, and they experience a less strict home surrounding than in the West (or than in the West of the not-so-distant past). Sexual restraints and taboos (with corresponding feelings of guilt and shame in this area) are not imposed on them, at least not in the same way or to the same degree as in the West up till recently. This gives them perhaps an easier and more harmonious early childhood than Western children. Very strict, even harsh discipline and competitiveness (and deep frustration) normally begin when East Asian children are sent to school. School discipline in the Confucian East is (normally) extremely strict, and competition for good marks is unlike anything known in the West.

Japanese school education seems to be of a much higher standard than Western school education. Japanese ambitions to excel in exams are so high that failure has often led to suicide. This may be regretted, but it has benefited the economy.

Discipline can have many causes and take many forms

Competitiveness and harsh discipline in the pursuit of excellence in education, combined with careful indoctrination in proper form and polite behaviour, have in the East led to personal discipline and self-control and individual exertion to reach the highest limits of one's capabilities. This has been an asset to economic life in ways similar to what strict early child-rearing and socialisation (in combination with less competitive mass education) have been in the West.

In socialist countries, the need to conform to the rules of a regimented society led to a kind of superficial "socialist morality". But external "force" without adequate incentives or inner motivation made people fall far short of their potentials in production and development in these countries. Discipline of this kind serves no progressive purpose.

Jewish parents seem to have been indulgent in their child-rearing practices. However, ambition or the necessity to succeed in life (an attitude strengthened by their "marginal" existence in many societies) has both disciplined them, driven them to make the most of their abilities, and together with various cultural and external pressures (including discrimination) induced them to enhance their determination to succeed. This "discipline" has evidently helped them to gain success in many areas of modern society.

The many faces of marginality

Marginality is in itself not always a (strong) motive to discipline oneself and to strive for success, but it can be.

Indians and Pakistanis in East Africa (more than "at home"), Lebanese in West Africa and Jews around the world have done well socially and economically for reasons like social cohesion (mutual support and co-operation as well as international networks of contacts), faith in themselves, and a certain desperate resistance to being submerged in a wider society.

Black people in the United States, the United Kingdom and elsewhere have (as already noted) succeeded best when they have been well integrated in society at large and accepted the majority culture. The desire to excel has given many of them a spur to great achievements in the societies in which they live. Attempts at creating or keeping separate cultural identities have in their case led to losses for themselves, to "apartheid" in practice if not in theory. If they become more aware and proud of their cultural uniqueness, their ability to keep their distinct identity and values and still succeed may be enhanced.

The ideal of letting each social group develop according to its own wishes and instincts without helping those who want to integrate in a wider society to do so may lead to social fragmentation, stagnation, ghettos and ghetto mentalities and underdevelopment for these groups.

Only minorities with self-respect, pride and the conviction that they can reach a high level of development "as they are" seem to be able to stay marginal and at the same time do well and even profit from their marginality. People who are being kept down and separate by external forces may have a hard time developing, but efforts at "preserving their soul" may not be in vain.

The child is father of the man

A stable childhood milieu develops reliability and predictability. This is the case if the home milieu has been trustful and fulfilled the child's expectations. Such characteristics are valuable for social and economic relations and development, which are built on trust and the fact that the vast majority of people knows and follows the "rules of the game" according to which developed societies function.

People coming into developed societies with different ethical orientations can profit and do very well by bending the rules, which is not very difficult where principles of freedom, honesty and trust are strongly established and expected to be respected in a society. However, if the majority, or a large number of people, behaves in this way, i.e., bending the rules, social and economic life will be undermined and decay. This seems to be happening in many developed societies where norms are disintegrating.

"Blessed" are the prudent misers, for they may be rich

Another characteristic of successful or developed societies where children have been strictly brought up is that people in such societies learn to plan and to delay the enjoyment of what they have access to and which is available to them, both in the areas of economics and of morals.

Western societies earlier frowned upon "too great" luxury, conspicuous consumption and "free living". People who earned well did not use all they could afford in order to acquire comforts and ostentatious possessions. Instead they saved. And so as not to let money lie idle and be useless, they invested. And where it became unfashionable to invest in "meritorious" works or to build too glamorous houses and furnish them extravagantly, people invested in productive enterprises. This was of obvious advantage to economic growth and development.

In Japan, the saving rate is high, and this allows the state and financial institutions to invest "saved" capital for development purposes. This partly accounts for the important role of the state and large financial corporations in Japanese development.

The ability to delay enjoyment, save and invest is necessary for development.

Learning to love what you hate

The kind of discipline that is most beneficial for development must become so internalised (and give shape to feelings, instincts and views) that it is not felt as something imposed from outside.

If the values taught or inculcated during childhood and early youth are so internalised that they become part of the subconscious and unconscious mind, as well as the more conscious forms of life and thought, then they will determine what people do naturally and easily ("live by") when they become adults. They will set their mark on everything they do. It becomes part of their "morals", almost instinctive.

If the majority of people in a society is brought up with more or less similar values, these values (the common social ethic or ethical orientation) will help to give shape to that society in many ways, including aspects that strongly influence and promote development.

5. A spirit of co-operation

This point shall be briefly stated.[5] In all developed countries people seem to be able to work together as a group towards common goals. This is not only so in a piecemeal way but it marks their attitudes and their total orientation to work.

Upbringing and education aim to help people to "fit in", to respect (but not fear) "authority" (those who decide and give instructions) and

5 Emil Durkheim sees discipline, social cohesion and co-operation as aspects of the same thing, solidarity, which in his view normally (but not for him personally) needs a religious basis (in a broad sense) if societies are not to disintegrate. If post-religious (which in Durkheimian logic would imply post-moral) Europe (or the West) can continue to prosper, Durkheim's thesis would be disproved. If the West stagnates and regresses, this would confirm Durkheim's views. History can apparently show no example of a society continuing to flourish after the moral base has collapsed.

to be able to take sensible "orders" because one believes that this is beneficial and necessary for the common good and for the task at hand. The "chain of command" is respected irrespective of the level of knowledge or skill: even a better qualified worker knows that things will fall apart if "orders" or instructions are not followed.

Unwilling or recalcitrant obedience of superiors in the working place, because one "has to", is a different thing from a co-operative spirit and will in the long run only serve to undermine the working morale and the ability to get things done.

The "willing spirit" seems to be the basic attitude that upholds the normal practice of co-operation in developed countries, although it is of course not always or universally present there either. It now seems to be on the decline in many countries in the West.

As this co-operative spirit is found in all developed societies, it is likely that these societies have developed partly because of this ethos.

But this spirit does not automatically lead to development: a country like China had for long such an ethos without developing. Now, however, it seems to be a strong contributing factor in its development.

On the other hand, in countries where people work competitively against each other, are suspicious of each other's motives and "obey orders" only half-heartedly or reluctantly, development seems to be slow, if not totally absent.

A voluntary, positive spirit of co-operation (but not submissiveness) is essential for the development of a nation.

Even when "classes" form, they have to co-operate if development shall have a chance to take off. Adjustment of economic and social differences must find other ways than a class struggle where one class tries to eliminate the other.

Nation states, or communities sharing a common language and a common culture, seem on the whole to be ideal entities or units for fostering co-operation.

6. Progressive attitudes

You become what you believe

The last point that shall be mentioned is that people in developed countries largely agree that progress or development is possible.

A much more common view in the world is, or was till recently, that things will continue to be much as they are, and if someone, or a country, gets rich, or gets an "advantage" above another, it is at the expense of someone else. As the total wealth in the world is, in this "static" ("zero-sum") view, thought to be (more or less, or absolutely) constant (without increasing or decreasing), a wealthy person is in a sense "unjust", or a "thief" who has acquired more than his or her fair share.

Those with a fatalistic outlook on life may think that economic imbalances are the natural order of things, the will of God and depending on his curse or blessing; or depending on certain "qualities" in people, such as noble blood or high caste or intelligence. Wealth is thus seen as a "reward" in economic terms of what is one's "right".

These views do not inspire exertions of a progressive kind.

Prizes for everyone?

The "modern" view of development - namely that total growth is possible, that one can progress by increasing the yield of the earth without "robbing" or depriving anyone or depleting the earth[6] - is recent and dependent on two interpretations of the world:

---

6 The very legitimate concern about the over-exploitation of resources, depleting them for future generations (non-sustainable development), does not contradict the view that equitable world-wide development is possible. "Sustainable development" does not mean that development is impossible or harmful.

- growth or development has taken and is taking place: this is a reasonable conclusion from the fact that modern development has come about in many countries in the world; and
- the "linear" view of history: this perspective on modern development sees history as moving "forward" and not as an eternal repetition of itself.

The history lesson made simple

There are some slight indications of a linear view of history in antiquity, but it was fully and clearly spelt out only in "Semitic" religions (Judaism, Christianity and Islam).

The Bible tells that God has created everything and "governs" the universe towards an end or goal. Man has been charged with obligations to serve God and people, and this service includes the duty to rule over ("subdue") the earth and everything in it (Genesis 1:26-28).[7]

Although these biblical injunctions were given long before any inkling of modern development took place, such exhortations were strongly stressed when development got under way, both to "justify" development and to show that development was in line with the will of God. Development could thus be seen as the fulfilment of God's

---

7 The Book of Genesis, chapter 1, verses 26 to 28, reads:

"And God said, Let us make man in our image, after our likeness: and let them have dominion over the fish of the sea, and over the fowl of the air, and over the cattle, and over all the earth, and over every creeping thing that creepeth upon the earth.

So God created man in his own image, in the image of God created he him; male and female created he them.

And God blessed them, and God said unto them, Be fruitful, and multiply, and replenish the earth, and subdue it: and have dominion over the fish of the sea, and over the fowl of the air, and over every living thing that moveth upon the earth."

purpose with the world. (In Islam, however, the linear view of history has led to fatalism and inertia.)

People's thoughts were increasingly shaped by progressive views in the West, and history came to be written in such a way as to explain the working out of the will of God. The historical process was "seen" to have a purpose and aim, and historical "laws" were "discovered". These same "laws" came to be explained in "evolutionary" terms when Westerners began to free themselves from the religious interpretation of history.

Same old belief on a new foundation

When religion lost much of its hold on "modern" people's minds, the teaching of history and science (first "scientific" Darwinism about the "evolution" of living things and the survival of the "fittest", then also "social" Darwinism about the "evolution" of society and the success - and dominance - of the "best") has been able to "explain" development without recourse to God or religion.

National and world history as taught everywhere today explains past events "empirically" (not religiously), and history is universally taught in such a way as to "explain", and give hope of, development - endlessly, to ever greater heights ("Up and up and up and on and on and on", in the "Whig interpretation of history"). Only recently are cautioning voices about the limits to the potentials for growth being clearly heard.[8]

"The modifiable character of fatality"

This book has tried to show that there are no inevitable laws leading to development, but that economic and technological development depends on the development of human capabilities in certain directions, under special circumstances, under full human control.

---

8 Loud early warnings came with Donella H. Meadows et al., *The Limits to Growth.* Cf. also their "sequel" 25 years later, *Beyond the Limits: Confronting Global Collapse; Envisioning a Sustainable Future.*

Development is not inevitable, and the development process may be reversed. However, history seems to have moved "forward" totally: we have not "forgotten" all the achievements of past civilisations even when these civilisations have collapsed.

Thus, history seems to have moved forward, and not in circles or cycles with an eternal repetition of the selfsame things. And with its ups and downs it has totally reached ever greater heights, at least technologically (although questions may well be asked whether this development is also reflected in improved human relations and/or greater happiness).

From a "linear" historical point of view, history should therefore not be represented as a circle.

From the same (linear) viewpoint, it could possibly be represented as a series of circles that are not concentric and not overlapping (indicating that each civilisation makes a new and independent start).

Or probably it could be better represented as non-concentric and partly overlapping circles, indicating that much is taken over from earlier civilisations by succeeding ones.

However, the best way to visualise the historical process as development may be as a series of generally upwards-moving waves (rather than as a straight line), with the point in history where we live now at a higher level than the starting point (the earliest known history), and higher than all previous civilisations, and also generally higher than preceding periods of our own civilisation (although reverses and even a total collapse may occur).

But, again, this model, illustrating the "linear view of history", represents only technological and economic development; that is what we are concerned with here.

Whether true or false, it works

Nobody can "prove" whether the "modern" view of history is correct or not. Reverses in the development process are quite possible and indeed likely. There may come a time when mankind, or a section of it, will "overreach" itself, or when it does not exert itself hard enough, and a downward trend or slide starts (or a steep plunge may occur). However, the belief that universal development is possible is widespread and spreading, and this belief is itself a stimulus to development.

*

It should be clear from the preceding pages that the view propounded here is that every nation can develop; development is universally possible. However, economic development takes place as a result of the development of specific human beliefs, attitudes and skills, and not according to irreversible historical or natural laws.

No time to sleep

Development is in our hands, and what people do will decide their speed and level of development. Development does not "come" of itself. It is a product of human ingenuity and effort - if these are applied and exercised in the proper way.

The "progressive" view is built into practically all modern educational systems all over the world. For many in developing countries it may still be only "book knowledge", without having become part of their conviction or so internalised as to influence their orientation and conduct. But the "linear" view of history and development is in the process of penetrating to all corners of the world and to each living person.

Breaking down our defences

Recently many people are registering objections to this "progressive" view, at least in its more mechanical form.[9] Still, "progressive" views are gaining ground.

---

9 We create the spiritual and intellectual and moral world we live in by our beliefs and convictions and the conduct that results from them.

Not only history but also the sciences (biology, astronomy, physics, etc.) are today taught in "evolutionary", "progressive" ways in schools and universities.

Even mathematics - besides contributing to precision and the development of logical thinking - promotes in practice a progressive view, in that it shows that (mathematical) problems have solutions, and that one can find solutions (solve problems) by applying logic and being persistent.

If mathematics is taught so that it is within the grasp of the average pupil or student, it helps to develop attitudes and habits of mind as well as skills that are beneficial to development generally. But if, in an attempt to "raise the level of education", it is taught so that only some of the pupils become "comfortable" with mathematics and learn to solve mathematical problems with ease and confidence, then the teaching of mathematics, whatever its other merits, is not a very valuable contribution to development. This is because development does not depend on a few exceptional brains but on mass participation. For this kind of participation, the masses must possess the required skills and attitudes, and they acquire them in programmes of popular (not elitist) education. However, a developed society can also make good use of the extraordinary gifts and achievements of "elites" and "geniuses" for further development.

Not all in the mind, but mostly there

Development is probably more a result of the acquisition of mental attitudes (and beliefs) and habits of thinking and doing things than it is of the learning of particular practical skills.

> Development presupposes order and belief in the possibility of order. Order is "discovered" and "created" when we imprint (or force) our views upon our surroundings (or the "world" or our "universe"). But disorder and chaos are also "there". If "chaos theories" determine our conduct, our "world" will also be(come) chaotic and cease progressing. Our beliefs form our existence. "Order" and "chaos" are not absolute entities.

Specific professional qualifications (skills) are useful and needed in order to do most jobs well, but most of the skills required for very many modern jobs, and for participation in development, are fairly easy to acquire (with exceptions, of course), if people's attitudes and habits have already, beforehand, been "conditioned" for development. In most underdeveloped countries, the problem is not that people lack skills (although still more are needed) but that those with appropriate skills so seldom make (or are given the chance to make) proper use of what they are trained for. The essential mental attitudes and the required social environment are lacking.

You are - and are shaped by - what you think and believe. This adage seems to be true perhaps especially in relation to development.

CHAPTER 9

A DEVELOPMENT MODEL FOR AFRICA

Africa is a bounteous and beautiful continent, and its people have developed social institutions and created cultural values that are admirable and that have served them well.

Every nation in the world is by nature equipped with more or less the same gifts and potentials for any kind of achievement in all fields of human endeavour: art, science, scholarship, politics, economics, development - as well as destruction, war, exploitation, etc. Africa has the same potentials for development as any other continent.

Starting from scratch

Africa has the poorest people and is the least developed of all the world's continents. The saddest part of it is that there is no indication that this situation is at present changing for the better.

Africa is not even on the way towards development. Africa is becoming poorer and more underdeveloped by the year. As Africa has not found the course that leads to development, the continent is in dire straits indeed.

Wanting to compete

The wish to develop is strong in Africa. Everyone seems to want the artefacts or products of developed countries, but nobody - in or out of

Africa - seems to know how Africa can develop and become self-sufficient and self-reliant in any area.

It is easy to see that Africa has made a false start towards development.[1] Actually Africa seems not to have really started to develop at all. However, there are many voices advising Africa how to do better.[2] When such advice is taken, by Africans or outside supporters (development agencies), Africa has been getting only ever deeper into the mire.

Africans have increasingly responded to theories and practices of development coming from outside the continent (largely imposed on them) with "theories of underdevelopment" or suchlike. This may be done in order to find alternative ways to go, but it may also be done so as to be able to pin the blame for Africa's economic and technological backwardness on someone else: capitalists or colonialists or neo-colonialists. When they think they have found the right target for their anger and frustration, many revert quickly and comfortably to inertia and do nothing; or they join a "revolutionary" or "reactionary" movement promising change. When "the revolution" (or whatever) is over and an alternative order established, the new republic usually becomes worse than the former. Again, capitalists or colonialists or neo-colonialists are blamed.

A country is as developed as its people

Africa is the least developed continent in the world - and Africa is as developed as its people.

It is always so: any country in the world - North or South, East or West - is as developed as its people.

---

1 Cf. René Dumont, *False Start in Africa.*

2 Cf. René Dumont's many books on Africa; Goran Hyden, *No Shortcuts to Progress*, etc. The International Monetary Fund (IMF) and the World Bank use both the carrot and the stick to get Africans to do their bidding.

Africa's present state of development is no indication of the intellectual level or professional quality of the continent's "elites". Nor is of course the present level of development in Africa an index of Africa's potentials.

Development takes place when it becomes a mass movement, involving nearly everyone in a country. Africa needs not remain underdeveloped. All the necessary human potentials and natural resources are available in the continent. If Africa is to develop, Africa's own people have to take charge of their own development.

It may be true what one perceptive person has said: "We Africans will never develop unless you developers (foreign development workers) get out of here." Whether that is so or not, Africa's future is in the hands of the Africans.

Development aid has been of help in countries where the population has already learned what development means and have found the right path to development. But in Africa, development aid has often been given in such a way that it may have made the situation worse and underdevelopment more glaring, inhuman and disastrous. The right kind of "enabling" or "capacity building" aid could, however, probably do some good.

Broken dreams

Many Africans have begun to look back with nostalgia to better times in the past. It is almost certain that Africans had more to eat and were generally "better off" and more content in the past than they are now. Many may therefore wish to turn their back on "modern development" and instead embrace, or hold on to, "traditional values". However, it may be difficult, probably impossible, to reverse the present trend towards modernisation.

At the present stage, many Africans seem to seek only the most superficial and least valuable aspects of what "modern civilisation" has to offer, to the dismay of the more "traditional" of them. If the turn towards modernity stops up now, it is likely that Africa will be left for a long time with this "surface development" and end in even greater chaos and poverty than it is in today. A radical return to past values and customs, to the exclusion of "modern" ones, would probably turn out to be detrimental even in the eyes of most of the "traditionalists". A healthy mixture of the best of the old and the best of the new would be the best solution.

Is there hope?

So what is to be done? I shall add one more voice to a chorus by trying to answer that question. However, my voice will not be singing exactly the same tune as others.

The persons who will be most strongly opposed to these views are those who have profited most from the present situation. This includes politicians, businessmen and intellectuals (most "elites"). As these are also among the best educated and most articulate of all Africans, practically wholesale condemnation of what is proposed may be expected from their side.

Hopefully some of the "common" or "ordinary" Africans will appreciate this challenge to the majority to take charge of their own development and benefit from it. On the other hand, there are also dedicated leaders and intellectuals who have the welfare of their country and people at heart.

Perhaps people from donor countries (politicians, tax payers and development workers who do not want to squander money) may react to the poor performance in development in Africa by rejecting present aid policies and practices. They may seek better ways to go or leave Africa to go its own ways. There are indeed other and better ways of doing things than perpetuating the mess we see today. However, it would be a big mistake to turn one's back on the wretched of the earth.

Aid benefits mostly those who help themselves to it

Aid is today largely a means of lining the pockets of the few. This happens partly through corruption. However, much (possibly most) of it ends up benefiting a few well-paid people who follow the rules and are not directly corrupt but may contribute little or nothing to development.

The majority of the people in African countries become comparatively worse off as a result of development aid as given today because it contributes to widening the gap between the rich and the poor.

The most effective aid for African development ought probably to be given almost exclusively directly from donors to or through reasonably small but efficient non-governmental (independent, voluntary) development agencies that work closely and directly with the people they want to help, or that are run by the beneficiaries themselves.

International organisations dealing with global aspects of the environment and health and international law, etc., are needed and can do useful work. The fact that global and regional political and economic organisations are essential for international relations is, however, another matter, not relevant in our context. They ought, on the other hand, not to function as aid or development organisations, as they cannot be efficient or avoid the misuse of funds (although they might be of some service by facilitating the international exchange of information and experience, e.g., through a limited use of "advisers").

Emergency aid through "neutral" global organisations may be justified, but food aid in crisis situations would be most beneficial to a country or region if food is bought from adjacent areas, so as to stimulate local food production. Droughts are often the result of unwise government policies and practices, but outside food aid may actually worsen the situation, as it may depress local food prices and frustrate local initiatives (and also lead to corruption).

Africa is no "special case"

Africa can develop if it follows the same path to development that has been followed by every country in the world that has developed. In spite of differences between developed nations, there is only one known road to development, and the differences that do exist between developed countries (e.g., with respect to the distribution of wealth) are irrelevant to or for development *per se*. Africa can only develop by taking the same path.

The situation in Africa today is such that the rich get richer and the poor poorer. By combining the worst of Western practices with the worst of African traditions (and adding more of their own invention), dictatorial or rapacious governments exploit their people more than any colonial government ever did.

The stakes up for grabs are very great. Lack of transparency and accountability and the use of "law and order" to protect ill-gotten gains make corruption so easy that few can resist it, and there are few or no mechanisms to prevent it. Ever more people try to get a piece of the cake, either through manipulation and dishonest practices, or by military might, or through "revolution", or by just becoming corrupt officials at a lower (and perhaps safer) level. Leaders try to stay in power by "rigging" elections and by creating and maintaining a middle class or other "interest groups" (for example by pampering to the "needs" of the military or an officer corps or businessmen or a swollen bureaucracy). These are given enough privileges to keep them in line and to support the powers that be. Aid may actually stimulate this tendency.

Instability is the order of the day in Africa. Still, stability is claimed by all in authority to be a necessary precondition for "development" - but to them it may just be a means of staying in power so as to be able to "eat" more. Many things need to change if Africa is to develop.

Aid for development?

One step in the right direction for donors who want to extricate themselves from participation in the tragedy of Africa would be to make sure that aid (money, loans, goods, experts, etc.) reaches the people in greatest need.

Rich Africans do not often become entrepreneurs, nor do they generally invest in productive enterprises. Wealth may be used for the acquisition of land (which they rarely developed well), status symbols (cars, etc.), or "real estate" - houses to rent out so as to earn money without having to produce anything. Ruthless "security forces" and strict laws against "theft with violence" (exempting embezzlement, etc.) are in place to protect the interests of the rich.[3] If these people can find ways to become large-scale beneficiaries of development aid, that is one way to join the class that oppresses the poor. This may be done legally and above-board because law-making is in the hands of those who use the state machinery for their own ends. Little aid reaches the really needy, and relative to the big beneficiaries they become poorer.

"Colonisation" from within

The educational structure in Africa also contributes to Africa's underdevelopment. The educated (including most leaders) have become the heaviest burden on African economies, drawing unreasonably high salaries for producing nothing and contributing little of value to Africa's development.

Productive peasants and workers are given the crumbs, which become fewer and smaller as the "elites" grow. The educated have become very capable of voicing their "cause": equal pay with Westerners

---

3 This is in many ways a replication of the situation in Europe soon after the Industrial Revolution; cf. *Les Misérables* by Victor Hugo.

for jobs requiring the same education - but without asking questions about comparable "productivity". No one stands up to claim the same pay for African as for Western peasants even if they work just as hard. Thus, things go from bad to worse.

There is still hope

What, then, is the way forward for Africa? We shall see how the points discussed in the previous chapter (about common features of developed countries) apply to the African situation. This should make it clear both where Africa has gone wrong and how it can change course so as to find and follow the path that leads to development.

1. Education

Colonising the mind

Modern education in Africa was earlier closely tied to foreign missions and foreign rule (colonialism). Also the few "indigenous" schools that grew up during colonial times largely followed foreign patterns. It is a pity that independence has brought so few changes for the better in this respect, in spite of the great expansion of education.

African schools try as soon as possible to reach a level where the school population can use a colonial language in all subjects taught, and mastery of this language is the key to success as well as a (if not the) principal sign of academic excellence. The foundation is laid in elementary school, and the foreign language is then often both the most important subject taught and the medium of instruction in all subjects from junior secondary school up to university level.

The reasons given for this vary. One is that it would be too expensive to make textbooks in "local" languages. Of course it is much more expensive to train teachers and students year out year in to know and use a foreign language well enough to learn and to teach all subjects in this language, with the added cost of importing foreign textbooks (where they are not produced or reproduced locally).

Another reason given is that the educational level ought to be the same as that in developed countries. And as education in developed countries is thought to have contributed to these countries' development, it is assumed that a faithful replication of the same educational system will help developing countries to develop. This is a total fallacy.

Education in a foreign language can never be kept at the same level as in the country where that language is the mother tongue of the population. This is one reason why educational levels are often low in Africa. Even where students have been able to cram a lot of knowledge or book facts, they are rarely able to make full practical use of their knowledge or education. Even where the level of education in such a situation is high and fairly close to its model, only an elite is able to keep up in such a system, and elite education - whatever its other merits - does not contribute to development. Mass education does.

Being different by being equal

Most important of all: by copying the educational system of a developing country very closely, a developing country stands the original pattern or system on its head. The educational system in every developed country starts with the principle of teaching the familiar, concrete and near things first, and only then proceed to the more remote and abstract. If an African country copies or imitates the school system of a European country, it follows the opposite principle: it starts with the remote, the abstract and the unfamiliar.

The start of education in a developed country is always made in the mother tongue, and this is the most important subject all through school. University education is also in the mother tongue. It is inconceivable for people in a developed country that it should be otherwise.

No country can develop by educating (or trying to educate) its population by using a foreign language as the principal means of instruction.

The primacy of the mother tongue

In a developed country, it is expected of all who write articles or books or whatever that they are able to express themselves with fluency and precision whatever their specialisation. Good and correct language is not the exclusive "domain" of linguists or literary people.

Fluent and easy command of one's primary means of expression is the most basic requirement of an educated person in a developed country.

In developing countries educating their people in a foreign language, it often happens that a person cannot express all thoughts easily and precisely in the mother tongue, let alone in a foreign tongue. Only a minority of people in developing countries can express themselves correctly and fluently in a foreign "national" or "official" language. Newspapers, radio programmes, books, even school and university textbooks are often badly written. One can thus easily understand the low level of precision and understanding among the majority of the school and university population. This must change if Africa wants or is to develop.

Crap!

The present state of education in Africa produces claims that it is content, not form, that counts. As one intellectual wrote in a book review, lambasting Western emphasis on correct form and good style: "The most important thing about literature is not style; it is the message conveyed." This could never be said about "literature" in any developed country or by any intelligent person fully educated in the mother tongue.

"Westerners" do not emphasise form or style at the expense of the content or message of a book or article. For a book to be printed or read at all, the author must aim at perfection in all aspects, in form as well as content. If it had been otherwise, Western scholarship and literature would be in poor shape indeed.

In every place where development has taken off, the aim with any kind of product is to make *everything* as correct and perfect as possible. This holds true with respect to writing and publishing, teaching, the execution of a job, etc. A car is bought as much for its appearance as its performance, and the same holds true also for clothes, houses, furniture, food, books, etc.

Development must be of one piece - just as scholarship and art must be of one piece - or it is not development (or scholarship or art) at all. Form is as important as content, content as form, especially in education, where so much is forgotten. It is the way one has learned to work with problems that endures and improves.

Decolonising the mind through the tongue

No developing country can develop unless it adopts a "local" language which is widely known and spoken "naturally" in the country as the "official" and "national" language and the means of mass education and communication.

In countries with many small tribal languages, it may be possible and advisable to adopt one of the most widely known languages as the national, official and educational language, without limiting people's right to use local, "tribal" languages when that suits their needs better. A well developed minority language may sometimes serve the same purpose. A "local", naturally used language chosen as the "national" language will help the process of "nation building", if the language is used continuously in a variety of contexts.

The most important thing is that a "national" language must have a natural base in the country, so that it can be heard *naturally* in its pure and correct form at all times. People are able to adopt a new language in this way, as has been the case with English in the United States and

Swahili in East Africa. This never happens with a language that is "naturally" foreign to the population, for example English, French or Portuguese in previous colonies in Africa (with the possible exception of South Africa).

If a language spreads widely through natural expansion, or even some pressure (as sometimes happened with for example Arabic), such a widely known language can be adopted as a "new" national language. But this expansion can benefit the process of development only if it takes place through the daily influence of "natural" speakers of the language.

English or French or Portuguese (or Italian or Spanish) has no chance of becoming a "natural" language in any previous colonies (except possibly where a large segment of the population speaks that language as their indigenous language - as for example English in South Africa). A kind of Creole has sometimes taken shape as a result of the meeting of languages, but that has no advantage over an "indigenous" national language. A Creole may, however, become a full-fledged language in its own right, and then it can of course also be a national, official and educational language where there is a natural base for it.

When fringe benefits matter most

If a national language with natural roots in the country becomes the language used for all nation-wide activities - education, communication, legislation, politics, etc., then many areas of life will benefit. A greater amount of information can be absorbed and far greater precision and understanding achieved than if a foreign language is used. Clear thinking and analytical depth are developed. It becomes easy to internalise what is taught and learned, and one can make good practical use of one's knowledge. It is a thorough absorption of ideas, attitudes and routines that counts most in the development process.

Who does it is more important than how it is done

A shortcut to development is sometimes attempted by emphasising skills training at the expense of formal training. This defeats all purposes of education for development.

The skills needed for development to take off are not very complicated. They are fairly easily learned or acquired. *The efficient way work is performed* in developed countries is the result of a long process of mass socialisation and internalisation that goes far beyond the learning of skills.

It is not the transfer of technical knowledge or technology that is the problem. There is enough know-how in Africa already for development to start. It is proper mass education that is needed. Developing countries can never side-step this part of the educational process and develop by stressing skills training at the expense of formal ("character") training.

Developing countries are surfeited with professionally trained or skilled people who are not able to get development started. These people therefore mostly drain the economy without putting sufficiently useful inputs back.

Educating those who really matter for development

Developing countries need a broad foundation for development in the form of an educated majority of their people (and not only many highly trained or skilled people) to reach a more advanced stage of development.

This can be achieved only by dropping foreign educational patterns and start with the near and familiar. Basic requirements are the use of a national mother tongue, stress on local and national history and geography and civics, phenomena studied in the immediate surroundings in science, and straightforward, practical mathematics using local concepts and examples and drilling students till they become thoroughly familiar with basic mathematical concepts and skills instead of reaching as high a level as possible quickly by learning theoretical mathematics the learner cannot properly apply outside the classroom.

Doing it your own way

The *principles* of education applied in developed countries also developing countries can learn something from. However, wholesale imitation of foreign patterns, without adaptation according to the same principles, turns the purposes and results of education topsy-turvy. The outcome is disappointing for developing countries because it is detrimental to modern development.

2. Mass involvement in development

As a result of having copied too much from foreign educational systems without sufficient adaptation, African nations have not been able to properly equip and mobilise the masses for development.

The few against the many

The belief that an elite or elites can bring about development has resulted in the training of a lot of technicians. They are on the whole overpaid, underemployed and a drain on the economy. If others (e.g. peasants) were paid according to their contribution, relative to that of the elites, the national economy would collapse. The demands of the elites have nearly managed to do that alone.

Of course it has been observed that the productivity of workers and peasants in developing countries is lower than in developed countries (making "cheap labour" quite expensive). However, this is not only the case with peasants and workers but also with highly trained professionals of all categories. One of the main concerns in relation to development must therefore be to raise the level of efficiency and productivity in all areas of work in developing countries. High salaries in poor countries contribute to inflation or the exploitation of the peasantry and the working class. This is in fact what is taking place on a grand scale, and it holds these countries back and makes development an ever more illusory dream. No developing country is served by producing and pandering to parasites.

Laying a firm foundation

One of the most important steps developing countries must take in order to develop is to give good elementary education (six to eight years) to the majority of their people, in their own national languages and in subjects relevant to their life and surroundings. Skills training can easily be added and suited to national development needs, and professionals can be fitted into the national economy as required. The masses must have a chance to contribute in areas where they can contribute most and be rewarded according to what they do to meet national needs. This should be true for workers as well as for "elites" of all kinds.

No "system" can bring about development

There has been much discussion of the advantages of democracy versus "strong(man)/one-man rule" and-party systems in Africa. In relation to development, this debate is largely irrelevant. Under whatever system, in practice the principle of "One Man One Vote" usually prevails, and the One Man With The One Vote is the top man, whether under the guise of democracy or in open dictatorship. Where dissenting voices are allowed to be raised and heard and "opposition parties" are tolerated, the outcome is mostly the same. Change often comes through a coup, but the same system goes on. The milder forms of tyranny may sometimes open ways for some development. However, genuine democracy and development come into existence together, more or less simultaneously. Autocracy and development are basically incompatible, but formal multi-party democracy does not cause development.

Democracy in a real sense can only exist when a population is reasonably well educated. Such a population can also help to further the development of the country. Democracy is not a cause of development, but the same people who can promote development can also take charge of political affairs. Democracy and development are twins.

Elites with an education largely unsuited to their countries' needs will cling to power and oppose changes in the educational system and the power structure, as the system by its very foreignness is the hallmark of their "uniqueness" and "right" to power and privileges.

But unless the education process changes so that it can equip, enable, mobilise and involve the masses properly, the present situation will go on, and little or no development will take place; and democracy will continue to be as illusory as ever.

Hidden forces for development

It may be that the first indication of a groping towards real "self-determination" and "self-reliance" appears under various disguises, such as an upsurge of certain religious expressions ("indigenous sects"). Often such sects urge their adherents to be well informed about their own religious position. This normally makes them seek more education.

Such sects are popping up all over Africa. It is probably a reflection of a wish to develop independently and find new and more rewarding ways of living than is the case at present.

Unless they are too odd and irrational, such sects may develop thinking, understanding and independence of thought and action, which are the first steps towards democracy and development.

If such aspirations are weird and fanciful, they may be the expressions of longings for sudden and miraculous transformations of society in such a way that the wealth ("cargo") of foreigners will be transferred in a moment to groups of Africans.[4] Even these seemingly irrational hopes may be reflections of deep desires for change and progress and thus be symptomatic of the times. These "sects" have great potentials for mobilising the masses, and if they stress education, they may even promote "indigenous" (that is, true) development.

In practice, a predominantly rational search for progress is likely to be more conducive to development than the primarily emotional aspirations of millenarian movements. If this "rational" search takes the form of careful and intensive study, it does not matter in a development context if the search is for "secular" benefits or if it is for enlightenment in scriptures regarded as sacred and authoritative (such as the Bible). This latter may also well prepare people for development and democracy, as it did in Europe prior to the Industrial Revolution, and which it seems to be doing in many parts of Africa (more so than abstruse and absurd ideologies that used to appeal to some intellectuals).

If the educational system fails to give the masses the help they need to develop, religious movements that stress knowledge and understanding may step in and be catalytic and provide the necessary lever for development to take off. This differs from the situation in the developed world, where secular education and information dissemination are everywhere replacing the influence of churches and other religious movements as spurs to development. Secular trends can perhaps be helpful for countries with forms of religion that are not particularly conducive to - and that may even be obstacles to - development.

In Africa, it seems as if a combination of secular and religious influences has helped to rouse people from a traditional way of life and made them long and search for and move towards modern development. In the end, the joint effects of both may help Africa to develop.

---

4 Such beliefs (millenarianism or chiliasm) are widespread in simple societies. See for example Peter Worsley, *The Trumpet Shall Sound* and T. O. Ranger, *Revolt in South Rhodesia: A Study in African Resistance.*

With the talent and zeal of its people, this can happen fast once they have found the right path towards development.

There is nothing to prevent African nations from becoming full partners and even leaders in development a few generations hence, once they get going in the right direction.

3. Nationalism and "nation-building"

"Nation-building" is a popular term among leaders and politicians in Africa. The expression seems to be a contradiction in terms: a "nation" exists, one does not create or "build" it. But what is meant by the term is the attempt to forge a number of nations (or nationalities or tribes) into a unity of sentiment and loyalty within common borders, and thus create a "nation" that geographically coincides with a country's or state's borders. This is done for example by "fighting tribalism", that is, ignoring or forbidding expressions of tribal differences or opposition; full freedom to use a variety of "vernaculars" may be denied, and only one (or none) of the "local" languages may be allowed for "official" use. For the latter purpose it is common to resort to a foreign language.

Widespread intermingling of peoples ("nations" or "tribes") in a country could perhaps result in a population mixture that promotes the desired kind of "nation-building"; but such mixing is not extensively practised as conscious government policy in the continent, although some movement does take place through intermarriage, movement for education and particularly in search of work or - latterly - of food due to frequent droughts or safety in areas of unrest, etc. Forced mixing of peoples is not advisable, as can be seen in the result of such policies in the former Soviet Union and Yugoslavia.

Bricks used in building a nation

The means used to "build" a "nation" in Africa have largely been (1) political: one national political party which is, or more than one party that are, countrywide (non-tribal) and fighting for common national interests and goals; (2) educational: a uniform educational system; and (3) linguistic: use of a common language for "official" business. Furthermore, trade, a common currency, a common flag and national anthem, common defence and security forces and foreign policy are of course also important factors in uniting tribes within a country.

This is the opposite of what happened in Europe in the formation of nation states, a process that practically coincided with the rise of modern development - and the nation state may have been an important element stimulating economic progress. Something similar to European nation-states (with one language and rather similar customs and values and much shared history) exists also in other developed parts of the world.[5]

Developed nation-states seem mostly to be reasonable units and arrangements conducive to co-operation for development. Africa is apparently seeking a different solution.[6] But in the end, "built" nations (or federations or confederations) may for Africa possibly bring the benefits of the "natural" nation states of the developed world; and eventually, "tribal" differences may be overcome, but the process is a long-term one.

The typical situation in Africa is that a number of tribes (or ethnic groups or nationalities) with different languages, customs, institutions and history are joined in one "nation" (state, country). Those who have not

---

5 The fact that these nation states always absorbed (and consist of) amorphous elements may give hope to developing countries that "nation-building", as practised all over Africa, is actually possible and perhaps a good idea.

6 There are exceptions: Somalia, Botswana and Swaziland have uniform populations, and Burundi and Rwanda have a common country-wide language. However, these nation states have not developed: the nation state alone is thus no guarantee or sufficient cause of development.

chosen or been able to agree to have one of their own local languages as the "national" language use a foreign language for "official" purposes (including education). Rivalries and suspicion (even violent conflicts) are commonplace in these countries, often inspired by tribal or clan differences.

Still, African leaders believe that they can build one nation out of a conglomeration of peoples; and perhaps they will succeed where others have failed. (This is a topic African leaders are reluctant to discuss. At present, the principle of keeping the artificial "colonial" boundaries is upheld and almost sacrosanct. Perhaps federal arrangements would work better in the long run.)

Elements of integration

(a) In order to "build a nation" into a unit suitable for development, every country needs to develop and spread a common indigenous language which everyone can understand, as a first and most important prerequisite. It *must* be a language that is spoken "naturally" in that country - no imported language will do to make a country "one nation". However, in addition to this "national" language, "tribal" languages should be allowed free development. The chosen "national" language must grow and develop "naturally" until it becomes the normal and natural means of communication in all contexts in a country, without any (feelings of) coercion - but with facilitation and encouragement from the government. Too rapid and mandatory introduction of one language may harm the cause of unity and hinder the general acceptance of the language. When it attains high prestige, people will love to learn and use it.

(b) A flourishing literature in the indigenous national language can also help to "build the nation". Here Africa has gone seriously astray.

There are very few rich national literatures in Africa. Most countries have preferred to write in European languages (mostly English and French). This literature will never serve to enhance unity in African countries, and it will not be of lasting interest.

Highest literary excellence can only be attained in the mother tongue. Africa has a rich and beautiful literature of its own, but still it is mostly oral - and written only in a few languages (e.g. Amharic and Swahili).[7] By promoting literature in national languages, great written (and modern) literatures can of course be created also in Africa, and a great service will in that case be rendered to the "nation" and "nation-building".

(c) Another important positive element in nation-building is to give everyone the same chance to share equally in national life: in education, politics, productive work, trade, etc. Easy movement from one area of the country to another will encourage people to think of themselves as part of a larger national unit, whatever "tribe" they come from.

Strong domination of a country by a single "tribe", however big numerically in relation to other "tribes", can only serve to stir up differences and antagonism and lead to conflicts harmful to national development. Power-sharing "builds a nation".

"Nation-building" may not be a bad thing

The advantage of "building a nation" for development is that people who have a fellow-feeling and share many values will work well together

---

7 Cf. Reidulf Molvaer, *Tradition and Change in Ethiopia. Social and cultural life as reflected in Amharic fictional literature ca. 1930-1974*, and *Creative Lives*; and Jan Knappert's many publications on Swahili literature.

to develop their country. Developed nation states have been able to do this, but in Africa, "natural" nations or tribes are often so small that the continent would become very fragmented if states were to be formed on the same principle as nation states in Europe. The smallest units could not function well on their own.

States should ideally have a certain size (difficult to quantify) to work well. Both too big and too small states seem to run into difficulties, and this could be true in Africa as well. To find the best solution for Africa is of course up to the Africans themselves, and perhaps the present situation is as good as any. There does not seem to be a perfect or "ideal" solution to the problem of state borders for Africa. Some think that federal solutions would work best, and they might be right. The future will tell.

At a difficult and confusing time, "nation-building" seems to be a necessary step for development in Africa. The quicker it is achieved (with the consent and willing support of the people, not with the use of force), and the better the arrangements found, the sooner Africa may reach the threshold from where development may take off.

But "nation-building", in one form or another, is only one of the conditions that can underpin the process of development.

4. Discipline

Discipline as a factor promoting development poses several problems for Africa. Although forces of "external discipline" abound, the motivation for *self*-discipline of the kind conducive to progress seems diffuse and is not easy to pinpoint, and it appears to be weak. It is probably one of the areas where obstacles to development will be hardest to overcome.

Development requires individual and social discipline - discipline shaped by external pressure (customs, laws, etc.) as well as (and particularly) personal (internal) motivation as a result of internalisation of certain values and character traits during the process of socialisation, starting early in life with child-rearing, upbringing and education, and reinforced throughout life.

Everyone a "policeman"

External discipline in Africa is largely imposed by authoritarian pressure from the family and the surroundings, later also from persons "in authority" (teachers, employers, the police, politicians, etc.). The authority of parents, especially the father, is great, and what the child is told to do, it learns to do without reservation, without asking or being told why, often without understanding. "Free" or moderately free ("modern") upbringing is largely frowned upon.

The child learns to be extremely sensitive about questions of honour and shame, and it learns to conform to social norms in order to avoid ridicule, insults or punishment. Deviations in the pursuit of individual interests, and also most forms of innovation, are avoided. Social behaviour thus becomes rather uniform, and conformity becomes the ideal. One has to fit in. This attitude is thought to be beneficial for the preservation of customs, traditions and values, and thus for social cohesion. Values expressed in folk-tales and proverbs that stress or exemplify ideal traditional behaviour are kept alive.[8] Many feel that there is a conflict between tradition and newer influences following in the wake of development.

"Policemen" are not enough

African leaders are normally good at organising and controlling people for obedience and conformity. "Good citizens" keep in line, and this (called "peace" or "unity") has also been extolled as a necessary prerequisite for progress and development. However, this view of total compliance and uniformity as conditions for progress may be contrary to historical facts, at least in developed countries: the tensions of opposing views, trials and

---

8 Cf. Reidulf Molvaer, *Socialisation and Social Control in Ethiopia*, Wiesbaden 1995.

errors, and debate - also political - have been the conditions under which development and progress have taken place in the world.

The loneliness of the long-distance runner

As means of promoting modern development, the normal forms and forces of social control and discipline in Africa may fall short of what a modern society needs, especially if external form is considered more important than internalisation. In such cases, people who move away from home will tend to abandon their "traditions" as soon as accustomed external pressures fall away. If there is little self-discipline, erratic and unpredictable behaviour patterns may take the place of "tradition". This is no basis for building a modern society.

A main reason for weak self-discipline is probably the role of the extended family that influences the child during its first and most crucial, formative years. The extended family system may perhaps have created free, happy and harmonious people and may (as some claim) have many psychological advantages over the nuclear family system typical of developed societies. But here we are interested in only one problem: how it relates to development.

Again it may be worth pointing out that modern development entails changes in or the loss of many cherished traditional values, and if people decide that these values are more important to them than development, they should be given a free option to remain as they are. There are more important things in life than development. Here we only discuss *how* and *under what conditions* development takes place and what obstacles must be overcome in order to develop.

In the extended family, the child receives different signals and influences about how to think and how to behave. Parents, sisters and brothers, grandparents, uncles and aunts, cousins, nieces and nephews and more distant relatives, servants and regular visitors to the family - all these and more leave their often divergent impressions on the child. Some are lenient and indulge the child ("spoiling" it with their "kindness"), whereas others are strict and authoritarian, etc.

Rather than becoming broad-minded and self-confident, such a child may grow up without firm norms, values and mores, and without a firm character. It learns to be "diplomatic" in order to please adults of different moods and characters. This "adaptability" tends to persist throughout life.

This is not the kind of child-rearing and character-training that helps the growth of self-discipline that is needed for development, where work depends on the contributions of individuals who act on their own "drive" and honesty, not only because they are supervised and afraid to be found out, "shamed" or "punished".

Modern economic life depends on a reliable work force, and the lack of it is one of the greatest shortcomings of underdeveloped countries, perhaps especially in much of Africa, where poor work, absenteeism, slovenly routines, time-wasting procedures and inefficient management are all too common.

The amorphous character easily resulting from child-rearing practices in the extended family is often reinforced by beliefs in higher (spiritual) powers of different and contradictory characters, creating uncertainty about ultimate values. From this follows an uncertain value system, with shifting social and ethical attitudes, reinforcing a pliable character trying to adapt to various and perhaps contradictory interests. Thus, external adaptation to or in, for example, new (foreign) societies is often easy, but acceptance of a new society's values is hard. Parasitism rather than development results from such attitudes. Could science help to remove some confusing superstitions? Could "higher" forms of religion do so? People must find their own way.

A strong nuclear family may help to overcome the "anti-progressive" influences of the extended family. This happens most effectively when both parents share in the rearing of the child and set firm and consistent norms for its upbringing.

Such a situation is now coming into existence in Africa. This is a natural consequence of having a paid labour force, more general education, rapid urbanisation and a cash economy. However, as many mothers have to take paid jobs or to work long hours on the farm and as fathers are often absent for work elsewhere, many children lack an ideal stabilising family atmosphere. Close-knit families would help children to develop character traits that would prepare them for development.

To create strong, independent individuals it may also be necessary for parents to begin to explain rules of behaviour and reasons for "orders". The lack of understanding of the rationale behind what one is told to do or not to do creates "mechanical" obedience and weak internal motivation to respect norms when external pressures fall away.

Rational behaviour as a matter of choice is encouraged when children learn to understand the reasons for a certain way of life.

Losing one's grip on the rudder

There is a danger that family life in Africa may be transformed without being "strengthened" in ways contributing to development. Modern parents everywhere are confused about new ways, and normlessness in family life, including child-rearing, often results. African parents also feel that they have been taken by surprise by "modern times", and may be at a loss what to do.

The abandonment of polygamy may for example have weakened rather than strengthened marriage ties and family life, as men are now more inclined to have extramarital relations and to change marriage partners more frequently, thus creating an uncertain, unstable atmosphere for the children.[9] The new situation is not better than the old, although polygamy is probably a main cause of amorphous and weak

9 One effect of the AIDS pandemic may be stronger family ties and closer family units (as a result of trying to avoid being infected). This may

norms in child-rearing, as views, interests and customs in the same family may clash.

Unless nuclear family ties are strengthened, it may take a long time to prepare people properly for development through character formation and self-discipline in the family. Additional ways of building discipline may have to be sought.

Run as fast as you can

Another way of training children in self-discipline, powerfully *supporting* family influences, is *a strict and competitive educational system*. Here too a stable nuclear family, interested in the progress and education of the children, can be of great help. In Japan, for example, a somewhat indulgent but stable and consistent home surrounding is suddenly "disrupted" when the child starts in school. The toughest and most competitive years of its life then begin.

Strict, exact and demanding routines in the acquisition of precise knowledge, clear understanding and the ability to apply new knowledge normally characterise(d) schools in developed countries, and in Japan perhaps more than elsewhere. If education follows the same principles in Africa, the same results will ensue, to the benefit of economic life.

There are numerous weaknesses connected with education given in a foreign language, stressing memorisation when understanding fails and more or less mechanical problem solving (techniques for passing exams may actually be taught as a subject!). This does not promote development.

The educational systems in most African countries accustom students to sloppy thinking, imprecision, vagueness, the acquisition of half-absorbed, vaguely understood, undigested and poorly co-ordinated

---

actually be of importance for the development of Africa. This depends on Africans' own reaction to the AIDS threat.

pieces of information, enough to pass exams but practically not very useful. This kind of education may be as much of an obstacle as a help to development. The system has to change drastically if it is to serve progress.

The requirements for development are not fulfilled by present educational systems and practices. Education needs to be overhauled and improved from top to root. This has been discussed earlier. If the schools become good and progressive (also with respect to discipline), it may be an advantage if children start early, at (about) the age of five, preferably preceded by a couple of years in good kindergartens of a modern kind.

There are possibilities of strengthening discipline among adults by strict demands concerning punctuality, precision and productivity at work; however, to take root, work discipline must be prepared in the home and at school.

Learning (the) tricks

In Africa today, competition to "succeed" is very hard. It normally requires deviousness, trickery, "diplomacy" and "patronage" (and luck) to get and keep a job and to advance in one's career. The picture is the same in the work place, politics, trade, even self-employment. It is often so even in education: good marks may be a "favour" in response to other "favours", or a very good student seen as a possible "threat" to (competitor for) a teacher's job may receive poor marks. The pervasiveness of such factors influences life to such an extent that the discipline that might result from learning to work hard and systematically is obviated because hard work is so seldom the road to success in Africa, and good education is not necessarily the best way to a good job.

The hard-working honest plodder is usually the loser in a world full of tricksters. Much African folklore makes the point: the spoils go to the smart guys, whereas those who have struggled hard to produce good results are left with long noses. This reflects real life.[10]

In poor countries, hard work is no guarantee of success. Few benefits accrue to those who try to contribute to the development of the country to the best of their ability. To succeed, one needs first of all "contacts", "help", "networks", the ear of someone in high places or with access to someone there. One needs access to "privilege". "Success" does not normally follow from work well done. There is no question of "equality" or of getting what one deserves, or of an equitable share of the nation's wealth, commensurate with one's efforts or contribution.

There is also little understanding of the way a developed democracy works. The ideas most people have of democracy is more like "mob rule", the absolute right (not restricted by any Bill of Rights) of the majority to decide over and for the minority in all questions. And "majority decisions" are often fabricated by manipulation. The question of "human rights", protecting the rights of minorities, is not generally appreciated and often ridiculed. One understands democracy when one develops, not before and not later.

Africa is far away from democratic practices in economic as well as in political life. It is hard to see how social life can serve as a "school" for discipline conducive to development under such conditions.

Asking the impossible?

The question of discipline serving development is perhaps the most difficult problem to find a solution to in Africa. A reformed educational system may give the greatest hopes of progress in the field of social discipline and self-discipline of the kind that furthers

10 There is a special genre of folk-tales called "trickster tales" illustrating this point. They are very common and popular in Africa. (Cf. Reidulf Molvaer, *Socialization and Social Control in Ethiopia*, Wiesbaden 1995.)

development. At least it can help Africa to start moving along the road that leads to development.

It needs to be stressed that this kind of discipline is basic and absolutely essential for all economic progress. The character formation and self-discipline that may result from a good, modern, rigid and competitive educational system must, however, be reinforced by firm norms of child-rearing in order to have a powerful impact on development. Public and private economic (and political and social) practices must be reformed so that work is rewarded according to its contribution to society and its value for development; and people must get employment for reasons of qualification and merit.

5. Co-operation

There are traditions of small-scale co-operation in "mutual aid associations" and in other ways all over Africa. Efforts are made to help each other in small communities, for example to plant or harvest a field, to build a house, to dig a well, etc. Those who help others expect to be helped again when it is their turn to ask for assistance. All this is good, of course; but it does not amount to much when it comes to developing a whole community or country. These traditions are very old, but Africa is still underdeveloped, and limited "mutual aid" efforts have not brought development about. Something more is needed.

Kissing the hand that hit you?

Africans are also used to "co-operate" under coercion. "Chiefs" in the past and at present, as well as former colonial masters and modern politicians, have implanted the mentality of obeying orders; and people usually "obey". But this forced co-operation does no more to help development than it did in societies from ancient to modern times that based their economies on slavery, forced labour, compulsory service, and so on.

Co-operation for genuine development must be voluntary and based on the realisation that it is to the mutual benefit of all. It has to be co-operation of a special kind, and specific conditions have to be fulfilled: the masses must have been "enabled" to do their bit in the extended network of people who together bring about national development.

"Don't forget who you are"

Excessive pride is an obstacle to development. If people are unwilling to be "corrected" or "told" what to do, co-ordinated development is difficult. Many have of course experienced that calls to co-operation are "traps", as people are often asked to do or help with tasks that lead to loss for themselves and benefit for those who give the orders. But pride preventing meaningful co-operation has also deeper cultural causes.

African politicians do not like "advice" or "criticism", unless it is "constructive", which normally means that they only welcome flattery. If one-party systems are seen as the most "suitable for Africa at the present stage of its development", this argument is used to silence all opposition. Only by overthrowing the government can dissenting voices be heard, until a new coup silences also them. At present there is another "wind of change" blowing over Africa: "multi-party democracies" and greater opportunities for "opposition parties" are in fashion. Without outside pressure, this would probably not have happened. However, in reality not much is likely to change for quite some time. Only when conditions are ripe for true democracy will there be conditions for genuine development, and the other way round. There is still some way to go.

Where's the leader?

Highly centralised power is not conducive to social harmony, co-operation or development. What is jokingly said in the West about a boss who is no good, that "The boss is always right", is often accepted as an advanced view of leadership in Africa. This reflects one reason for poor leadership for development.

Africans have great problems with efficiently administering, organising and leading development programmes. That is one cause of the high rate of failure of development projects. African leaders are not so good at guiding people towards maximising their efforts and achievements as they are at keeping people "in check" so as to limit their performance.

Local and national development initiatives usually fail. The enabling process has not taken effect. The right basis has not been laid.

The blind leading the blind?

On the whole, few Africans seem fully to understand what development means. How can they then be expected to bring it about? They need first of all to acquire a proper understanding of and attitude to development and learn the processes that lay the foundation for and lead to development. Few Africans have had the chance to gain the necessary experience. Therefore it has been easy for Western aid agencies to lead them up the garden path with their faulty development policies and theories. It is high time they begin to think, decide and act by and for themselves.

Biting off one's nose to spite one's own face

Envy is a great leveller in Africa.[11] People who want to improve their material life will be suspected of wanting to be better than others and

---

11 There may originally have been good reasons for this. If an "advantage" was given to someone in a traditional society, added "power" thus gained was likely to be used to oppress others. This is what has happened in political life, and caution is appropriate. African age-grade systems represent a more democratic tradition than for example democracy in ancient Greek city-states. However, for a modern society to take shape, a new spirit of hard

accused of pride, and they will be thwarted in their efforts to make a better life for themselves. People who work harder than usual may be suspected of doing so in order to put others in a bad light. They experience a hard time being accepted.

Perhaps Africans will deny that envy and jealousy are particularly strong in Africa, but in a comparative perspective there can be little doubt that this is so. People even destroy opportunities for themselves so as to deny others an "advantage" - or even an equal opportunity.

Jealousy and envy often develop into morbid suspiciousness, so that people ascribe all kinds of doubtful motives to others. Even "good deeds" may look suspect. A "benefactor" (e.g., a "donor") is thus usually disliked, as the motives for "good deeds" are thought to be selfish: the benefactor "does good" for his own personal advantage or gain. The fact that some or much aid is given as political "bribes" (and perhaps most aid actually serves the same purpose) reinforces this belief. Aid only benefiting leaders and elites (as it very often does) makes this a common conviction.

"I'll scratch your back if you'll scratch mine!"

Positive, willing co-operation of the kind that leads to development can only occur if people believe in progress and have a forward-looking view, develop positive attitudes to each other as human beings (beyond the scope of family relations), and have the required skills.

The "right" attitude to co-operation may perhaps be fostered if people are "taught" more positively about "human nature" in the home, schools, churches, and through the mass media. Before that can happen, one must

---

work and competitiveness (as well as more suitable forms of democracy) must be accepted. If this is done voluntarily, a willing co-operative spirit may also grow up and gain strength. This will be of great benefit for economic development.

of course have parents and teachers who themselves believe in such values. As long as one's own attitude and motives are negative, it is hard if not impossible to impart positive values, views and attitudes to others.

Demonstration of the benefits of positive co-operation in development activities may instil more positive attitudes to work and to one another. Religious, philosophical and psychological influences (instruction) can help to improve the situation. But probably people will change only when they see that co-operation "pays", when they come to believe in co-operation for "selfish" reasons. This can only be achieved through an intense process of observation and participation, training and education, till new views and attitudes are internalised - and then externalised: put into practice.

6. Progressive views

African intellectuals have discussed the time concepts prevailing in African cultures. Whereas some cultures have a view of the past and the present that can span long periods, other cultures have "short memories" and may even have made it a taboo to mention dead people, including past leaders and heroes. This has led to the loss of much historical knowledge and contributed to a diminished historical consciousness and perspective.

How far can you remember?

Detailed and long historical memory and consciousness could not have been well nurtured where writing was unknown. But even in such societies there were often special "historians of the tribe" whose duty it was to remember and pass on the history and traditions of the people.

However, in whatever way the historical time aspect - its depth and meaning - is recognised, there is in "traditional" Africa no concept of history as leading from a "simple" past and better present to an even more advanced future. Rather the opposite is the rule: some period in the past (or the past generally) is seen as better than the present (perhaps there are "memories" of a "golden age"), and things are normally thought to be going from bad to worse.

Changing perspectives

The progressive view of history and development came to Africa with Christianity, capitalism and (later) socialism. The last of these was for long the most popular version among intellectuals, often in a simple, utopian form, whereas the former (Christianity and capitalism combined) has probably been more acceptable to the masses.

A "diluted" popular and superficial belief in "progress" is spreading with modern education. However, this belief does not exclude claims to "special privileges" for a few at the top.

It is hard to say if this progressive view is a belief in the possibility of general progress, progress for all, i.e. that it is possible to extract more from nature, and that nature may be nurtured to produce more totally without depleting it for future generations, and to the potential benefit of all. In practice, Africans unfortunately still accept that progress should mostly benefit the few who are "lucky" and "smart" and able to "help themselves" to "a piece of the cake".

"Your gain is my loss"

It is a common view in Africa that some people can "progress" only at the expense of others: one person's gain is another person's loss. The resources in the world are widely thought to be constant, and in their distribution, some may get more and others less; it is thus not considered possible to increase total resources - or the accumulated yield of nature[12] - to the benefit of all in such a way that everyone and anyone

---

12 This is of course true for non-renewable resources (e.g. minerals and fossil fuels), but the zero-sum view of development holds that even renewable

can improve living standards (or the quality of life) without harming nature and/or reducing the standard of living of others.

This "zero sum" view of development is not helpful in the struggle to achieve economic growth. It goes against the belief that development is furthered for example through hard, systematic work and scientific methods. In a country wanting to progress, this static view and its attendant attitudes will hinder the fostering of habits beneficial to development, such as predictability, honest business dealings, reliability, precision, a desire to do one's best, pride in a job well done, etc.

New lamps for old

How can more Africans acquire a genuine belief in the possibility of progress and development? There are a few ways that seem helpful to achieve this.

(a) Progressive views may result from the rapid expansion of Christianity in Africa at present. New "sects" with a local flavour may be more important in this respect than some of the tamer imports from the West. Democratic attitudes in social, political and economic life will normally go together with this religious orientation. Religious freedom and economic freedom normally come together, and "reasonable" (non-exploitative) "capitalism" may well follow upon a spread of Christianity.

(b) Another possible shaper of progressive views is some form of socialism. Socialism in Africa has appeared in many forms, but it is not likely that such views will become popular, especially now that socialism is not such a fad. The former adulation of

---

resources (e.g. forests, fresh water and arable land) and their yield (e.g. agricultural products, fuel wood, water for drinking and irrigation) are constant.

forms of socialism by many elites is in itself perhaps a good argument against socialism as a solution of Africa's development problems. Grassroots social democracy may, however, have a chance. Combined with older traditions in Africa ("African socialism"),[13] one main concern of many socialists, namely social and economic justice and equality, could perhaps now be realised without the dead weight of doctrinaire Marxism.

(c) A surer way to spread ideas of progress is through the education system and the mass media, for example in the way history and "current events" are presented. News about progress at home and elsewhere can demonstrate that progress is possible and actually taking place in many areas of the world.

It's easy to believe what you want to believe

It is not necessary to inundate people with ideological garbage or gobbledegook to get them to believe in the possibility of progress. People want to believe that it is possible to improve their life situation, and straightforward presentation of for instance history as progress, and information about how people elsewhere have improved their living conditions can easily instil a belief in progress.

This belief has spread to very many already. What people need to be better informed about is *how* and *under what conditions* development takes place, and *what is required of a people* who want to develop. Unless the right ideas are communicated, people will have unrealistic expectations and may want to take shortcuts to development by means of, for example, such gimmicks as revolution and progressive dictatorship. In spite of past disastrous outcomes of revolutions, the idea continues

---

13 This ought to be based on the "age-grade" systems, not the chiefly traditions unless chiefs are chosen by and held accountable to the people. (Even age-sets choose leaders who become the first among equals.)

to appeal to many immature minds, especially among intellectuals. Autocratic leaders also like to think that they are doing their countries a service.

Revolution - the violent overthrow of the existing order and the establishment of a self-styled "progressive" government - may have many causes and results. However, development does not come out of the barrel of a gun. There are faster, better and surer ways to bring about changes furthering development, as has been demonstrated in all developed countries.

Don't give up hope

One can work towards and bring about development everywhere. It needs the involvement and participation of the majority of the population in a country. Participation that leads to development will be possible when people have come to believe that development is possible and that their efforts can and will lead to economic advantages for themselves. They will succeed if they have been enabled to contribute meaningfully and constructively to the development process.

*

SHREDS AND PATCHES

Do it yourself! - no one will do it for you

Africa will develop when Africans themselves are ready to develop the continent. This will happen when they acquire the appropriate beliefs, attitudes and skills required for development.

Skills training in not enough, as clearly shown by Africa's failure to develop after so many have acquired skills thought to be useful and necessary for development.

Money (capital) has also little direct relation to development in Africa. The vast sums invested by national governments and from abroad in support of development have not improved the economic situation or furthered development. Africa is worse off now than it was before the massive pursuit of modern development started. This is because the "pursuit" has been made in the wrong direction.

Unless attitudes and beliefs change, Africa will not develop. Child-rearing practices and educational policies and practices will also have to change. Many other things will then fall in place.

Up to now, the trend has been in the opposite direction: skills are imparted, money supplied, programmes and projects made and new systems of government introduced, in the belief that this would lead to development. But *people* must be "developed" before a *country* can develop.

Development is a human question more than it is a technical problem. When people are ready for development, a country will develop, not before - and not later.

No more excuses!

Africa has all the human and natural resources it needs to develop. North-western Europe started the development process when it was relatively poor, and development started to take off first in some of the most exploited and impoverished parts. The acceleration started c. AD 1500, not so very long after devastating plagues and endless wars had reduced the European population much more than slavery depleted the population of Africa. Japan has developed in spite of a scarcity of natural resources. Development still took off when people had gone through the right preparatory phases.

Markets are not closed to African products. They are open enough, not least internally in the continent but also outside, if Africa has something valuable to offer, not only of unfinished but also of finished products. There is no reason at all why Africa cannot develop. But it will not take place unless or until Africa starts at the right end: by training, educating and preparing its people for development in the correct way.

Why don't they eat cake?

What about development assistance? Is it all a waste?

Development aid has not been able to start a process towards development where people in the receiving country have not been prepared and equipped for development. How can this state of affairs (stagnation or even a turn for the worse) be changed and the trend reversed?

There are a number of things that could be done to help underdeveloped countries develop without causing actual harm and without wasting money.

Helping people to help themselves

Developing countries need, as stressed already, to develop their own national languages for general communication and as a means of instruction in all its educational institutions, including university education. After a country has made its free choice of a national language (or more than one if it is not possible to agree on one), help could be given with linguistic technicalities and the writing and printing of textbooks for all educational levels.

Experts in relevant fields could, if necessary and if wanted, be supplied by and from donor countries. Adequate local staff must be supplied by the "host" country. No harm need be done if such staff is paid by money from a donor country if their salaries are more or less at the same level as other similar jobs there. If they are much better paid, it easily leads to corrupt practices. For example, influential people in developing countries will try to get their own "favourites" into these jobs instead of the most qualified ones. Payment of salaries by a donor country should be made only for the duration of people's employment in such a project. No staff ought to be so long with a supported project that such employment comes to be seen as "permanent". Expertise and chances of promotion in one's previous career (or the place of work from where one is "on loan") may be lost if one returns to one's previous job after a very long absence. One condition for taking on local staff by outside agencies from for example local (government) authorities must be that they can return to their previous jobs without loss of seniority, promotion or other opportunities as soon as the project, or their involvement in it, is over.

What words can do

Help with general, popular education ought to have a high priority among both givers and receivers of development aid.

A national literature should also be promoted in order to build and strengthen a national language both for unity and for a higher quality of education in the country. Paper could be supplied and printing subsidised by donors so that the cost of books can be within the range of what students and readers can afford. Printing can even be done abroad if opportunities for corruption in the process cannot be eliminated in the assisted country, or if the facilities are lacking.

Training in book writing and book production can be given to achieve objectives in this field. If a country refuses such help without other "benefits" ("handouts"), so be it: no help need be given (and the reason for it should be made public).

Support could well be given for the translation or original creation of literature promoting national development, progressive ideas, co-operation and appropriate skills. This need and should not, however, lead to massive scholarship programmes for training abroad: when the time is ripe, practically all skills training can be done locally. Some experts (e.g. to train local trainers) can well be supplied from donor countries as needed and wanted, till local experts are trained.

All needs (of experts, literature, training, etc.) must of course be seen as real needs both by givers and receivers of aid. Some vigilance must be exerted to avoid that expressed "needs" are not only the whims or selfish wishes of politicians or the head of state.

Some help with health and environmental matters can be justified, particularly the international aspects of them. Emergency aid can also do much good. However, such aid is of course meant to meet special needs or patch up problems in a precarious situation and is not directly linked to real *developmental* goals.

Small is sometimes beautiful

Bilateral aid (understood here as aid from one country to another, not only from one government coffer to another, and including most particularly aid from, through and/or to non-governmental, voluntary, independent development organisations) can best fulfil the conditions of aid that is genuinely helpful to a developing country. Bilateral donor organisations do of course not understand better than multilateral or global ones the problems of developing countries or what development is, but they are much more efficient (unless one believes the many totally fictive reports of some of the bigger development agencies), and they can more easily be held accountable for their use of funds and staff. Proper assessment of needs, monitoring of projects and programmes, control with and accounting for the use of funds, genuine evaluation and reporting of achievements can also best be done if the aid given is bilateral.

Ask no questions and hear no lies

Global organisations and agencies can never fully control how aid is used, and it is easy to misuse it. The bigger the donor organisation, the more potentially harmful can its influence on development be and the more damage can it do. No actual or conceivable mechanism can properly monitor the activities of global development agencies or control the use or misuse of funds or goods given as aid. Reporting can only be done with the full consent of (even clearly corrupt) governments. These organisations are therefore not the best tools for development.

A better way to give global development agencies a positive influence on development in the Third World is to channel most of their funds for development through independent (voluntary, non-governmental) organisations. However, much money can be saved if governments channel development funds through voluntary, non-governmental organisations in the first place, without going through wasteful global organisations.

"Trust me!"

Aid must be given on strict conditions, for specific purposes, and not paid out unless the conditions are fulfilled. Deviations from original plans should be agreed upon before they are implemented. The main condition must be that aid shall benefit the really needy.

Development "planning" at present often serves only as a basis for requests for aid. When it is given, the plans may well be forgotten and the money used for something else, and perhaps not properly accounted for. This does not promote development, nor does it benefit those one intended to help.

Reports on development activities are often fictive and designed to "cover up" the facts. Monitoring to check results is therefore absolutely necessary. Global organisations are often happy to close their eyes to the facts, so that they "truthfully" (in line with figures supplied to them by recipient governments) can report fine achievements. Many bilateral donors are, however, also reluctant to accept and learn from unpleasant truths.

"Inspection" and monitoring should go on all the time and not only at the end of a project. There are many ways to hoodwink donors.

At the end of a project, deceived donors are not always willing to face up to the saddest facts and to report them. So the deception goes on.

Properly controlled aid is sure to meet with much resistance from some governments (or government officials) of recipient countries. There will be complaints about donors imposing their will from outside the country, forcing certain development policies on developing countries, neo-colonialism, etc. The real reason for such complaints about "strings attached" is usually different: the wish to have a free hand to misuse funds. "Conditions" attached to aid cannot be avoided if one wants aid to do some good.

There is no need for developing countries to accept unwanted aid or aid on unacceptable terms. Only aid benefiting the needy people in a country should be requested and given. Developing countries should also set conditions for accepting aid: it must be clearly seen to help common, needy people and not serve the political ends of those who give the aid. Most donors will agree to that.

Loans benefiting the rich are repaid by the poor

Aid ought to be direct and given as grants. Loans seem regularly to be misused, and since their use is in practice almost totally under the control of the receiving country, this money is used so that the upper crust gets (nearly) all the advantages. But those benefiting most from loans (i.e. those who are best off in society) are not the ones who will repay the loans.

Foreign loans are repaid from money which comes from ordinary taxpayers. The powerful often have ways and means of avoiding taxes, and "progressive" taxation does not much affect the purses of the wealthy. Peasants and workers "pay" the debts of poor countries, but mostly indirectly - by being poorly paid for their work and products, while such products are largely resold for much larger profits on outside markets, open and accessible only to the rich and powerful. Some of the surplus of such transactions is used to pay foreign debts. The powerful are often reluctant to give up even this money, and that is one reason for requesting cancellation or rescheduling of debts (so as to have more money for themselves or let future leaders worry about the national debt); this is the newest way to humiliate their countries for the sake of personal profit (the old way is to always beg for money abroad).

Loans to poor developing countries thus make, on the whole, the burdens of the poor heavier. All debts incurred in such ways ought to be cancelled for the sake of the poor, and loans for development ought be given with the greatest caution - if at all.[14] Grants ought to be specific and for purposes that are manageable. Transfer and use of funds should be transparent, and accounting strict - and projects monitored. This is not the same as being stingy and mean to developing countries. It is a policy based partly on the realisation that it is limited what can be done from outside to promote development, and partly on the fact that aid does not at present always (or often) reach the intended beneficiaries.

Wake up, nice guy!

Development is the achievement of a country's own people. What can be done with outside assistance may be to prepare the ground for development to take off; or the development process can be slightly speeded up with outside assistance where the population has already acquired the necessary attitudes and skills.

---

14 It is questionable whether a country is (morally) obliged to repay loans given for specific purposes when they are not actually used for these purposes: the donor may have a duty to find out if this is so. When donors continue to give aid to governments that regularly misuse funds, they may not be morally justified in claiming this money back from taxpayers who have not received any benefits from such loans.

Aid can, however, also slow down the development process, as it seems to have done in many parts of Africa, if it comes into the wrong hands and is used for anti-developmental purposes (e.g. to build up strong armies or security forces).

Development aid ought to be reconsidered, restructured and given only on special conditions for specific purposes - and then properly monitored and accounted for.

If one really wants to help developing countries, one ought to help them help themselves, and then let them find their own way and pace towards development. When the conditions are right, carefully considered aid (especially to promote general education and self-help) can do much good if it is channelled so as to benefit those in real need of it.

Don't interfere!

Africa will develop when it learns to develop on its own accord. Perhaps Africa will develop fastest by following the Japanese or moderately socialist practice of much government involvement in development, if the political leaders are competent and can be held to account for their deeds. Individuals in Africa are used to spending money at hand on pleasures, status symbols and consumer goods rather than saving and investing (which also means risking) their private capital in productive enterprises. State inputs into development activities may therefore help to get the ball rolling. Gradually increasing private involvement in productive enterprises will probably be an advantage for development if the owners and managers of industries, etc., are truly "progressive". This is likely to be increasingly so as levels of general education are raised.

Private enterprise is of course better than corrupt government practices in the development process, and it is always good to have alternatives to choose between. But this problem will be sorted out when Africa is ready to develop. The present common practice of letting foreign or multinational companies run many enterprises, with kickbacks or perks for politicians, does not help the development of developing countries.

Meanwhile, it would be profitable for African countries to reduce their bureaucracies, to pay politicians and intellectuals proportionately to their contributions to the national economy and no more, and to encourage the masses (including educated people) to work in productive enterprises, not least in agriculture.

Enabling (capacity building) policies and processes must take pride of place in the long haul to help Africa to gain a place among progressive and genuinely developing continents. Their time will come, but two things can in the meantime be done to make the road less arduous:

- for supporters: to stop interfering negatively with Africa's development, especially support of reactionary leaders and governments and exploitative and harmful "development" programmes, and instead help the poorest to help themselves;
- for Africans: to find their own way, to learn from experience at home and abroad, to develop on their own, and not to attempt unrealistic shortcuts;
- for all: to care more about people than about money and power.

Africa will develop when it finds and follows the road that leads to development.

Africa will have its day.

CONCLUSION

All that glitters is not gold

Every country in the world is searching for ways to improve the life of its citizens. Some have succeeded fairly well, and the less successful look to these "rich" countries for inspiration to achieve similar levels of development. But no country is perfect, and many in developing countries are rather put off by various aspects of life in developed countries; therefore they are looking for alternative ways to realise their ambitions.

The variety of cultures and ways of solving the problems of living and of human happiness in the world adds to the interest and richness of human existence and widens the possibilities for human beings to order their lives in meaningful ways and according to their deepest wishes and aspirations. However, there seems to be only one path or "model" that leads to development.

There are many aspects of social, cultural, spiritual and individual life that are not directly related to development and which can be preserved even as a country modernises, although indirectly they will be influenced by the level of development a society has reached. People in developed countries are not all of a piece. In these countries there is ample room for experimentation, variety and personal choice. Such freedom also a people attempting to escape from grinding poverty can have.

It would be a pity if economic development should destroy or diminish the differences between people, cultures and nations. Differences compatible with development should be encouraged and seen as an enrichment of the human scene.

It is not necessary to destroy in order to progress

Today everyone seems to aspire to ever higher levels of development. Due to impatience and a poor understanding of development, much of the rich variety of human cultures is being destroyed.

Everyone and every nation can develop, and it is not necessary to impoverish cultural and social life in order to achieve one's development goals. Some aspects of life, especially in relation to child-rearing, education and tribal or national allegiances, will often have to be modified. But this modification ought not to lead to cultural impoverishment or conformity.

Most "traditional" social and cultural values in a country undergoing change ought to be retained and reinforced - even when they are modified - so that people do not lose their identity during the development process. True development requires that more - not less - attention is paid to individual, local and national values, norms and customs.

Something has to go

It may be irksome for some that strong stress has to be placed on co-operation, wider national rather than tribal units, delayed enjoyment of possessions and opportunities for purposes of investment, etc.; but there are also positive things to be said for such development-related changes, and they are not foreign impositions. For most sacrifices there are compensations in the wake of development.

In the end, development should lead to greater "enjoyment" (even if it is "delayed" for a time) and freedom of choice, and better opportunities for self-realization. And the kinds of mutual interdependence and co-operation that benefit the development process emphasise values that are found in most cultures - they only need to be expressed in new ways and given shapes that fit the ends of progress and modernisation.

Don't blame it all on development

Some may regret the turn towards individualism and the nuclear family that follows in the wake of development. But this change is taking place anyway as a result of population increase, urbanisation, salaried employment, a cash economy and a greater demand for skills and education. Some may say that this is part of development - but this is not always so: most of these changes are taking place also where people are sinking into greater and greater poverty. This is change, not development.

Something to gain for all

Genuine development will lead to greater welfare for the majority of people in a country. Changes that do not (at least eventually) lead to a better life for the majority are not part of true development.

Such development should not only lead to higher incomes. In every really developed country there is an increased demand for education, books, music, art, sports, entertainment, social services, leisure, or anything that is thought to make life richer and more meaningful. A greater number of things is not enough to satisfy the needs of people who have absorbed the values and advantages of development. An improved quality of life and wider freedom of choice are more important than a higher standard of living in purely monetary terms.

In developed societies, individual choices and freedoms and rights are cherished and respected, in spite of shortcomings. There are aspects of developed countries that many find "ugly", but the need to conform is less there than in developing countries; that means that there is no need to adopt what repels. There are probably as many people in developed countries who are opposed to these "ugly" aspects of their societies as there are people outside who may reject "development" for such reasons. In developed countries there are usually very good opportunities for people to choose less ugly alternatives, as "deviant" patterns of behaviour (both "good" and "bad") are widely accepted. Deviant views are also often listened to, more so than in developing countries.

No place to hide

Development is not a "part" activity but something that influences all areas of life. It is not possible to develop one part of society and leave the rest untouched. Development influences all forms of work and all areas of economic, socio-cultural and political life.

If development is properly "organised", and if people co-operate wisely, it can lead, not to conformity but to enrichment of all aspects of life, a greater number of choices and a varied, interesting and rich life. "Elites" should thrive in such surroundings - they benefit in many ways from living in developed societies, as they have many choices open to them, are appreciated more than in developing countries, and can contribute much to the common weal.

Development is not an unquestioned good. Wisdom and good judgement are required to give shape to the kind of life people want and value in modern societies. The beginning of the Industrial Revolution led to much misery, and so does the beginning of development everywhere. But we can learn from past mistakes and make the development process more humane. And the end result should be greater satisfaction for the majority.

More to gain than to lose

Development is a human more than it is a technical question and problem. Developing countries should take care to preserve their most cherished values; otherwise they may find that development becomes an evil master and tyrant rather than a servant and benefactor. Economic development without moral values becomes a monster, and it will not be national development but a skewed and halting development benefiting only the few with power to control the economy.

True development should enrich, not impoverish life for the masses. Development can and should be felt as a gain, not as a loss. Development that creates mostly misery is not worth having. Genuine development frees man from many shackles.

*

Summa summarum

Development does not come automatically, of necessity, or by any law(s) of nature or history. Systems, structures or ideologies cannot bring about development. And development is not achieved only because people want it, value it or work hard for it.

But people can prepare or be prepared for development and in a sense train or be trained for it. People can get set for development somewhat like a football team training or being drilled to score goals and win matches. In preparing for development and in bringing it about, the whole nation must take part.

To achieve their goals, the participants have to practise at six different things, all at the same time, namely:

(1) education (motivation, instruction, drill),
(2) mass involvement (all must play their part),
(3) nation-building (creating a team-spirit),
(4) discipline (self-control, ball-control),
(5) co-operation (team-work),
(6) looking ahead (being goal-oriented).

There is no time limit to this "game". It may last for ever, and a team will have good days and bad. If the players go tired of the game, they may try to keep it up artificially (e.g. through doping), but that will only postpone the downfall a while, and the fall may then be the more fateful and final.

The whole world is made up of such teams, and some score more goals (reach higher levels of development) than others; but all will have the chance to score some if they are well trained.

For want of a better name for this development model, I propose to call it "the football match model of development", underpinned by "the match theory of development".

ADDENDUM

DYNAMIC FUNCTIONALISM AS SOCIAL THEORY

A Sociodynamic Model of Society

By Reidulf K Molvaer[1]

Shortcomings of functionalism

Functionalism and its main derivative, structuralism, as well as modifications of these, have been guiding theories and models for much social research, and the dominant theories and models in social anthropology. They have been of great help in obtaining valuable data about

1 The author is a social scientist with twenty years' experience in development work. During his work, he has felt the need for a theory of society that can explain social change not only as an acceptable but as an inevitable and therefore desirable process. The observations made here are the result of the author's work and accumulated reading in social science and psychology over many years, and he thinks that the theory presented helps to give a useful perspective on society. The viewpoints borrowed from psychology are so simple and self-evident, and in line with 'common sense', that they can be understood and applied without any specialised training in psychology, and although only quite elementary elements of psychological theory are involved, the author finds them helpful for an explanation of societies in change, i.e. of all societies. The intention with this article is to present some suggestive, and hopefully seminal, points that can be further developed if social scientists find that they have explanatory force and are useful for research.

human communities, and they have advanced our understanding of society and social life. Since these theories - functionalism and structuralism, etc. - are variations on a theme, they can for our purpose here be treated as one theory. I shall use the term functionalism to comprise both, or all.[2]

The greatest problem with functionalism is that it cannot explain social change in a satisfactory manner. Many functionalists have described social change well and intelligently, but somehow it seems as if change is an anomaly not quite fitting into the theory, whereas social change is in fact the normal state of affairs in all societies.

The fundamental weakness of functionalism is that it is built on, or combined with, the organic model of society: all parts of society hang together - are interrelated and interdependent, and each and every

---

2 Action or interaction theory is not discussed here, but from the theory presented, one could infer and 'mend' some of its weaknesses. The treatment of 'goals' and 'means' in action theory points to some resemblance with the theory of 'dynamic functionalism'; besides, both borrow elements from psychology. However, because the *origin* of goals, and particularly the origin of *common* goals and norms and values or a common social goal-orientation, i.e. shared systems and standardised values, is not well explained by this theory, it is not satisfactory: it does not properly explain how social phenomena come about; and, although it may explain social acts, it does not explain the social phenomenon, society, as such, or the 'fact' of society. Although this is said to derive from the conditions of social action and interaction, it does not explain where social life originates. Neither does is explain the many similarities in societies very far apart, nor similarities in all societies. The theory leads one to expect a higher degree of disparities and conflicts than do in fact occur. It borrows very much from psychology, without, however, taking full account of the elements which give 'dynamic functionalism' greater explanatory power than the (inter)action theory.

part of society - institutions, modes of production, rebellions, myths, rituals, beliefs, ideas and values - are equally important parts of the fabric, and they all serve the purpose of social cohesion. As all parts are thus regarded as equally important, a change in one part entails a change in other parts, and this disturbs the social harmony, and that is normally regarded as undesirable and harmful to the unity and welfare of the society. Functionalists have therefore often shown a conservative bent in their conception and descriptions of society. Modernisation, development and 'progress' are thus often considered undesirable 'disturbances' of the social idyll.

Since change is not an anomaly but the 'rule' - the normal experience of each and every society, it would be desirable to find a model that takes account of change and gives it prominence, while the model must also be suitable for explaining the status quo - to take a 'snapshot' as well as to make a 'movie' of the scene.

It should, however, not be necessary to jettison all aspects of functionalism in order to achieve this: one could fit it, or parts of it, into another model or analogy than the organic one.

A Human Model

As human societies consist of humans, *society should be explained on a human model*, and not purely on the model of a biological organism. An organic model may explain a 'society' of lower animals, but not all aspects of human society: it can explain a static society or a society ordered by instincts, but it cannot explain change or changing societies.

The best parallel, analogy or model to explain human society must be the human person, i.e., the model should take into account aspects of the human being beyond the purely organic ones, but not exclude these. Human society should be likened to human beings in all their aspects - physical, emotional and cognitive - rather than to 'mindless' organisms. Human society is, as it were, the human person 'writ large'.

A human, i.e. partly psychological and partly organic, model, or a schematic model borrowing elements from both psychology and biology, is much more helpful than the purely organic one.

(A) Needs and Drives

On the human, psychological-organic model, society must be considered as a unity, as the person is a unity. But a person is not a mindless creature that has only needs, reflexes and instincts. There are other aspects of the person social scientists must consider and take into account.

The concept of *need*, i.e. something necessary for a particular purpose, has been important in social science,[3] but the human, psychological-organic model provides us with the useful *distinction between drives and needs.* A *drive* is a strong inner, innate urge which is not learned, although it can be canalised and otherwise modified, e.g. by learning, in order to satisfy a need, attain a goal, or avoid pain in ways that are learned, although some reflex actions, e.g. withdrawal from a source of suffering, are triggered more or less 'automatically' by the reflex system.[4] One could also say that drives are inner motivations for actions, purposeful striving, to avoid frustration or pain, or noxious stimuli. Many 'felt needs' trigger or activate drives that 'need' to be satisfied, whereas other 'needs' can be satisfied 'automatically' by reflexes. Needs alone do no move people to act: reflexes and drives to. When hungry, one is stimulated to eat, and the activity of eating gives satisfaction

3 Early functionalists, including Malinowski, talked of "needs and drives" as if they were phenomena of the same kind, covering what in the following is termed "needs". The disctinction between needs and drives was not drawn in the way done here, following common psychological usage.

4 Both reflexes and drives can be somewhat modified by experience, except reflexes connected to the autonomic nervous system, e.g. digestion or the heartbeat, but even these can respond to emotional changes.

till the hunger is stilled; but work needed to produce food or to earn money needed to buy food may or may not be pleasurable and thus may and may not be undertaken 'willingly'. Much human activity goes into easing the struggle for survival. Reasoning, the intellect, is to a large extent employed to find ways and means not only to satisfy drives but also to reduce work or effort needed to produce or achieve what is required to satisfy drives. Direct satisfaction of drives is always enjoyable or pleasurable, whereas discovering and employing the appropriate means to satisfy drives is not always so - they are in fact often unpleasant: a 'struggle'.[5]

The satisfaction of drives is necessary for the survival *and/or* well-being of the individual and the race - and of society. The drives are rather constant, persistent, although they can to a limited extent be modified by learning or persistent habit or experience, and they are, with limited variations, common to all of mankind, inherited in the common gene-pool, and can therefore explain and form a basis for social life. Needs not directly connected to drives, e.g. the need for iodine, beer, or a new pair of shoes, are less strong or 'basic' than needs related to drives, but this is not always so, as in the case of addiction, or even - at the unconscious level - of iodine, and need-satisfying activities may take many forms (drives are not linked to rigid behaviour patterns) and are easier to modify or change than drives. Thus, the hunger drives are more or less constant, but the need for a specific mode of production

5 Social scientists have used the concepts primary and secondary needs, and one could also talk of basic and derived needs: because one needs food - a primary or basic need, therefore one needs to work - a secondary or derived need, etc. But the concepts 'primary or basic needs' are not normally used as equivalents or substitutes for 'drives'. Primary or basic needs are usually defined as needs that must be satisfied for survival, whereas not all drives are related to survival. However, they could be 'redefined' and used in the sense of drives.

or type of food is not. Hunger 'activates' drives by triggering food-seeking or food-scanning behaviour that aims at stilling the hunger, and a drive persists till it is satisfied, and it does not change its nature in its 'dormant' stage, because it is stilled. However, a drive can be satisfied in many ways, although acculturation and canalisation and conditioning establish preferences for certain foods, and only these foods may make one *feel* satisfied.

(B) Dynamics of The Human Model

To be practically useful for social scientists, it is convenient to group the drives in a few clusters or classes related to basic and dominant needs and urges that seek satisfaction and which manifest themselves clearly also as social phenomena. Such a 'classification' of drives can look for example like this:

(1) *the self-preservation drives, or the drives for physical survival, or the 'hunger drives'*. These drives 'aim' at satisfying a society's - as well as a person's - need for food, drink and the elimination of noxious waste - 'social waste' can be criminals, etc., as well as harmful substances which need to be replaced by 'fresh air' - and, by extension, for security, which may express itself in a tendency to plan, hoard, try to develop or progress, avoid danger, seek power, build defences, go to war, conquer, steal, rob, go cattle rustling, be angry, fight, etc.; conflicts can be considered as attempts to obtain greater security of survival, etc.; stimuli for some of these tendencies may be feelings of insecurity, fear, perception of danger, etc.;

(2) *the self-perpetuation drives, or the drives for racial survival, the procreative or 'species drives'*. At the personal level, this manifests itself primarily in the sex drive combined with the parental drive. The satisfaction of the sex drive is not a condition for

individual survival - people can live long lives in permanent celibacy, and the sex drive is not equally strong in all or at all ages; also the strength of the parental drive varies considerably (and in isolation, the sex drive may rather come under point 4 below). But without reproduction, neither a society nor the human race can survive. Therefore we have social institutions - primarily marriage, which, as a lasting relationship, is based on the parental rather than the sex drive but which does not function well without also satisfying the sex drive - and various safeguards of these for the purpose of securing the survival of the community;

(3) *the drives for meaning or understanding, or the 'exploratory drives'.* These give rise to religion, philosophy, morality as a cohesive and integrative force (which may, however, also be part of other drives), science, research, the pursuit of knowledge, curiosity, physical exploration, adventure, discovery, experimentation, risk-taking - also in relation to modification of experience, social change and development - but this aspect of the drives may be counteracted by the self-preservation drives and the need for security, sometimes expressed as resistance to change and social inertia: people at the margin of existence will not - cannot afford to - take unnecessary risks and may therefore seem to oppose progress,[6] etc.;

(4) *the aesthetic drives.* These trigger artistic creations, the pursuit of pleasure, fun, festivities, entertainment, leisure activities, play (*homo ludens*), exercise (e.g. sport), the acquisition of luxuries, a search for beauty, comfort and rest - although this latter,

6 Many experiments or attempts at adaptation are unsuccessful. Therefore there is, especially in times of stress or decline, a tendency for ideas of a Golden Past, the Lost Paradise, the Good Old Days, etc. to pop up.

> including sleep, may also be part of the self-preservation drives: no one can work or survive without rest - it is perhaps best understood as a drive to get rid of fatigue products; among these drives may perhaps also be included care and protection of the weak, tenderness, etc.

Associated with the drives listed above, some would add various *social drives*, as everyone experiences a craving for company, a need to do things together: to reproduce, to find common security, to co-operate in production, to share in fun and grief and worship, etc. However, 'social drives' are probably not independent 'drives' but rather a 'principle', more like an instinct, that penetrates all (other) drives; there is a 'social factor' in all drives: one cannot reproduce nor continue one's existence in isolation; neither can one find much meaning in life without company - life becomes meaningful in society; and aesthetic experiences most people want to share, and many activities - fun, play, sport - find their expression only as group, i.e. social, activities. However, the social aspects of drives are as strong as the drives themselves (except perhaps the drive for physical survival), as human experience - in addition to psychological research - demonstrates, e.g. religion ('it is not good for man to be alone'), philosophy ('man is a political creature, or social animal'), common sense ('no man is an island'), as well as ethology (the herd instinct, etc.). The social factor, principle, or instinct is what *makes* society, it is the unifying or unitary 'element' that makes society both possible and necessary; it is more than 'social cues' or 'social codes' (which we can conclude for example from the fact that infants brought up without 'love' or social warmth usually soon die, however well they are otherwise cared for): it is the *sine qua non* of society. But even the social 'instinct' has limits: beehives, hunting bands, or human settlements do not grow endlessly but are limited to or by what serves the purpose of satisfying drives and needs most efficiently.

(C) Organic and Dynamic Aspects

By taking the drives into account and projecting them on to society, social scientists can explain human society both as a 'state' (the status quo) and as a changing 'organism'. The *organic* aspect of society is seen in the interrelationship of the different 'parts', and the *dynamic* aspect is reflected in the need to rank the parts 'hierarchically', as it were, in relation to how well and 'efficiently' they satisfy needs that activate drives, or in view of their role in satisfying drives.

The drives are of various kinds: biological, psychological, and 'auxiliary' (the 'emergency drives'). Each drive or 'cluster' of drives, may help to explain different aspects of society and social life. The drives are limited in number, whereas ways and means to satisfy drives are much more multifarious. The drives are more or less constant, but the ways and means to satisfy them vary from person to person, from society to society, and from time to time. It is therefore necessary to postulate two qualitatively different categories of social events and processes: (1) the satisfaction of drives and (2) ways and means to satisfy drives. A few examples can serve to illustrate this:

- The hunger-drives are constant and must be satisfied for a society to persist, but modes of production - economic activities - to satisfy these drives vary and change over time, and modes of production are thus *subordinate* to the hunger-drives.
- Marriage in one of a variety of forms may be felt as a personal or social 'need', but even marriage may go out of fashion; however, the sex and parental drives do not change or die out so easily. In a society, there are almost always regulatory mechanisms to ensure its perpetuation or survival, but forms or ways to secure this vary considerably.[7]

---

7 Social survival drives may not always be able to cope with 'emergency situations'. Thus, whole villages may die out due to AIDS because the

- Order is necessary for society to exist and function, and it satisfies the self-preservation and self-perpetuation drives and the need for security both of individuals and societies; but the shapes of 'government' and laws to maintain order vary, and they change over time, in line with changes in the perception of what is most beneficial for the society and in line with the ability of the society to change - but there are always also 'conservative' or 'reactionary' forces at work; etc.

Schematically, the sociodynamic theory and model can be simply illustrated like this:

The Community/Society		
Drives: Innate, constant Explain 'why' Activated by frustration Result: scanning-behaviour	⇒	*Ways and means to satisfy drives:* Learned, variable, changing Explain 'how' Activated by drives Aim (desired result): satisfaction of drives
Self-preservation drives Need: food, drink, voiding	⇒	Hunting and gathering, fishing, pastoralism, mixed farming, agriculture, industry, services; power, security, etc.
Self-perpetuation drives Need: offspring	⇒	Promiscuity, concubinage, cohabitation, family life: polygamy (polyandry, polygyny), monogamy (permanent, serial), etc.

members are not able to change their reproductive traditions soon enough to stop the disease from exterminating the community. Two interests are here in conflict. One should think that the survival drive was primary, but in this case the facts may throw some doubt on this assumption. It may therefore not always be helpful to range the drives in a strict 'hierarchy': sex may be as important as food for some, artistic achievement as important as life for others, some risk their lives for new discoveries, etc.

Drives for meaning Need: understanding	⇒	Religion (animism, Shintoism, Hinduism, Buddhism, Taoism, Judaism, Christianity, Islam, etc.), philosophy (Platonism, Stoicism, Epicureanism, Existentialism, Marxism, etc.), magic (black and white), science (nuclear physics, space exploration, search for the source of the Nile, social theories, etc.), etc.
Aesthetic drives Need: pleasure	⇒	Sex (heterosexual relations, homosexual relations, prostitution, etc.), play (tennis, football, chess, etc.), art (drawing, painting, mosaics, etc.), music (flute playing, folk melodies, symphonies, etc.), oral and written literature (folk-tales, novels, poetry, etc.), good health (avoidance of illness, harm, pain), etc.

The inevitability of change

How can *social change* be explained on this model? Changes that facilitate the satisfaction of drives are 'good' or positive changes, those that make such satisfaction more difficult are harmful changes - and accustomed ways that once served a useful purpose may become harmful, or at best 'neutral', if they no longer achieve what they used to do. Thus, with reference to the clusters of drives listed above, if food becomes more abundant, racial perpetuation more secure, the acquisition of useful information easier, and leisure activities healthier and richer - these are all beneficial changes; those that have the opposite effect are negative or noxious changes.

However, 'progress' must be seen in a social context. If more food comes into the hands of only a few at the expense of others, if a greater number of surviving children is mostly due to the polygamous habits of rich men who empty the market of wives for the majority, if knowledge is monopolised by a certain caste or class and used to manipulate the majority, or if increased leisure for a few is due to the exploitation of the many by the few, then these changes do not constitute or contribute to progress but to social imbalances, oppression, underdevelopment - and may lead to rebellion, etc.

This means that this social model - dynamic functionalism - can be used to advocate equality, anti-exploitative measures, equitable distribution of resources, democracy, justice, respect for human rights, etc. It is not the drives of individuals but of society as a whole that must be satisfied[8] more or less equitably for society to persist, function well, be in balance and harmony.

Societies persist because they change and adapt to changing circumstances - if they do not, they will fall apart. Normal change does not in itself act *against* but *for* the persistence of a society - and if a society does not change 'with the times', it will disintegrate, lose the commitment, consensus, solidarity, participation and co-operation of its members. If a society stagnates, cohesion decreases and conflicts increase. But here it should of course be added that not all changes are for the good of society; e.g., many failed attempts at development have been harmful.

A change in an organism, e.g. loss of a limb, is mostly 'unhealthy' - only a few changes or mutations are beneficial, although cross-breeding and genetic manipulation may occasionally bring about positive changes. The same could be said about social change on the organic model.[9] On the 'human' model, change is a good thing if it facilitates

---

8 We are speaking in terms of our model, which is an abstraction. It is individuals that have drives that must be satisfied - society does not have drives; and hunger etc. is individual - a society is not hungry, unless we speak figuratively or refer to all individual members of a society. The same applies when we talk of 'social needs'.

9 Researchers who investigate a community over a limited period of time may find the organic model satisfactory because few societies change much in a short time, and if great changes do occur, they may be the result of

the satisfaction of drives. The drives do not change in any fundamental way; ways and means to satisfy them may and do. The functionalist hypothesis, on the organic model, that a change in one part of society, one institution, leads to changes in all the other parts - as a change in an organism leads to an overall change in the whole organism - is not satisfactory, although it points to an important aspect of society as 'a whole', because it does not explain, or help to understand, whether such a change, or changes following from it, is (are) good or bad, although the underlying assumption - and one often expressed by anthropologists - is that it is bad; neither does the theory give criteria by which to evaluate particular changes. Changes not directly, or only peripherally, related to the efficient satisfaction of drives - e.g. shortening of the initiation period, change from polygamy to monogamy, or conversion from animism to Islam - lead to fewer beneficial or harmful changes in other areas of society than changes more directly or closely related to the efficient satisfaction of drives, e.g. loss of food-producing capacity by a farming community due to drought or land expropriation, better health - and thus productivity - in a community due to immunisation and improved sanitation in place of magical healing and witchcraft, or the introduction of schools and modern technology.

In times of rapid change, the need for understanding ('meaning') increases, and people may for example become more religious in an attempt to make sense of and adapt to the new situation. Such mental or psychological changes are helpful in coping with the new without too great loss of security and without too much social disruption.

---

drought, famine or war, i.e. they are harmful changes. This may incline some to think that change, and particularly rapid change, is always or mostly bad. But in a comparative perspective and with a longer time view, it becomes clearer that change is inevitable and very often beneficial - it shows people's ability to cope with and adapt to changing needs.

Modification of drives and of ways and means to satisfy drives

Although *drives*, and communal needs 'corresponding to' drives, are innate and rather constant, they can be and are *modified* - canalised, conditioned - by learning and experience,[10] but this is a slow process, and the range is limited.[11] *Ways and means* to satisfy drives, and communal needs 'corresponding to' drives, *vary and change* much more frequently and rapidly, and sometimes drastically and extensively, and they are mostly totally dependent on learning and experience.[12] Both external forces - 'impersonal' or social pressure, socialisation, social sanctions, etc. - and deliberate choice - through communal decision-making processes, creative innovations, etc. - can *to some extent* modify a society's 'drives' or basic social needs and *very extensively* alter ways in which they are satisfied.

How are drives or 'basic social needs' modified? It seems best to consider this question in conjunction with the question of how ways and means are found to satisfy drives. *Perception*, i.e. cognition, coding, understanding, reasoning, motivation, *learning*, i.e. socialisation, acculturation, canalisation, conditioning, memory, and *choice*, i.e. volition, experimentation, change, are fundamental concepts in this context.

By using a human, i.e. psychological-organic, model to explain social function and processes, one can 'presuppose' and accept the influence and importance of even a society's perception - in processes like consultations, achieving consensus, elections, etc. - and therefore

10 This is the case also for reflexes regulated by the autonomic nervous system.

11 However, neuroses may develop, e.g. irrational and exaggerated fear, sex fetishism, etc.; in society, this may appear as fascism, racism, religious fundamentalism, etc.

12 Sucking to satisfy hunger is 'instinctive' in babies, and there may be other examples of ways and means to satisfy drives that do not depend on learning and experience.

choice. Identical drives and social needs need not lead to attempts to satisfy them in identical ways. One problem may have many solutions, and people with the ability to think have a choice between different options, resulting in the variety of social institutions that exist even under otherwise similar conditions, and of course even more so under dissimilar conditions. Only if people were purely mindless organisms could one defend a strict determinism and expect the same kind of society as a result of similar external conditions.

Our model makes it necessary to conclude that some social phenomena (corresponding to human drives) are more important than others, and that derived needs (ways and means to satisfy drives) are secondary and can and should be adapted to serve the more important. Thus, mode of production should ideally correspond to the most efficient ('best') way to still a society's hunger or food needs. However, security considerations may obviate risk-taking where the outcome is uncertain or not clearly perceived, and this may slow down changes beneficial to meeting social needs, etc. Such inertia can be both good ('wise') and bad ('reactionary').

The human, psychological-organic model makes it also necessary to postulate memory and the ability to learn.[13] People and communities can build on previous experience and retrieve from memory, but they can also experiment and hit upon new ways of doing things, i.e. reason and learn - by trial and error as well as success. Whether they choose to go on with the old or to try new things, they can pass on their experience, skills, knowledge and beliefs to new generations through socialisation processes - child-rearing, acculturation, teaching. And they - the society as a whole or some sections of it - can, on the other hand, try to prevent experimentation and change - social control mechanisms usually serve to prevent or delay change.

---

13 Learning is both a means to modify reflexes and drives and a means to acquire flexibility in the pursuit of means to satisfy drives.

Why do some societies borrow - adopt and adapt - some elements from another culture and reject others, while other societies borrow other elements? To answer this question, one cannot only take technology, i.e. what is most efficient or what is most beneficial technically or economically, into account, but one must also understand people's perception - what they foresee as the most likely outcome, the 'cost-benefit', of any borrowing from outside, or of innovation generally. This is not a one-dimensional problem. People may accept changes they clearly see as beneficial, i.e. as contributing to the satisfaction of any or all of their 'drives' or basic social needs; but when 'novelties' are untested, perception or expectation or considerations of risk-minimisation are as important as, or more important than, technical or economic aspects, especially as these latter are seen through the eyes of outsiders who may have experience of the 'new' situation from their own societies and whose evaluation may therefore be different. The poor need to be sure.

Mechanisms of change

Biologically oriented psychologists are trying to find material, physi(ologi)cal bases for all mental processes. In a similar way, some social scientists try to find material bases (mostly expressed in economic terms) for all social phenomena. But psychologist with this orientation, no less than others, also stress that learning can modify drives; and perception influences the way people try to satisfy their needs. Something similar applies in the analysis of society. It may not always be helpful to say that social phenomena can only be explained by other social phenomena, although that is generally true.[14] Riverine civilisations can partly be explained by

14 It may be helpful to be more precise in one's use of terms. Social phenomena are not phenomena as much as concepts or abstractions: they 'exist' only in the eye or mind of the beholder. Social 'facts' or 'phenomena' are logical constructs, conceptions 'invented' by the perceiving person. Since *perception* is the constituting element in any social 'fact' or 'phenomenon', it is not

environmental conditions, etc., although rivers do of course not create societies: only 'perceptive' human beings do. If conflict breaks out where there is a sudden change in the environment, e.g. limiting the amount of food available, some links between natural causes and social behaviour seem likely, although such links can only be perceived by a logical process in the minds of people, and perceived 'linkages' may be the result of past experience, reasoning, or ideas coming to a community from outside. Perception of causes determines the choice of measures taken, e.g. conflict with the government if bad government is seen as the cause of hardships; but expected outcome is also important - one will fight only if there is a reasonable chance of winning. Both the social and the natural environments influence perception, just as perception influences the choices that are made in attempts to solve problems of managing one's material and social environments. This way of looking at things - stressing the importance of perception - should, however, not lead to the opposite conclusion of the ones mentioned above (viz., that there is a material base for all beliefs and social phenomena - *à la* Marx, or that only social phenomena can explain social phenomena - *à la* Durkheim), namely that perception - beliefs, expectations, etc. - alone can explain social phenomena - *à la* Max Weber, at least in his 'Protestant Ethic and Capitalism' phase. There is a place for *all* such explanations, but each in their proper area and circumstance. On our model, this is so because not all drives are of the same nature: some are biological and some are psychological, and some may be a combination of both,

---

difficult to see that the same perceiving subject can see social possibilities (the possibility to create social life or facts or phenomena) in the natural environment. Thus, the idea of a social phenomenon can be suggested to the perceiving (thinking, imaginative, logical) individual by a natural phenomenon, fertile land can give a person the idea that this is the place to build homes and start community life. This definition may make the following observations in the main text more comprehensible.

e.g. some of the 'emergency drives', such as fear and anger, connected to the autonomic nervous system; and it is possible to be 'taught' conditioned reflexes. Thus, societies as well as individuals *must* have food and water and get rid of noxious waste - this is necessary for survival, but people in society and as individuals *like* sex and art and religion and cornflakes - which are not necessary for survival, and societies as well as individuals may *wish* to go on being pastoralists or farmers - and a particular mode of production may become the only *viable* means of survival in certain situations, and we *feel* hunger when 'meal-time' arrives - just as societies may 'feel' hostile to strangers, with or without cause. Mode or choice of behaviour, i.e. social activities, as well as material or psychological motives for behaviour - community decisions, etc. - will vary according to circumstances.

It is obvious that environmental - material no less than social - conditions influence social life. History makes it just as obvious that ideas and beliefs have on occasion changed the course of events. The difficulty has been to find a theory or model that can explain all these phenomena, and for lack of it, some have become very one-sided in their attempts at explaining social facts; thus Marx and Weber stress mostly one or the other of the above-mentioned causes of change. Dynamic functionalism makes it possible to embrace both these, as well as Durkheim's, ways of explaining social facts or phenomena: some social phenomena have material causes, some ideological or perceptual ones, some result from a combination of both, and some social phenomena originate from other purely social phenomena.

The main and common feature of all attempts at explaining social phenomena must be the demonstration that they satisfy or aim at satisfying basic human needs based in the drives, or that social phenomena are manifestations of efforts to satisfy these drives in the best way the society has hit upon, or the way that best serves this purpose without obviating the satisfaction of other drives. A society is likely to reject any, not only the most efficient, way to satisfy a drive when this would reduce or hinder the satisfaction of other drives. Thus, indiscriminate sex may satisfy one (psychological) need but harm the interests of social cohesion, stability and perpetuation - the latter due for example to sexually transmitted diseases; therefore totally promiscuous societies do not exist (or may have perished for this very reason).

Uses of a sociodynamic, human model of society

The sociodynamic, human (i.e. psychological-organic) model can thus explain why societies are as they are just as well as the organic, functionalist model: existing social arrangements satisfy its members' needs in acceptable ways; but it can also explain why societies change, which is not easy on the classical functionalist model: they change in the pursuit of better ways of satisfying their members' drives. Our model can also, by the same token, explain the purpose of the rich variety of human activities, institutions, ideas, beliefs and values: they are the ways and means perceived by the members of various societies as the ones best suited to satisfy their basic needs or drives; and it can explain why previously 'purposeful' arrangements cease to be useful: they do not satisfy basic human needs as well as they used to do; and it can also show why social arrangements often persist after they have lost their usefulness: there is an element of inertia in all societies (perhaps due to unclear perception) that serves to prevent undue risk-taking. This model can also explain peaceful coexistence and co-operation: they are beneficial for the satisfaction of basic needs; and it points to the meaning of conflict: it is a tool in the search for better and safer ways to ensure the satisfaction of basic needs or a fair distribution of resources.

The sociodynamic model may also help to bridge the gap between social and cultural anthropology because it places equal emphasis on institutional and other social phenomena. Socialisation and culture (the latter understood as learned behaviour, or socially acquired knowledge, skills, customs, beliefs and values) are as important as - and may influence and give shape to - social institutions or structures, and vice versa:

social conditions (e.g. institutions or social crises) may give rise to ideas (e.g. religious beliefs about how to cope with crises), which in turn may give shape to social institutions (e.g., religious beliefs may not only give rise to rituals and objects of art used in religious contexts but produce social charters justifying power structures, such as priestly authority and divine kingship, or regulate community behaviour to avoid future crises, etc.). The importance or value of any aspect of society - an idea as well as an institution or the natural base of life - and its modification is determined by what it contributes to the satisfaction of basic human and social needs and how these relate to drives.

'Dynamic functionalism'

As 'traditional' or 'classical' functionalism has given rise to much excellent fieldwork, it would be a loss to break with it completely, in spite of its shortcomings; but one could adapt or modify it so that it fits and explains reality as we experience or 'see' it and help to correct or improve our understanding or perception of reality in a more satisfactory manner. The model outlined in this paper is a sociodynamic model and can be called the theory of sociodynamics; but instead of giving it a totally new name, it may be just as well to stress its links with past theories and (also) call it 'dynamic functionalism'. The word 'functionalism' will still point to the 'organic' or 'holistic' interconnectedness of various institutions and other social phenomena; the word 'dynamic' shows that social phenomena are best explained as manifestations of attempts to satisfy basic human and social needs corresponding to drives, and that some 'things' are therefore more and others less important than others for social life - according to the degree to which they satisfy or fail to satisfy drives, and that 'things' can and sometimes must change if a society shall be able to continue to satisfy the same old drives and needs or perhaps to satisfy them more efficiently and/or abundantly.

The 'old' functionalism was and is a good tool for explaining static societies - which are purely imagined constructs as no society is static, or societies 'as if' they were static, or perhaps societies (if such exist) which are changing only in circular ways, along traditional, preordained, totally predictable cyclic patterns. The advantage of this model, 'dynamic functionalism', over classical functionalism is that it can explain both societies as they are at any given moment, as well as social change, and why societies change and must change, as well as why some societies change more rapidly and others more slowly than others. It recognises change as the normal state of affairs in any society - and it does not make one regret change as such, but only harmful changes.

Societies are 'going concerns', and they can now keep going, i.e. changing, without distracting or distressing social scientists or confusing their theories, and their theories need no longer be at odds with social change or human aspirations for change - or for 'stability' and perhaps stagnation. For some, the Golden Age lies in the future. The whole of the Third World hopes that it does just that.

Appendix

VARIOUS USES OF THE SOCIODYNAMIC MODEL

In the main article, I have included an illustrative model to show the ongoing processes to satisfy social "drives". Individuals are "satisfied" and can then "rest" from "scanning behaviour" that were activated in order to satisfy their drives, till a need arises again. However, in a society, there are always members who feel a need that they seek to satisfy; therefore drive-satisfying processes are as constant as the basic needs. Thus, food-producing or food-processing activities are always taking place somewhere in that society. Similarly with activities to satisfy other drives. Therefore all the arrows point only in one direction in that illustration: from drives towards means to satisfy these drives.

However, the model can also be used to illustrate various states of societies, and unequal situations for different societies, whether there is balance or imbalance between drives and their satisfaction. Below, I add some examples of uses that can be made of the basic, "general" model.

Figure 1: Illustration of the ongoing processes of satisfying basic needs or drives - the arrows point only one way, from basic to derived needs, from drives to means of satisfying them. This is the "general" model used in the article.

The Community/Society		
Drives: Innate, constant Explain 'why' Activated by frustration Result: scanning-behaviour	⇒	*Ways and means to satisfy drives:* Learned, variable, changing Explain 'how' Activated by drives Aim (desired result): satisfaction of drives
Self-preservation drives Need: food, drink, voiding	⇒	Hunting and gathering, fishing, pastoralism, mixed farming, agriculture, industry, services; power, security, etc.
Self-perpetuation drives Need: offspring	⇒	Promiscuity, concubinage, cohabitation, family life: polygamy (polyandry, polygyny), monogamy (permanent, serial), etc.
Drives for meaning Need: understanding	⇒	Religion (animism, Shintoism, Hinduism, Buddhism, Taoism, Judaism, Christianity, Islam, etc.), philosophy (Platonism, Stoicism, Epicureanism, Existentialism, Marxism, etc.), magic (black and white), science (nuclear physics, space exploration, search for the source of the Nile, social theories, etc.), etc.
Aesthetic drives Need: pleasure	⇒	Sex (heterosexual relations, homosexual relations, prostitution, etc.), play (tennis, football, chess, etc.), art (drawing, painting, mosaics, etc.), music (flute playing, folk melodies, symphonies, etc.), oral and written literature (folk-tales, novels, poetry, etc.), good health (avoidance of illness, harm, pain), etc.

Figure 2: Illustration of a society in harmony or equilibrium: means to satisfy drives are adequate; order is maintained; political power is used to distribute "products" equally to the satisfaction of the whole society; peace prevails. However, even where there is enough, and especially where there is plenty, power can be used to secure more than is needed for some and less than is needed, or less than a "fair share", for others. "Class formation" and "power struggle" may result.

The Community/Society		
Drives: Innate, constant Explain 'why' Activated by frustration Result: scanning-behaviour	⇒ ⇐ or ⇒	*Ways and means to satisfy drives:* Learned, variable, changing Explain 'how' Activated by drives Aim (desired result): satisfaction of drives
Self-preservation drives Need: food, drink, voiding	⇒ ⇐	Hunting and gathering, fishing, pastoralism, mixed farming, agriculture, industry, services; power, security, etc.
Self-perpetuation drives Need: offspring	⇒ ⇐	Promiscuity, concubinage, cohabitation, family life: polygamy (polyandry, polygyny), monogamy (permanent, serial), etc.
Drives for meaning Need: understanding	⇒ ⇐	Religion (animism, Shintoism, Hinduism, Buddhism, Taoism, Judaism, Christianity, Islam, etc.), philosophy (Platonism, Stoicism, Epicureanism, Existentialism, Marxism, etc.), magic (black and white), science (nuclear physics, space exploration, search for the source of the Nile, social theories, etc.), etc.
Aesthetic drives Need: pleasure	⇒ ⇐	Sex (heterosexual relations, homosexual relations, prostitution, etc.), play (tennis, football, chess, etc.), art (drawing, painting, mosaics, etc.), music (flute playing, folk melodies, symphonies, etc.), oral and written literature (folk-tales, novels, poetry, etc.), good health (avoidance of illness, harm, pain), etc.

Figure 3: Illustration of a surplus-producing society, i.e. a society producing more than necessary to satisfy basic needs or drives. The "surplus" may be traded or exchanged to obtain means to satisfy other "needs" (or wishes) the society's own production does not meet, e.g. the desire for "luxuries"; or it may lead to accumulation to meet future needs or give feelings of security ("money in the bank"), etc.

The Community/Society		
Drives: Innate, constant Explain 'why' Activated by frustration Result: scanning-behaviour	→ ⇐	*Ways and means to satisfy drives:* Learned, variable, changing Explain 'how' Activated by drives Aim (desired result): satisfaction of drives
Self-preservation drives Need: food, drink, voiding	→ ⇐	Hunting and gathering, fishing, pastoralism, mixed farming, agriculture, industry, services; power, security, etc.
Self-perpetuation drives Need: offspring	→ ⇐	Promiscuity, concubinage, cohabitation, family life: polygamy (polyandry, polygyny), monogamy (permanent, serial), etc.
Drives for meaning Need: understanding	→ ⇐	Religion (animism, Shintoism, Hinduism, Buddhism, Taoism, Judaism, Christianity, Islam, etc.), philosophy (Platonism, Stoicism, Epicureanism, Existentialism, Marxism, etc.), magic (black and white), science (nuclear physics, space exploration, search for the source of the Nile, social theories, etc.), etc.
Aesthetic drives Need: pleasure	→ ⇐	Sex (heterosexual relations, homosexual relations, prostitution, etc.), play (tennis, football, chess, etc.), art (drawing, painting, mosaics, etc.), music (flute playing, folk melodies, symphonies, etc.), oral and written literature (folk-tales, novels, poetry, etc.), good health (avoidance of illness, harm, pain), etc.

Figure 4: Illustration of a society which does not produce enough to satisfy drives. This can be remedied for example by exchanging "things" that do not satisfy drives (e.g. oil) for means to satisfy drives. If no means of exchange exist, unrest and war may ensue.

The Community/Society		
Drives: Innate, constant Explain 'why' Activated by frustration Result: scanning-behaviour	⇒ ←	*Ways and means to satisfy drives:* Learned, variable, changing Explain 'how' Activated by drives Aim (desired result): satisfaction of drives
Self-preservation drives Need: food, drink, voiding	⇒ ←	Hunting and gathering, fishing, pastoralism, mixed farming, agriculture, industry, services; power, security, etc.
Self-perpetuation drives Need: offspring	⇒ ←	Promiscuity, concubinage, cohabitation, family life: polygamy (polyandry, polygyny), monogamy (permanent, serial), etc.
Drives for meaning Need: understanding	⇒ ←	Religion (animism, Shintoism, Hinduism, Buddhism, Taoism, Judaism, Christianity, Islam, etc.), philosophy (Platonism, Stoicism, Epicureanism, Existentialism, Marxism, etc.), magic (black and white), science (nuclear physics, space exploration, search for the source of the Nile, social theories, etc.), etc.
Aesthetic drives Need: pleasure	⇒ ←	Sex (heterosexual relations, homosexual relations, prostitution, etc.), play (tennis, football, chess, etc.), art (drawing, painting, mosaics, etc.), music (flute playing, folk melodies, symphonies, etc.), oral and written literature (folk-tales, novels, poetry, etc.), good health (avoidance of illness, harm, pain), etc.

Figure 5: Illustration of a society that produces little but has managed to "modify" its needs to circumstances, live at subsistence level or in eternal poverty, having accepted its lot, and which therefore lives in peace and "harmony", or equilibrium, if means to satisfy basic needs are reasonably equitably distributed. Classes can of course also arise in such societies, for example where a ruling class has been able to build up a strong myth or "ideology" "justifying" inequality and obtain general acceptance of it.

The Community/Society		
Drives: Innate, constant Explain 'why' Activated by frustration Result: scanning-behaviour	→ ←	*Ways and means to satisfy drives:* Learned, variable, changing Explain 'how' Activated by drives Aim (desired result): satisfaction of drives
Self-preservation drives Need: food, drink, voiding	→ ←	Hunting and gathering, fishing, pastoralism, mixed farming, agriculture, industry, services; power, security, etc.
Self-perpetuation drives Need: offspring	→ ←	Promiscuity, concubinage, cohabitation, family life: polygamy (polyandry, polygyny), monogamy (permanent, serial), etc.
Drives for meaning Need: understanding	→ ←	Religion (animism, Shintoism, Hinduism, Buddhism, Taoism, Judaism, Christianity, Islam, etc.), philosophy (Platonism, Stoicism, Epicureanism, Existentialism, Marxism, etc.), magic (black and white), science (nuclear physics, space exploration, search for the source of the Nile, social theories, etc.), etc.
Aesthetic drives Need: pleasure	→ ←	Sex (heterosexual relations, homosexual relations, prostitution, etc.), play (tennis, football, chess, etc.), art (drawing, painting, mosaics, etc.), music (flute playing, folk melodies, symphonies, etc.), oral and written literature (folk-tales, novels, poetry, etc.), good health (avoidance of illness, harm, pain), etc.

Figure 6: Illustration of a "typical" society, where means to satisfy drives are adequate in some areas, inadequate in some, and more than adequate in others. Several examples can be given of this, with different sets of arrows. This is only one example.

The Community/Society		
Drives:	⇔	*Ways and means to satisfy drives:*
Innate, constant	→	Learned, variable, changing
Explain 'why'	←	Explain 'how'
Activated by frustration		Activated by drives
Result: scanning-behaviour		Aim (desired result): satisfaction of drives
Self-preservation drives Need: food, drink, voiding	→ ←	Hunting and gathering, fishing, pastoralism, mixed farming, agriculture, industry, services; power, security, etc.
Self-perpetuation drives Need: offspring	⇔	Promiscuity, concubinage, cohabitation, family life: polygamy (polyandry, polygyny), monogamy (permanent, serial), etc.
Drives for meaning Need: understanding	→ ⇐	Religion (animism, Shintoism, Hinduism, Buddhism, Taoism, Judaism, Christianity, Islam, etc.), philosophy (Platonism, Stoicism, Epicureanism, Existentialism, Marxism, etc.), magic (black and white), science (nuclear physics, space exploration, search for the source of the Nile, social theories, etc.), etc.
Aesthetic drives Need: pleasure	↔	Sex (heterosexual relations, homosexual relations, prostitution, etc.), play (tennis, football, chess, etc.), art (drawing, painting, mosaics, etc.), music (flute playing, folk melodies, symphonies, etc.), oral and written literature (folk-tales, novels, poetry, etc.), good health (avoidance of illness, harm, pain), etc.

Figure 7: The lines separating the four categories of drives in the model are not continuous. This means that some drives can be satisfied by means normally applied to satisfy other drives. This can lead to, for example, sublimation (sex deprivation may lead to charity work or artistic or scientific excellence) or its reverse (sex deprivation may lead to crime, food deprivation to war), etc. This could be illustrated by using the basic model but with arrows crossing the broken lines of the figure (and not only lines separating contiguous "areas" in the model).

The Community/Society		
Drives: Innate, constant Explain 'why' Activated by frustration Result: scanning-behaviour	⇔ → ←	*Ways and means to satisfy drives:* Learned, variable, changing Explain 'how' Activated by drives Aim (desired result): satisfaction of drives
Self-preservation drives Need: food, drink, voiding	→ ←	Hunting and gathering, fishing, pastoralism, mixed farming, agriculture, industry, services; power, security, etc.
Self-perpetuation drives Need: offspring	⇔	Promiscuity, concubinage, cohabitation, family life: polygamy (polyandry, polygyny), monogamy (permanent, serial), etc.
Drives for meaning Need: understanding	→ ⇐ □	Religion (animism, Shintoism, Hinduism, Buddhism, Taoism, Judaism, Christianity, Islam, etc.), philosophy (Platonism, Stoicism, Epicureanism, Existentialism, Marxism, etc.), magic (black and white), science (nuclear physics, space exploration, search for the source of the Nile, social theories, etc.), etc.
Aesthetic drives Need: pleasure	□ ↔	Sex (heterosexual relations, homosexual relations, prostitution, etc.), play (tennis, football, chess, etc.), art (drawing, painting, mosaics, etc.), music (flute playing, folk melodies, symphonies, etc.), oral and written literature (folk-tales, novels, poetry, etc.), good health (avoidance of illness, harm, pain), etc.

Comparison of societies.

By means of this model, it should be possible to compare societies and institutions in more meaningful ways than just comparing institutions "by themselves", which may appear rather meaningless and pointless. Processes and institutions can be analysed for their fitness to meet basic needs (satisfy drives), and their effectiveness in this respect can be compared with similar processes and institutions (and their efficiency) in other societies. Two factors need special attention in such comparisons: (1) resources, or the environment, and (2) human perception. The first gives the opportunities and sets the limits. Thus, one will normally find agricultural communities where the soil and the climate make this a suitable way to satisfy basic needs; but pastoralism develops much more likely where the soil is less fertile and the climate hotter. Fishing is a normal activity for people living near seas, lakes and rivers; and hunting is "normal" for forest dwellers. Human perception plays a role in all such choices that are made, but the environment presents certain options as more immediately "obvious". In more technologically developed societies, perceptions have overcome many limits set by the environment, and more efficient means of satisfying basic needs are found. However, if experience from developed societies is applied in improper ways to unsuitable environments, the result may be short-term gain but long-term loss, i.e. less effective satisfaction of basic needs; this is particularly clear where governments in "developing" countries desperately try to "settle nomads" (under the pretext of giving better social services but which is mostly done for purposes of political control). However, the environment does not set absolute limits even in less developed societies (and not all efforts at development are misguided, even though much has gone wrong in this respect in the past). The environment is not deterministic in the sense of cancelling out human perception and choice. But in a general way, comparison of the (effectiveness of the) ways found to satisfy basic needs (drives) in different societies/communities is possible by using the sociodynamic model.

A note on literature

A full bibliography will not be given here. In the article I have tried to reconsider some of the theories of some of the great thinkers within the social sciences over the last couple of centuries, and I have relied on well-known basic texts in English translation. Marx's theoretical views can be studies in for example *A Contribution to the Critique of Political Economy* and *Economic and Philosophic Manuscripts of 1844*. Max Weber's views are set forth in, e.g., *The Theory of Social and Economic Organisation* and *The Methodology of the Social Sciences*. Durkheim has set out his position in for example *The Rules of Sociological Method* and *Sociology and Philosophy*. Raymond Aron has given well-written summaries of the views of these and other theorists in *Main Currents in Sociological Thought*. Functionalism as it is often understood and practised was advanced by Malinowski, e.g. in *A Scientific Theory of Culture*. He as well as his followers realised the inadequacies of his theory and the need to make it "dynamic", and in 1945 there appeared an edited version of his theories in *The Dynamics of Culture Change*, but one does not make his theories dynamic just by "throwing in" haphazardly a "need" here and a "drive" there to explain change, and his attempts in that direction were not satisfactory. Both Lévi-Strauss with his structuralism (e.g. in *Structural Anthropology*) and Radcliffe-Brown (e.g. in *Structure and Function in Primitive Society*), as well as Talcott Parsons (e.g. in *Essays in Sociological Theory, The Structure of Social Action* and *The Social System*) and others have tried to improve on Malinowski's theories, but critical objections still remain strong (P S Cohen's criticism in *Modern Social Theory* is still valid). One clear shortcoming is the lack of scientific rigour in making use of the psychological concepts "need" and "drive". The first great advance in the study of drives and needs came already 1938 with Henry A Murray's *Explorations in Personality*. Since then the study of drives and needs has been fairly well exhausted, so that textbooks on psychology today rarely discuss them very deeply: they are taken for granted, and dictionaries and glossaries of psychological terms (the latter often appended to psychology textbooks) just define the terms without further elaboration. The concepts would be fairly useless for social scientists other than psychologists if it had been necessary to undertake a professional study of psychology in order to make use of them in for example sociology and anthropology. It is an advantage for such scientists that there is general agreement on them and that they can be used with confidence and without expecting a radically new interpretation of drives and needs with the next textbook on the market. One popular book of general psychology that was first written as an introductory university textbook in psychology and then rewritten as a Penguin book was C J Adcock's *Fundamentals of Psychology*. This has been reprinted many times and read also by social scientists. As it makes use of the terms drives and needs throughout, it can be considered a sufficient and accessible summary of the issues also for social scientists. Any expansion of one's knowledge of these theories, as well of the theories of the social scientists noted above, will of course deepen one's understanding. These notes are just a help to get started. Social theory has become fashionable, and so many books on theory are being produced that much time and energy are required to keep up with the flow of new books: one would have little time for reflection on new theories and new aspects of old theories if one should read them all. Most of them are, however, not innovative but give summaries of old and more recent views and theories.

100224-200-1-60W